444 EPIC WORLD WAR I & II FACTS

The Ultimate Collection of Shocking War Stories, Hidden History, and Trivia-Winning Facts

SCOTT MATTHEWS

The more that you read, the more things you will know. The more you learn, the more places you'll go.

- Dr. Seuss

Contents

Introduction

In the early years of the twentieth century, much of the world believed it was entering a new age of progress.

Cities were growing fast. Trains crossed continents. Telegraph wires carried messages in minutes instead of weeks. Electricity lit streets that had once gone dark at sunset. Medicine was improving. Industry was booming. Empires felt confident, modern, and powerful.

To many people living in Europe in 1914, war felt like an outdated idea. Something from the past. Nations had fought before, of course, but the belief was that modern diplomacy, technology, and shared culture would prevent anything truly catastrophic.

They were wrong.

Beneath the surface, the world was tightly wound.

Countries had spent decades building massive armies and navies, convinced that strength alone would guarantee safety. Military plans were drawn up years in advance, timed to railway schedules and mobilization orders that could not easily be slowed or stopped. Alliances bound nations together so rigidly that a conflict between two countries could pull in half the world within days.

National pride ran hot. Old rivalries simmered. Borders were disputed.

Empires feared decline. Politicians made promises they could not easily back away from.

The system looked stable, but it was brittle.

All it needed was a spark.

In June of 1914, that spark appeared in the city of Sarajevo. A single assassination, carried out in a crowded street, set off a chain reaction no one could fully control. Within weeks, Europe's great powers were issuing ultimatums, mobilizing armies, and declaring war.

Many believed it would be over quickly.

Young men rushed to enlist. Some smiled for photographs. Some treated it like an adventure. Newspapers spoke of glory, honor, and decisive victories. Soldiers packed light, expecting to return home within months.

Instead, the world fell into a war unlike anything it had ever seen.

World War I was not a war of sweeping cavalry charges and heroic duels. It became a war of trenches carved into mud, stretching for hundreds of miles. A war where machine guns could cut down entire units in seconds. Where artillery shells fell day and night, sometimes for weeks without pause.

It was the first truly industrial war.

New technologies appeared almost as quickly as soldiers could adapt to them. Poison gas drifted across battlefields. Submarines hunted unseen beneath the sea. Airplanes, once a novelty, became weapons of war.

Millions of soldiers lived underground like animals, surrounded by rats, lice, and constant fear. Civilians far from the front lines were pulled into the conflict through rationing, propaganda, forced labor, and bombing raids. Entire societies were reshaped by the demands of total war.

And when it finally ended, the cost was staggering.

More than sixteen million people were dead. Entire empires had collapsed. Borders were redrawn. Families were shattered. The psychological wounds would last for generations. The world that emerged afterward was not safer or more stable, but fragile, angry, and unsettled.

In many ways, the modern world was born in the trenches of World War I.

This book is not a traditional history lesson.

It does not move carefully year by year or battle by battle. It does not ask you to memorize dates, maps, or lists of generals. Instead, it focuses on the moments that reveal what this war truly was.

The strange facts.

The brutal realities.

The human stories.

The overlooked details that textbooks often skip.

You'll hear about soldiers, spies, nurses, and civilians. About inventions created out of desperation. About decisions that changed history in ways no one intended. About courage, fear, ingenuity, and unimaginable loss.

Some facts will surprise you.

Some will disturb you.

Some will change how you think about war entirely.

Each stands on its own, but together they paint a picture of a conflict that reshaped the world in ways we are still living with today.

This is not just a story about how World War I began.

It is a collection of moments that show what happened when a modern world collided with industrialized violence for the first time.

This is *Epic World War I Facts*.

167 EPIC
WORLD WAR I
FACTS

Scott Matthews

ONE

World War I

1. The Assassination That Sparked World War I

On a bright, hot Sunday in June 1914, a man named Archduke Franz Ferdinand was riding through the streets of Sarajevo in an open-top car. He was a powerful man, the heir to a massive empire, and he was dressed in his finest military uniform, complete with a hat decorated with green feathers. Beside him sat his wife, Sophie. It was their wedding anniversary, and despite the political tension in the air, they wanted to show the people they were friendly and unafraid.

But hiding in the crowds were six young men with a dark plan. They were nationalists who wanted their people to be free from the Archduke's empire, and they had come armed with bombs and pistols. Earlier that morning, one of them had already thrown a bomb at the car. It missed, bouncing off the folded-back roof and exploding under the car behind them, injuring several people. Most people would have fled the city right then, but the Archduke was stubborn. He insisted on going to the hospital to visit the people who had been hurt.

This is where history took a strange and deadly turn. The Archduke's drivers weren't told about the change in plans. As the motorcade sped through the city, the lead driver took a wrong turn onto a narrow side street. When the Archduke's driver realized the mistake, he slammed on the brakes to try and reverse. The engine stalled, and the heavy car came to a jerky stop right in front of a deli.

Standing outside that deli was nineteen-year-old Gavrilo Princip. He had been part of the assassination plot earlier that morning and thought he had failed. He was likely standing there wondering what to do next when, suddenly, his target literally stopped right in front of him. Princip didn't hesitate. He stepped toward the car and fired two shots from just a few feet away. One bullet hit the Archduke in the neck, and the other hit Sophie.

In the chaos that followed, the Archduke's last words were a plea to his wife: *"Sophie, Sophie! Don't die! Live for our children!"* But it was too late. By the time the car reached help, both were dead. Those two small pieces of lead didn't just kill a couple on their anniversary; they acted like a spark in a room full of gunpowder. Because of the complicated promises different countries had made to protect one another, this one local tragedy began to pull the entire world into a war that no one truly knew how to stop.

2. The Rivalries and Alliances Behind World War I

To understand why a single shooting in a far-off city could set the whole world on fire, you have to look at Europe like a giant playground full of bullies and nervous friends who had all made secret pacts with one another. By 1914, the continent was split into two main "teams." On one side was the Triple Entente, made up of Britain, France, and Russia. On the other side was the Triple Alliance, which included Germany, Austria-Hungary, and Italy. These weren't just friendly handshakes; they were "all-or-nothing" promises. If one country got into a fight, their partners were forced to jump in and help, whether they wanted to or not.

The biggest "bully" on the block was Germany. It was a relatively new country, but it was growing incredibly fast. They had the best factories, a massive army, and they were starting to build a navy that made Britain, the king of the seas, very worried. Germany felt surrounded by enemies and believed that the only way to be safe was to be the strongest. Meanwhile, France was still bitter and angry over a war they had lost to Germany forty years earlier. They wanted their land back and were looking for any excuse to take it. Then there was Russia, a massive but struggling empire that saw itself as the "big brother" to smaller Slavic nations like Serbia.

Adding to the tension was the race for "Empires." The powerful countries of Europe were like collectors, trying to grab as much land as possible in Africa and Asia. They wanted the gold, the rubber, and the glory that came with owning colonies. This made everyone suspicious of everyone else. If France took a piece of land in Africa, Germany felt they had to take two pieces just to keep up. It was a never-ending competition that made every border in Europe feel like a tripwire.

By the time 1914 rolled around, these countries weren't just talking about war; they were preparing for it with industrial precision. They had built thousands of miles of special railways just to move soldiers to the front lines. They had filled warehouses with millions of uniforms and rifles. Every general had a "plan" tucked away in a desk drawer, a step-by-step guide on how to invade their neighbors. The atmosphere was so thick with distrust that people started calling Europe a "powder keg." It was a room filled with gunpowder, and all the leaders were walking around holding lit matches, hoping they wouldn't be the one to drop theirs first.

3. Germany's Plan for a Two-Front War

Once the alliances were triggered and the "Great Rush" of soldiers began, the generals finally got to use the secret plans they had been perfecting for decades. The most famous and dangerous of these was Germany's Schlieffen Plan. The German leaders were terrified of a "two-front war," the idea of having to fight the massive Russian army in the East and the powerful French army in the West at the exact same time. It would be like a person trying to fight off two different attackers from opposite sides. To avoid this, they decided they had to knock France out of the war in just six weeks, before the slow-moving Russian "steamroller" could even get its boots on.

To make this work, the German army didn't march straight toward the heavily defended French border. Instead, they swung like a giant hammer through the neutral, peaceful country of Belgium. This move shocked the world. Belgium was a small nation that just wanted to be left alone, but the German plan required their flat roads and railways to get to Paris quickly. This "rape of Belgium," as the newspapers called it, changed the politics of the war instantly. It turned the conflict from a local dispute into a moral crusade. In London, the British government, which had been hesitating, now felt it had no choice but to enter the war to protect the "sanctity of small nations."

As the German "hammer" swung through Belgium and into Northern France, the maps in the war rooms of Paris and London were covered in red ink. The French army, dressed in outdated bright blue coats and red trousers, suffered staggering losses as they tried to stop the grey-clad German tide. By September 1914, the Germans were so close to Paris that the French government fled the city, and the sound of German heavy guns could be heard by civilians in the streets. It looked like the war might actually be over by Christmas, just as everyone had predicted, but with a German victory.

Then came the Battle of the Marne, a moment that changed everything. In a desperate, last-ditch effort, the French and British managed to find a gap in the German lines. They threw everything they had into the fight. The German advance was finally halted. Exhausted and running out of supplies, the German army retreated a few miles and did something no one expected: they dug in. They shoveled out long, shallow ditches to protect themselves from the deadly machine-gun fire. The Allies did the same. Within weeks, these simple ditches began to stretch and grow, forming a solid line of earthworks that would eventually run from the sea all the way to the mountains. The "War of Movement" was over, and the era of the trench had begun.

4. The Race to the Sea and the Birth of Trench Warfare

By the late autumn of 1914, the grand plans for a quick victory had vanished into the damp earth of Northern France. After the massive movements of the summer, both the Allied and German armies found themselves in a desperate situation. Neither side could move forward against the power of modern rifles and heavy guns, so they began a frantic series of maneuvers that historians call the "Race to the Sea." This was a high-stakes game of leapfrog on a continental scale. Each army tried to outflank the other, moving further and further north toward the coast of Belgium, hoping to find an open path to get behind the enemy lines. But at every turn, they found their path blocked by fresh troops and ready defenses.

When they finally reached the cold waters of the North Sea, there was nowhere left to run. The two massive forces were now locked in a line that stretched for hundreds of miles, from the sandy beaches of the coast all the way to the rugged mountains of the Swiss border. To stay alive in this open landscape, the soldiers did the only thing they could. They used their small shovels to dig shallow holes in the dirt. Over the following weeks, these holes were connected and deepened, turning into a permanent system of earthworks that would not move significantly for the next four years. This was the moment the world realized that the war had changed from a contest of speed and skill into a static, industrial struggle.

In the grand palaces and government buildings of London, Paris, and Berlin, the mood shifted from excitement to a heavy, calculated determination. The leaders had to accept that the "short war" they had promised was an illusion. This political realization led to a massive change in how nations were run. They began to look at the map not as a series of battlefields, but as a giant balance sheet of resources. They needed more coal, more steel, and more men than anyone had ever imagined. The home fronts were now just as important as the front lines, and the governments began to take total control over every aspect of civilian life to keep the war machine running.

The birth of this continuous line of defenses created a new and strange reality for the world. For the first time in history, two of the most powerful military forces ever assembled were staring at each other across a narrow strip of wasted land, unable to move. This stalemate forced the scientists and the generals to start looking for new, more terrifying ways to break the deadlock. The war was no longer about who had the best cavalry or the bravest chargers. It was now a cold, political battle of endurance. As the first winter of the war approached, the world was settling into a long, dark period of waiting, and the hope of a quick resolution was replaced by the grim reality of a struggle that would consume an entire generation.

5. The War Expands Beyond Europe

As the year 1915 opened, the war underwent a massive transformation that pulled the map of the conflict far beyond the borders of Europe. The most significant political shift occurred when the Ottoman Empire decided to join the side of Germany and Austria-Hungary. This decision was a strategic earthquake for the Allied powers. Suddenly, the British and French had to worry about their vast interests in the Middle East and the safety of the Suez Canal, which was the vital artery connecting Britain to its colonies in India and Australia. The war was no longer just a struggle over the fields of France; it had become a contest for the control of the ancient world and the vast oil resources that were beginning to drive modern industry.

The entry of the Ottoman Empire opened up several new and difficult fronts that required the Allies to divert hundreds of thousands of soldiers away from the Western Front. In the rugged, freezing mountains of the Caucasus, the Russians found themselves locked in a brutal struggle against the Ottoman forces. Meanwhile, in the hot, dusty plains of Mesopotamia and the deserts of the Sinai, British and colonial troops began a long campaign to protect the edges of their empire. These new theaters of war were incredibly challenging because they required different types of supplies, different clothing, and a different kind of endurance. The high-level planners in London and Paris were forced to juggle multiple crises at once, stretching their navies and their logistics to the breaking point.

This expansion of the war also had a profound effect on the global political atmosphere. It turned the conflict into a truly world-wide struggle between different types of empires. In the big cities of the Middle East, such as Cairo and Baghdad, the arrival of modern war brought a sense of upheaval and change that would eventually redraw the borders of the entire region. The British and French began to make secret promises to various local groups, hoping to stir up internal rebellions against the Ottomans. These political maneuvers were designed to win the war, but they were also planting the seeds for future conflicts that would last for a century.

By the middle of 1915, the "Bird's Eye View" of the war showed a world that was becoming increasingly entangled. The oceans were now just as dangerous as the land, as the German U-boats began to target merchant ships in an attempt to cut off the flow of supplies to the Allies. The conflict had become a giant, interconnected system where a battle in a desert could affect the food prices in a European city. The leaders of the major powers realized that they were no longer just fighting a war of armies, but a war of entire systems. Every corner of the globe was being pulled into the gravity of the conflict, and the hope of a local, contained resolution had completely vanished.

6. The Dominions and the Rise of the ANZAC Spirit

To understand the global scale of the war in 1915, you have to look at the unique and powerful bond that tied the people of Australia, New Zealand, and Canada to the British Isles. At the time, these countries were not just allies; they were Dominions of the British Empire, and most of their citizens still viewed Britain as the "mother country." Many families had only emigrated a generation or two earlier, and their sense of identity was deeply rooted in British culture, law, and history. When the King declared war in London, the people in Melbourne and Toronto felt as though their own homes were under threat. There was a widespread belief that if the heart of the empire fell, their own young nations would be left defenseless in a dangerous world.

The motivations for these young men to join the "Great Rush" were a complex mix of duty, adventure, and a desire to prove themselves on the world stage. In Australia and New Zealand, there was a feeling that their countries were still "children" in the eyes of the world, and that by fighting alongside the great powers, they would finally earn their place as mature, independent nations. For a young man in the Australian outback or the Canadian wilderness, the war was a chance to escape a quiet life of hard labor and see the legendary cities of the old world. They joined because they were told the empire was in danger, but they also joined because they wanted to be part of the greatest event in human history. They were often the tallest, healthiest, and most enthusiastic soldiers on the battlefield, and they brought a sense of rugged confidence that stood in stark contrast to the exhausted armies of Europe.

This loyalty was put to the ultimate test on the rugged, sun-scorched cliffs of the Gallipoli Peninsula. The high-level strategy behind the attack was to knock the Ottoman Empire out of the war by seizing the narrow Dardanelles strait, but the reality on the ground was a disaster of planning and geography. The Australian and New Zealand forces, famously known as the ANZACs, were landed on the wrong beaches and found themselves trapped under the guns of a determined Ottoman defense. As the months dragged on in the heat and the dust, the casualty lists grew longer and longer. Back in the big cities of the Dominions, the initial excitement turned into a heavy, national grief. This was the moment the relationship with Britain began to change. The people of the colonies began to realize that their lives were being spent by British generals who were often disconnected from the reality of the front lines.

The political legacy of 1915 was a shift in the very soul of these nations. While they remained loyal to the empire, the shared tragedy of Gallipoli for the ANZACs and the brutal battles in France for the Canadians created a new kind of national pride. They began to realize that they were not just "British people living overseas," but something new and distinct. They had their own way of speaking, their own way of leading, and their own incredible resilience. The war, which was supposed to protect the old empire, was actually planting the seeds of independence. By the time the survivors of 1915 were moved to other fronts, the world had learned that the "colonials" were among the most effective fighting forces on the planet, and the young nations they represented would never be the same again.

7. Verdun and the Somme: The Year of Attrition

As the calendar turned to 1916, the war rooms of Europe were filled with a new and chilling kind of mathematics. The generals and politicians realized that the defensive lines were so strong that a traditional victory might be impossible. Instead of looking for a way around the enemy, the German high command decided to lean into the horror. They developed a strategy of pure attrition, designed not to capture land, but to destroy the enemy's soul. They chose the ancient, symbolic fortress city of Verdun as their target. They knew the French people viewed Verdun as a sacred symbol of their national pride, and that the French army would be forced to defend it at any cost. The goal was to create a giant "meat grinder" where they could simply bleed the French army until it had no men left to fight.

For nearly ten months, the maps of northern France remained frozen while the landscape around Verdun was transformed into a moonscape of craters and ash. The scale of the artillery fire was unlike anything humanity had ever seen, with millions of shells being fired into a tiny area of land. The high-level politics of this battle were incredibly intense. The French government made it clear to their generals that losing Verdun was not an option, as it would cause the entire country's morale to collapse. This forced the French to rotate almost their entire army through that single, terrifying sector. The battle became a national obsession, a test of which society was more willing to sacrifice its children for a few square miles of ruined earth.

To take the pressure off the gasping French army at Verdun, the British launched their own massive offensive further north, near a river called the Somme. This was the moment the world saw the true cost of the "Total War" that had been building since 1914. The British government had spent over a year preparing for this attack, building up a massive force of millions of volunteers. In the planning rooms in London, there was a hope that this would be the "Big Push" that would finally end the war. But when the attack began in the summer of 1916, it resulted in the bloodiest day in the history of the British military. The high-level reports coming back to the capital were so shocking that they were initially kept secret from the public to prevent a total panic.

The year 1916 changed the very atmosphere of the war. The "Great Rush" and the excitement of the early days were replaced by a heavy, silent endurance. In the big cities like London, Paris, and Berlin, the casualty lists were no longer just names in a newspaper; they were a presence in every home and every street. The politics of the war shifted toward a grim, industrial determination. Governments realized that they were now in a race to see which nation would break from the inside first. The war was no longer about grand maneuvers or heroic charges; it was a cold, mathematical contest of industrial production and human sacrifice. As the winter of 1916 approached, the leaders of the world were looking at a map that had barely moved, even though millions of lives had been spent to change it.

8. Conscription, Industry, and the Strain of Total War

By the middle of 1916, the political landscape in London and Paris was undergoing a massive shift as the true scale of the industrial slaughter became impossible to hide. The British government, which had started the war with a small, professional army, was now forced to confront the reality that a conflict of this size could only be sustained by the entire nation. This led to one of the most significant political decisions of the war: the introduction of conscription. For the first time in history, the British state claimed the power to force its citizens into military service. This move sparked intense debate in the halls of Parliament and in the streets of the big cities, as it challenged the very idea of individual liberty that Britain claimed to be fighting for.

The mood in the capital cities was also changing as the "Total War" began to hit the kitchen tables of ordinary families. In London, the government created a new Ministry of Munitions to take control of the country's factories, turning them into giant workshops for the front. Women flooded into the workforce to replace the men who had been sent to the Somme, working long hours in dangerous conditions to fill the endless demand for shells and explosives. This was a social revolution happening in the middle of a global catastrophe. The sight of women in trousers and overalls, doing jobs that had previously been reserved for men, was a sign that the old world was disappearing forever. The politics of the home front were now just as vital as the tactics of the generals, as the leaders realized that they had to keep the workers fed, housed, and motivated to prevent a total collapse of society.

In Paris, the atmosphere was even more strained. Because the war was being fought on French soil, the nation felt like it was being slowly consumed by a giant, hungry beast. The government had to manage the millions of refugees who had fled the occupied north, while also trying to keep the economy from falling apart. The "Sacred Union" of political parties that had formed at the start of the war was beginning to show cracks, as the mounting losses at Verdun led to finger-pointing and accusations of incompetence. The French leaders were walking a tightrope, trying to maintain the public's will to fight while the country's young men were being fed into the "meat grinder" by the hundreds of thousands.

By the end of 1916, the "Bird's Eye View" of the Allied powers showed a world that was being pushed to its absolute limit. The high-level coordination between Britain and France was becoming more formal, with the leaders meeting regularly to try and sync their strategies. They were no longer just two countries fighting the same enemy; they were becoming a single, massive war machine. But beneath the surface of this unified front, there was a growing sense of exhaustion and a realization that the old ways of governing and fighting were no longer enough. The war was forcing a total reorganization of human society, and the people in the big cities were beginning to wonder if the world would ever return to the peace they had known before the summer of 1914.

9. Jutland, Blockade, and the War at Sea

While the armies were locked in the mud of the Western Front, a different kind of war was being fought on the cold, grey waters of the North Sea. For decades, Britain and Germany had been locked in a massive arms race to build the most powerful navy in the world. Britain, as an island nation, relied on the sea for its very survival, while Germany saw a powerful fleet as the key to becoming a true global superpower. By 1916, these two giant forces finally met in the largest naval clash in history, the Battle of Jutland. On a bird's-eye map of the ocean, it looked like a choreographed dance of steel, with hundreds of ships and thousands of heavy guns firing across miles of open water. Although the battle was a chaotic and bloody mess that didn't result in a clear, crushing victory for either side, its political consequences were enormous.

The result of the battle confirmed a terrifying reality for Germany. Despite their incredible technology and bravery, they could not break the British naval blockade. This blockade was a silent but deadly weapon that was slowly strangling the German Empire. By stopping almost all ships from reaching German ports, Britain was cutting off the flow of food, fertilizer, and raw materials that the country needed to survive. In the big cities like Berlin and Vienna, the "Total War" was no longer just about soldiers on a map; it was about the empty shelves in the grocery stores. The German people were being forced to eat "ersatz" or substitute foods made of sawdust and dried turnips, and the health of the civilian population was beginning to decline rapidly.

The politics of the blockade were incredibly controversial. The German leaders argued that it was a crime to starve millions of innocent civilians, and they used this as a justification to launch their own desperate counter-attack at sea. They decided to use their U-boats to sink any ship, even those from neutral countries like the United States, that tried to bring supplies to Britain. This "unrestricted submarine warfare" was a massive political gamble. The German high command knew it might bring the United States into the war, but they were so desperate to break the British blockade that they were willing to take the risk. They hoped they could starve Britain into surrender before the Americans could even get their boots on.

By the end of 1916, the war at sea had turned the entire Atlantic Ocean into a battlefield. The high-level strategy was no longer just about sinking warships; it was about the survival of entire populations. The British were racing to build more merchant ships and find new ways to hunt submarines, while the Germans were racing to sink them. This was a cold, mathematical struggle of logistics and endurance. The world was witnessing a new kind of conflict where the hunger of a child in Berlin was directly connected to the path of a torpedo in the middle of the ocean. The blockade was a slow-motion catastrophe that was hollowing out the Central Powers from the inside, forcing their leaders toward even more radical and dangerous decisions in the year to come.

10. The Russian Revolution and the Collapse of the Eastern Front

As 1917 began, the most significant political earthquake of the war occurred in the East, where the massive Russian Empire finally reached its breaking point. For three years, the Russian people had endured unimaginable hardship. Their armies had suffered millions of casualties, and the country's economy was in total ruins. In the grand palaces of Petrograd, the Tsar and his advisors were increasingly disconnected from the reality of the streets, where the lack of bread and fuel had turned frustration into a boiling rage. The high-level view of Russia showed a nation that was no longer a functioning empire but a hollow shell, held together only by habit and fear. In March, that shell finally shattered.

The revolution began not with a grand military plan, but with thousands of hungry women and workers flooding into the streets to demand food. When the soldiers were ordered to fire on the crowds, they refused and instead joined the protesters. Within days, the Tsar was forced to give up his throne, ending centuries of imperial rule. This was a moment of incredible political chaos that changed the entire map of the war. At first, the new government tried to keep Russia in the fight, but the spirit of the army was gone. The soldiers began to walk away from the trenches by the thousands, heading back to their villages to take part in the redistribution of land. The Eastern Front, which had tied down half of the German army for years, was effectively disappearing.

The German leaders saw this as a golden opportunity and made a daring political move to ensure Russia's total collapse. They helped a radical revolutionary named Vladimir Lenin return to Russia from his exile in Switzerland, hoping he would stir up even more trouble. The plan worked perfectly. By the end of the year, Lenin's group, the Bolsheviks, seized power and immediately asked for a ceasefire. The Treaty of Brest-Litovsk, which followed, was a total surrender. Russia gave up vast amounts of land, including what is now Ukraine, Poland, and the Baltic states. For Germany, this was the ultimate strategic victory. They could now take their entire Eastern army and move it to the West for one final, crushing blow against Britain and France.

The collapse of Russia sent a wave of terror through the Allied capitals. In London and Paris, the leaders realized that they were about to face the full, undivided weight of the German military machine. The politics of the war had shifted from a struggle of two fronts to a desperate race for survival on one. But the revolution in Russia also sent a different kind of shockwave across the world. It was the first time a major power had been completely destroyed by the internal pressure of the war. It served as a chilling warning to every other government that there was a limit to how much a population could sacrifice before they would turn on their own leaders. The map of the East was being redrawn in the fires of revolution, and the world was watching to see if the same flames would spread to the rest of Europe.

11. The United States Enters the War

While the Russian Empire was collapsing in the East, a different kind of power was rising in the West. For the first three years of the war, the United States had maintained a careful and profitable neutrality. The American President, Woodrow Wilson, had even won re-election on the slogan that he had kept the country out of the war. However, the high-level politics of the conflict were making it increasingly impossible for America to stay on the sidelines. The German decision to resume unrestricted submarine warfare meant that American ships were being sunk and American lives were being lost. To the people in Washington, this was no longer just a European quarrel; it was an attack on the freedom of the seas and the rights of all neutral nations.

The final straw for the American government was a secret message known as the Zimmerman Telegram. In a desperate attempt to keep the United States busy at home, Germany had sent a coded proposal to Mexico, offering to help them reclaim lost territories like Texas and Arizona if they would attack the Americans. When the British intelligence services intercepted this message and shared it with the United States, the political mood in the country shifted overnight. The idea that a foreign power was trying to stir up a war on the American border was a step too far. In April 1917, the United States formally declared war on Germany, a decision that fundamentally changed the math of the global conflict.

The entry of the United States was a massive psychological and industrial boost for the exhausted Allies. While the British and French were running out of money and men, the Americans had a nearly limitless supply of both. The high-level view of the Atlantic showed a bridge of steel beginning to form, as thousands of troop ships and supply vessels started to move toward the ports of France. This wasn't just about soldiers; it was about the vast industrial power of the American Midwest, the oil of Texas, and the financial strength of Wall Street. The war had become a race against time. The German leaders knew that they had to win the war with their newly freed Eastern armies before the full weight of the American "crusade" could land in Europe.

By the end of 1917, the world was locked in a frantic, high-stakes competition. In the war rooms of Berlin, the generals were working day and night on a plan for one final, massive offensive. They knew that every day that passed brought more Americans to the front lines. In London and Paris, the leaders were doing everything they could to hold on, praying that their tired armies could survive one last German storm. The politics of the war had reached a fever pitch, as the conflict was now a battle between the old empires of Europe and the rising democratic power of the New World. The stage was set for the final, decisive year of the war, where the fate of the century would be decided by which side could move their resources across the map the fastest.

12. Germany's Last Great Offensive in 1918

As the spring of 1918 arrived, the German high command launched the most ambitious and desperate military operation of the entire war. With the Russian front closed, they had managed to move nearly fifty divisions of veteran soldiers to the West, giving them a temporary numerical advantage that they hadn't enjoyed since the very first weeks of 1914. The German leader, General Ludendorff, knew that this was the final window of opportunity. The bird's-eye view of the Western Front showed a massive concentration of German power aimed directly at the junction where the British and French armies met. The goal was to punch a hole through the Allied lines, drive the British into the sea, and capture Paris before the American army was large enough to intervene.

The offensive, which began in March, was a tactical masterclass that initially shattered the long-standing stalemate. Using new methods of surprise and speed, the German forces broke through the trench lines that had been frozen for years. On the maps in the Allied headquarters, the red lines of the German advance began to move with terrifying speed, swallowing up territory that had been fought over for years in just a few days. The political atmosphere in London and Paris reached a point of near-panic. The threat was so great that the Allies finally agreed to do something they had resisted for years: they appointed a single supreme commander, the French General Foch, to coordinate all their forces. This was a major political turning point, as it allowed the Allies to finally act as a unified machine rather than a collection of separate national armies.

Despite their initial success, the German gamble began to fail because of the very "Total War" conditions they had helped create. As their soldiers advanced, they outran their supply lines and their heavy guns. The German troops, who had been living on starvation rations for years due to the naval blockade, were shocked to find Allied supply depots filled with white bread, chocolate, and fine wine. Many soldiers stopped to loot these supplies instead of continuing the attack, a sign that the discipline of the German army was beginning to erode under the weight of years of deprivation. Meanwhile, the first large groups of American soldiers were finally entering the lines, providing a fresh and enthusiastic wall of defense that the exhausted Germans simply couldn't break.

By the early summer of 1918, the German offensive had ground to a halt. They had gained a lot of ground on the map, but they had failed to achieve a decisive victory. More importantly, they had lost their best, most experienced soldiers in the process. The high-level view of the war now showed a German army that was overextended and physically spent, facing an Allied force that was growing stronger and more unified every day. The gamble had failed, and the initiative had passed permanently to the Allies. The German leaders realized with a sinking heart that they had thrown their last pair of dice and come up short. The war was no longer a contest that Germany could win; it was now a question of how long they could hold on before the inevitable collapse.

13. The Hundred Days Offensive and the Collapse of the Central Powers

By the summer of 1918, the momentum of the war had shifted in a way that felt like a physical weight lifting off the Allied powers. Sensing that the German army was finally at its breaking point, General Foch launched what would become known as the Hundred Days Offensive. This was not just one single battle, but a series of coordinated strikes across the entire Western Front that hit the German lines like a succession of hammer blows. On the high-level maps in the Allied war rooms, the static lines that had defined the conflict for four years were suddenly in constant, fluid motion. The Allies were now using their industrial superiority to its full effect, coordinating their infantry with hundreds of tanks and thousands of aircraft in a way that the exhausted German forces simply could not match.

As the German army was pushed back, the political foundations of the Central Powers began to crumble with stunning speed. In the big cities of Germany and Austria-Hungary, the years of starvation and loss had finally pushed the people beyond their limits. The high-level view of these empires showed a total internal collapse. In Austria-Hungary, the different ethnic groups (the Czechs, the Poles, the South Slavs) were all declaring their independence, effectively dismantling the empire from within. In Germany, the news of the military retreat triggered a wave of strikes and mutinies. The sailors in the German fleet, ordered to sail out for one last suicidal battle, refused to obey, sparking a revolution that spread to the factories and the streets of Berlin.

The politics of the war had reached their final, desperate stage. The German leaders realized that they were no longer fighting for victory, but to prevent a total social and political disintegration of their country. They began to send frantic messages to the American President, hoping to negotiate a peace based on his idealistic promises of a fair settlement. But the Allied leaders in London and Paris, who had sacrificed so much, were in no mood for a gentle peace. They demanded a total military surrender. The German Kaiser was forced to give up his throne and flee into exile, ending the German Empire that had been born in the fires of a previous war forty-seven years earlier.

By early November 1918, the maps showed the Central Powers in total retreat on every front. Bulgaria, the Ottoman Empire, and Austria-Hungary had all signed separate agreements to stop fighting, leaving Germany completely alone. The world was witnessing the simultaneous collapse of three of the most powerful empires in history. The high-level view was one of total upheaval, as the old order of kings and emperors was being swept away by a tide of military defeat and internal revolution. The war that had begun with such excitement and grand plans was ending in a chaotic, desperate scramble to stop the violence before it consumed what was left of European civilization.

14. The Armistice of 11 November 1918

The end of World War I did not arrive with a final, climactic battle, but with a quiet meeting in a railway carriage hidden deep within the cold, misty woods of the Forest of Compiègne. In the early morning hours of November 11, 1918, the representatives of a broken German Empire sat across from the Allied commanders to sign a document that would finally stop the slaughter. It is important to understand that what they signed was not a peace treaty, but an armistice. In the high-level language of international politics, a peace treaty is a permanent agreement that settles all the reasons why a war started in the first place. An armistice, however, is simply a formal agreement to stop the fighting; a massive, global "time-out." The German leaders were so terrified of a total revolution at home and a complete military collapse at the front that they needed the guns to stop immediately, even if it meant accepting humiliating terms.

The timing of this ceasefire was chosen with a sense of poetic drama that would be remembered for centuries. It was decided that the guns would fall silent at exactly eleven o'clock in the morning, the eleventh hour of the eleventh day of the eleventh month. This was a bird's-eye decision made by the top generals to ensure that the news had enough time to travel across the hundreds of miles of front lines. But for the men in the mud, those final six hours between the signing at 5:00 a.m. and the actual ceasefire at 11:00 a.m. were a surreal and tragic experience. Because the war was still technically "on," some commanders continued to order attacks, and artillery continued to fire right up until the final second. Thousands of men were killed or wounded on that final morning, their lives spent for ground that would be surrendered just a few hours later.

When the clock finally struck eleven, a strange and haunting silence swept across the world. For more than fifteen hundred days, the air in Europe had been filled with the constant, low-frequency rumble of heavy guns and the sharp crack of rifles. Suddenly, there was nothing but the sound of the wind and the occasional bird. On the maps in the war rooms, the red and blue lines that had pulsed and bled for years simply stopped moving. In the big cities like London, Paris, and New York, the news triggered a wave of celebration so intense it was described as a kind of madness. People danced in the streets, church bells rang out for hours, and total strangers embraced. But in the trenches, the mood was often one of numb disbelief. Many soldiers simply sat down where they were, unable to process that the world they had known, a world of constant death and fear, was actually over.

The "Long Shadow" of this moment would stretch far into the future. Because the war ended with an armistice rather than a total invasion of Germany, a dangerous political myth began to grow in the minds of the defeated. Many Germans felt that their army hadn't actually been beaten on the battlefield, but had been "stabbed in the back" by the politicians and revolutionaries at home. This sense of bitterness and unfinished business would eventually poison the politics of the next twenty years. Meanwhile, the four-year struggle had dismantled the very foundations of the old world. Four massive empires had vanished, and the maps were being redrawn by diplomats in Paris who were trying to build a new world out of the ruins of the old. World War I had ended, but it had left behind a globe that was fragile, grieving, and deeply unsettled. A world that was no longer at war, but was not yet truly at peace.

TWO

Making a Soldier

At the start of the war, the rush to join the military was driven by a mix of excitement, social pressure, and a deep sense of duty. Ordinary men who had spent their lives in quiet offices or on family farms suddenly found themselves standing in long lines to sign their names to the cause. This chapter looks at the reality of those early days, from the clever ways people were encouraged to volunteer to the first, often difficult steps of military training. It was a massive shift that turned millions of civilians into a new kind of army, changing their lives and their communities forever.

15. The Medical Exam That Decided Who Went to War

Before a man ever reached the trenches, he first had to pass through the army's medical board, a process far stricter and more methodical than most recruits expected. The exam wasn't just a quick glance. It was designed to filter out anyone who might break down under weeks of marching, digging, or carrying heavy loads. Men lined up half-naked in cold town halls or depots while doctors worked down the row like mechanics inspecting parts. Height and weight were recorded. Chests were measured during deep breaths to check lung capacity, because weak lungs meant poor endurance or higher risk of pneumonia. Hearts were listened to for murmurs or irregular rhythms, since long marches and battlefield stress could trigger collapse. Pulse rate was taken at rest to spot nervous or unhealthy candidates. Eyesight was tested against charts across the room, hearing checked with whispered commands, teeth inspected because untreated infections could disable a soldier in days. Even feet were closely examined. Flat feet were a common reason for rejection, not because they looked unusual, but because the army knew men with collapsed arches developed crippling pain and blisters after marching 10–20 miles (16–32 km) a day under load. A soldier who couldn't walk couldn't fight.

Recruits were graded into categories: fully fit for front-line duty, fit only for labor or support roles, or unfit entirely. Roughly a third failed their first exam. Knowing this, some desperate men tried to manipulate the results. They starved themselves to weigh less, sprinted in place to spike their heart rate, pretended not to hear instructions, memorized eye charts incorrectly, or complained loudly of back pain and "weak nerves." A few stuffed cotton in their ears or deliberately limped. Most attempts failed, but the fact that so many tried shows how terrifying the alternative seemed.

16. Training Camp: Turning Recruits Into Soldiers

Soldiers who passed their medicals were issued rough wool uniforms, heavy boots, rifles, and kit, then sent almost immediately to training camps, vast muddy cities of tents and wooden huts that could hold tens of thousands of recruits at once. Many had never been away from home before, yet within days they found themselves living shoulder to shoulder with strangers in crowded barracks that smelled of damp canvas, boot polish, and coal smoke. Life began before sunrise. Bugles (a small brass wind instrument used to signal commands in the army, its loud, clear notes carried across camps and battlefields to wake soldiers, start drills, announce meals, or sound alarms when shouted voices couldn't be heard) blasted around 5:00 a.m., dragging everyone from their blankets. Within minutes men stood outside for roll call, boots half-laced, breath fogging in the cold.

Days followed a relentless rhythm built around repetition and exhaustion. Route marches of 8–12 miles (13–19 km) were routine, and longer marches of 15–20 miles (24–32 km) were common to harden legs and feet. All of it was done carrying a full kit weighing 60–70 pounds (27–32 kilograms), sometimes more with extra ammunition. Shoulders blistered. Hips bruised. Straps cut into skin. Recruits quickly learned how physically heavy war really was.

Hours were spent drilling with rifles until every movement became automatic: load, aim, fire, cycle the bolt, fire again. Instructors demanded speed and rhythm, sometimes timing volleys with a stopwatch, pushing men to fire fifteen or more aimed rounds a minute until their shoulders throbbed and fingers cramped. Bayonet practice was even more brutal and personal. Recruits charged rows of straw-filled dummies while sergeants screamed inches from their faces to "thrust, twist, withdraw," teaching them not only how to stab but how to overcome hesitation. The goal was to remove fear and replace it with instinct. Some camps built mock trenches where men leapt in and out while lunging at targets, shouting battle cries to build aggression.

Grenade training took place in deep sandbagged pits where live explosives were handled under supervision. Recruits practiced pulling pins, counting seconds, and throwing fast before the fuse burned down. Mistakes could be fatal, and accidents occasionally injured or killed trainees, a grim reminder that even preparation was dangerous. Gas-mask drills were sudden and frightening. Without warning, whistles blew and instructors released tear gas or chlorine simulants. Men had only seconds to fit their masks. Anyone too slow felt their eyes burn and lungs seize, sometimes collapsing coughing in the dirt while others scrambled to help. The lesson was simple: hesitation meant death.

Entire afternoons were devoted to trench practice. Soldiers dug full-scale trenches by hand with entrenching tools, reinforced them with sandbags and duckboards, built fire steps and parapets, and learned drainage so the trench wouldn't flood. Then they moved through the maze under simulated fire, hauling ammunition, carrying stretchers, or rushing messages from one end to the other. Often, after hours of exhausting labor, they filled the trenches back in, only to dig them again the next day, repeating the cycle purely to build strength and muscle memory.

Lectures filled whatever time remained. Men were taught map reading, signaling with flags and lamps, first aid for bleeding wounds, how to recognize gas clouds, how to clean rifles properly, trench etiquette, disease prevention, and even how to write letters that wouldn't reveal military secrets. Veterans freshly returned from the front sometimes spoke bluntly about what to expect: mud, lice, fear, and the constant thunder of artillery.

Most instructors were professional sergeants or hardened veterans rotated back from the front, men already shaped by combat and impatient with mistakes. Discipline was harsh by design. The smallest error could mean punishment. Late for parade brought extra drill. Dirty boots meant confinement. Talking back cost pay. "Fatigue duty" meant endless chores like hauling water or digging pits after everyone else rested. "Pack punishment" forced a man to march for hours carrying full gear. Some were given Field Punishment No. 1, strapped upright to a post or wheel for hours under guard, exposed to wind and rain. It wasn't meant to injure, only to humiliate and deter. The message was clear: obedience had to be instant.

Training length depended on the war's urgency. Early in 1914–15, recruits might spend three to six months preparing. By 1917–18, as casualties soared, some men were rushed through in six to eight weeks or less, arriving at the front barely trained.

17. Specialist Roles and the Journey to the Front

After basic training, recruits were no longer treated as one mass of identical men. Officers began sorting them by ability, temperament, and simple physical build, quietly deciding who might survive longest in each role. Most became ordinary infantry riflemen, the backbone of every army, expected to march, dig, shoot, and hold the line under any condition. Better shots or calmer personalities were often chosen as scouts or snipers, men who worked in pairs, crawling ahead of the trenches to observe enemy movement or waiting motionless for hours behind a scope. Larger, stronger men were assigned to machine-gun crews, hauling heavy weapons and thousands of rounds of ammunition, or to stretcher-bearer teams who carried wounded soldiers through mud and shellfire, often unarmed and exposed. Engineers became sappers or tunnel diggers, some of the most claustrophobic and dangerous jobs in the war, burrowing underground for weeks to plant explosives beneath enemy trenches while listening for enemy miners doing the same. Others trained as signalers laying telephone wire, runners carrying messages across open ground, medics treating the wounded under fire, artillery gunners loading massive shells, drivers operating trucks and ambulances, or pigeon handlers caring for the birds that sometimes served as the only reliable communication during battle. Officers either came from separate academies or were promoted from the ranks after extra leadership courses, suddenly responsible for the lives of dozens of men they had once stood beside. A few volunteers stepped forward for especially dangerous specialties like flamethrower units or bombing squads, roles with frightening casualty rates but critical tasks in assaults.

Once assigned, recruits were grouped into companies and battalions that often stayed together for the rest of the war. Then came the journey to the front. Trains rattled them toward coastal ports, kit bags piled high, rifles stacked in corners. Ships carried them across the Channel in crowded holds smelling of oil and seasickness. Bands sometimes played and civilians waved flags, cheering as if sending men to an adventure rather than a slaughter. Many soldiers still imagined glory at this stage, postcards and photographs tucked into their pockets.

Yet even after reaching France or Belgium, they did not go straight into battle. New arrivals usually spent days or weeks in reserve or base camps behind the lines, drilling again, unloading supplies, filling sandbags, and learning practical trench habits from veterans who spoke quietly and without drama about what to expect: how to keep your head down, how to sleep through shellfire, how to spot gas, how to survive. It was called "seasoning," a final adjustment period meant to toughen nerves before exposure to the front.

18. The Heavy Load Every Soldier Carried

Before a soldier ever fired a shot, he first had to lift the war onto his back. In "full marching order," a British or Commonwealth infantryman carried far more than just a rifle. Slung over one shoulder was his rifle and bayonet, along with 120–150 rounds, roughly 8–10 pounds (3–4 kilograms) of bullets of ammunition packed into bandoliers and pouches that thumped against his chest as he walked. Around his neck hung a water bottle and a small canvas bag holding his gas mask, a constant reminder that poison gas could come without warning. Strapped to his belt was an entrenching tool, a short-handled shovel used to dig trenches, graves, or cover in seconds. Tied to his pack sat a mess tin, a battered metal container that served as his entire kitchen, used to boil tea, heat stew, or eat whatever rations he could get.

On his back he carried spare socks and underwear, soap, a razor, toothbrush, sewing kit, knife, letters from home, photographs, cigarettes or tobacco, matches, and any small comforts that made life feel human. Rolled tightly on top was his greatcoat, a thick wool overcoat that doubled as winter jacket, blanket, pillow, and sometimes even a mattress. Dry, it was heavy; soaked with rain and mud, it could feel like carrying another person. Add one or two days of hard rations (biscuits, tinned meat, jam, tea, sugar), and the weight kept climbing. Before attacks, extra gear piled on: several Mills bombs, the iron "pineapple" grenades that weighed nearly 1.5 pounds (0.7 kilograms) each, often two to four as standard and sometimes six or more stuffed into pockets, plus extra ammunition or tools.

Altogether, the load typically reached 60–70 pounds (27–32 kilograms), and sometimes more than 80 pounds (36+ kilograms), roughly the weight of a large suitcase or a small child. Soldiers didn't wear it every minute in the trenches, but whenever rotating between lines, marching to the front, or preparing for battle, everything went on at once. Men climbed ladders out of trenches, crawled under wire, and slogged through knee-deep mud with that weight dragging at their shoulders. Straps rubbed skin raw, backs ached constantly, and boots sank deep into the ground with every step. By the time they reached the fight, many were already exhausted. Some quietly discarded gear along the way just to move faster. The burden also explained why many experimental ideas, like steel body armor or wheeled shields, failed immediately: most soldiers were already carrying as much as the human body could endure.

19. Fighting for Pennies at the Front

Many soldiers carried sixty or seventy pounds of gear, slept in mud, and faced artillery every day, yet were paid barely more than pocket change. A regular British private earned just 1 shilling a day. Adjusted for modern value, that equals roughly $8–$10 USD per day in today's money, about the price of a sandwich and coffee. A full week at the front brought in only $55–$65, and a month's pay barely reached $250. From that small amount, deductions were sometimes taken for damaged equipment or small comforts, leaving even less. Corporals and sergeants earned only slightly more, while officers paid for many of their own uniforms and expenses out of pocket. German and French infantry wages were similarly tiny. Many soldiers joked that the cigarettes or chocolate in a parcel from home were worth more than their official pay. In reality, money mattered little at the front, there was almost nothing to spend it on, but the numbers reveal something striking. Millions of young men risked their lives daily for what would now amount to minimum wage.

20. From Bright Uniforms to Mud-Colored War

Before World War I, soldiers often marched into battle in bright colors meant to impress rather than hide, but the trenches quickly erased any trace of parade-ground style. By 1915, nearly every army had switched to dull, muddy tones designed to blend into earth and smoke. British and Commonwealth troops wore khaki wool tunics and trousers, the French abandoned their famous blue coats and red trousers for "horizon blue," and German soldiers adopted field gray uniforms that disappeared easily against mud and concrete. From a distance, and especially after a few days in the trenches, everyone looked roughly the same: brown, grey, and filthy. Rain, clay, and smoke quickly coated uniforms until color barely mattered.

The clothing itself was heavy and uncomfortable. Thick wool was chosen for warmth and durability, but when soaked by rain it absorbed water like a sponge, doubling in weight and drying slowly in the cold. Tunics scratched, seams rubbed skin raw, and lice thrived in the fabric. Around their lower legs, many British troops wrapped long cloth strips called puttees to support their ankles and keep mud out of their boots, though these often trapped moisture instead. Boots were stiff leather with iron hobnails hammered into the soles for grip, tough but slippery on duckboards and loud on hard ground. Steel helmets gradually replaced soft caps after the first year of the war, protecting men from falling shrapnel and debris rather than direct bullets. Each army developed its own shape, the shallow British Brodie, the deep German Stahlhelm, the French Adrian, giving the front lines a forest of strange metal silhouettes bobbing above the trenches.

Despite these differences, identity blurred quickly. In fog, smoke, or darkness, uniforms lost all meaning and soldiers fired at movement rather than color. A man crawling through mud at night looked like any other shadow. By the end of a week in the trenches, coats were torn, knees patched, and everything stained the same dull brown. The carefully issued uniform became something more primitive: just another layer between a soldier and the cold, the lice, and the war.

21. Killed by Their Own Side

Not every shell that killed a soldier came from the enemy. In the chaos of trench warfare, thousands of men were wounded or killed by their own side, a grim reality that soldiers bluntly called "short rounds" or simply "our own guns," because the modern phrase "friendly fire" didn't yet exist. Artillery batteries often fired from miles away using rough maps and smoke-obscured targets, and even small errors in range could drop shells directly onto friendly trenches. During attacks, creeping barrages were meant to land just ahead of advancing infantry and slowly move forward, but if the timing was wrong or the guns fired too short, explosions tore into the very men they were supposed to protect. At night or in fog, units sometimes fired on their own patrols, mistaking movement for the enemy. Signal flares were misread, coordinates confused, and messages lost when runners were killed. Gas attacks occasionally drifted back with the wind, choking the troops who released it. Even aircraft bombed the wrong lines.

Exact numbers are impossible to calculate, but historians estimate that friendly fire accounted for a significant percentage of battlefield casualties, in some battles reaching 5–10 percent or more. Soldiers grew grimly accustomed to it. Diaries mention the bitter irony of surviving enemy fire only to be shelled by their own artillery minutes later.

22. The Rifles That Kept Soldiers Alive

By the time a soldier climbed onto the fire step and raised his rifle over the parapet, the weapon in his hands might determine whether he lived through the next ten seconds or not. Although all sides carried bolt-action rifles that looked similar from a distance, their performance varied dramatically. British troops used the Short Magazine Lee–Enfield (SMLE), a rugged .303 rifle with a large 10-round magazine and an unusually smooth, fast bolt. It could be reloaded with two 5-round stripper clips in just a few seconds, and trained infantry were expected to fire 15–25 aimed shots per minute. Some could fire even faster. During training, British soldiers practiced the famous "Mad Minute," trying to hit a target fifteen times at 300 yards (275 meters) in sixty seconds. Skilled marksmen sometimes doubled that, firing so rapidly that Germans occasionally mistook concentrated rifle fire for machine guns.

German soldiers carried the Mauser Gewehr 98, one of the strongest and most accurate rifles of the war. It fired a powerful 7.92 mm cartridge and had a long barrel that made it excellent at distance shooting. But it held only 5 rounds, and the longer, stiffer bolt meant reloads were slightly slower. A typical German infantryman managed around 10–15 aimed shots per minute. The rifle was famously reliable and precise, which made it a favorite with snipers, but in the chaos of close trench fighting, its smaller magazine could feel limiting.

French troops began the war with the outdated Lebel 1886, which loaded cartridges one by one into a tube magazine under the barrel. Topping it off could take twenty or thirty seconds, an eternity under fire. Later they replaced it with the Berthier rifle, which used 3- or 5-round clips and loaded much faster, though still not as quickly as the Lee–Enfield. Across the front, soldiers quickly learned that rate of fire mattered just as much as accuracy when an enemy charge appeared through the smoke.

A rifle was only part of the load. Ammunition came in bandoliers and pouches, usually 120–150 rounds carried as standard issue, sometimes more before attacks. Bayonets fixed to the muzzle turned the gun into a spear for close quarters. Mud, rain, and trench grit constantly jammed actions, so men cleaned and oiled their rifles obsessively, sometimes sleeping with them tucked under their coats to keep rust away. A jam at the wrong moment could mean death.

In practice, these differences shaped the battlefield. British units could unleash rapid, sustained volleys that pinned attackers down. German rifles excelled at deliberate, accurate fire from cover. French troops compensated with grenades and aggressive tactics to make up for slower reloads. To the soldiers themselves, the debate was simple and personal. The best rifle wasn't the most elegant or powerful. It was the one that could be reloaded fastest, fired the most times, and still worked when soaked in mud at dawn, because in the trenches, a few extra rounds and a few saved seconds could be the thin line between firing back or never firing again.

23. The Specialist Weapons That Controlled the Battlefield

Not every soldier in the trench fought as a simple rifleman. Some belonged to specialist teams whose weapons could shape entire battles. The most feared were machine-gun crews. Instead of a light rifle, they hauled heavy, water-cooled guns like the British Vickers, the German MG08, or the French Hotchkiss, mounted on sturdy tripods and fed by long fabric belts of ammunition. A single gun weighed around 30–40 pounds (14–18 kilograms), and with tripod, spare barrels, water cans, tools, and thousands of rounds, a full team's load could exceed 100 pounds (45 kilograms). It usually took four to six men to operate: one firing, one feeding the belt, one spotting targets, and others carrying ammunition and cooling water. Once set up, the gun could fire 450–600 rounds per minute, fast enough to sweep entire fields in seconds. The goal wasn't precision shooting but area denial, creating invisible walls of bullets that could cut down charging infantry or pin enemies in place. During major attacks, machine guns often accounted for more casualties than rifles or artillery, turning open ground into killing zones.

Alongside them were bombing squads, the close-quarters fighters of the trench system. Armed not just with rifles but with satchels of hand grenades, extra ammunition, and sometimes clubs or trench knives, these men specialized in clearing enemy trenches one corner at a time. A typical British "bomber" might carry 10–20 Mills bombs (each about 1.5 pounds / 0.7 kilograms), tucked into pockets or sandbags slung over the shoulder. In raids, they moved ahead of riflemen, lobbing grenades around bends or into dugouts before rushing forward through smoke and debris. Fighting was often at arm's length, chaotic and brutal. It was considered one of the most dangerous jobs in the war, requiring speed, strength, and nerves of steel. Casualties were high, but these squads were essential for breaking through trench lines where rifles alone couldn't reach.

Together, machine-gun teams and bombers formed the heavy muscle of the infantry, one dominating the battlefield at long range with relentless streams of fire, the other smashing through tight trench corners with explosions and shock. While the average soldier carried one rifle, these specialists carried the weapons that truly controlled the ground.

24. The Fragile Wires That Held the Front Together

Despite the scale of artillery and machine guns, most communication on the Western Front depended on something surprisingly fragile: thin copper telephone wires stretched across the ground. Radios were bulky, unreliable, and rarely used at the front, so armies relied on field telephones connected by miles of cable linking trenches, headquarters, artillery batteries, and observation posts. Signalers spent hours unspooling wire reels through mud, shell holes, and barbed wire, sometimes laying lines at night while bullets snapped overhead.

The problem was that these lines broke constantly. Shellfire shredded them. Tanks crushed them. Passing soldiers tripped over them. Rain and mud shorted them out. A single bombardment could cut every connection in minutes, leaving entire sectors suddenly silent. When that happened, small teams nicknamed "wire soldiers" or "linesmen" crawled out with repair kits, following the cable by hand across no man's land to find the break. They often worked under active fire, kneeling in mud to twist the ends back together while artillery continued to fall around them. It was one of the most dangerous jobs in the trenches, because the wire itself led straight toward command posts that the enemy was already targeting.

THREE

Life in the Trenches

For the millions of men who served on the Western Front, the war was not defined by grand movements on a map, but by the narrow, muddy world of the trenches. These deep ditches in the earth became the permanent home for an entire generation of soldiers, stretching for hundreds of miles across the landscape of Europe. Life in this underground world was a constant struggle against the environment as much as the enemy. This chapter looks at the daily reality of that existence, from the constant battle with mud and water to the strange and difficult conditions that soldiers had to endure just to survive from one day to the next.

25. The Dawn and Dusk Ritual of the Trenches

Trench life followed a strict daily rhythm built around the most dangerous hours of the day: dawn and dusk, when visibility was poor and surprise attacks were easiest. In the half-light of early morning or fading sunset, shadows were long, fog hung low, and it was difficult to tell whether movement in no man's land was a patrol or an advancing assault. Commanders knew many attacks began at these moments, so twice a day the entire line went on full alert for "stand-to." Often around 4:30 or 5:00 a.m. in summer and closer to 7:00 a.m. in winter, every soldier climbed onto the trench's "fire step," a narrow ledge built into the wall that allowed them to stand high enough to shoot over the parapet (the raised wall of packed earth and sandbags at the front of the trench that protected soldiers from enemy fire). Rifles were loaded, bayonets fixed, and men waited silently, scanning the mist for shapes or sounds. The same tense ritual repeated at sunset. Between those alerts, the day filled with repairs, cleaning weapons, hauling supplies, and "sentry duty," where individuals took turns standing watch for an hour or two at a time, peering over the trench while everyone else tried to rest. The routine created a strange contrast: hours of boredom and chores interrupted predictably by two daily moments when everyone expected the war to explode without warning.

26. When Weather Became a Weapon

Weather often proved as dangerous as the enemy, and mud became one of the most constant enemies of trench life. Heavy rain could fall for days without stopping, turning carefully dug trenches into brown canals of standing water. Walls collapsed, duckboards floated loose, and men sometimes sank calf-deep or even waist-deep when they stepped off the wooden walkways. Boots were sucked off by the mud, rifles clogged with grit, and supplies delayed because wagons and horses simply could not move forward. In winter, the same ground froze solid, coating sandbags and uniforms with frost and leaving fingers too numb to pull triggers easily. In summer, the mud baked into cracked earth that smelled of rot and decay. Soldiers often joked that they weren't fighting for land so much as drowning in it. Many veterans later said the mud, not the bullets, was what they remembered most.

27. The Disease That Rottted Soldiers' Feet

Constant moisture created one of the most feared non-combat injuries of the war: trench foot. Soldiers' boots were rarely dry, and many men stood for hours in cold water or mud that seeped through seams and soaked their socks day after day. Without circulation or warmth, feet first turned pale and numb, then swollen and blotchy, the skin softening and peeling like wet paper. Blisters formed, infections set in, and a sour, rotten smell often followed. In severe cases the flesh blackened and died, sometimes leading to gangrene and amputation. Commanders quickly learned that entire units could be crippled without a single shot fired, so soldiers were ordered to change socks frequently, rub their feet with whale oil (a thick waterproof grease made by boiling whale fat, cheap and widely available at the time), and stand on duckboards whenever possible to keep out of standing water. Inspections became routine, with officers checking feet the same way they checked rifles. Even so, thousands were evacuated each year with damaged feet, proof that the mud itself could be as dangerous as the enemy.

28. Sanitation, Smell, and Disease in the Trenches

Sanitation was another constant struggle, and the smell of the trenches became something many veterans said they could never forget. Toilets were usually nothing more than shallow slit trenches dug a short distance behind the line, sometimes screened with sandbags or scraps of canvas for privacy. Men balanced on wooden planks or simply crouched over the pit, which quickly filled and had to be covered with earth and replaced. In crowded sectors or during heavy fighting, proper facilities broke down entirely, forcing soldiers to use buckets or improvised containers that had to be emptied by hand. Flies gathered in thick swarms, spreading germs between waste, food, and living spaces. When the wind shifted, the odor of mud, smoke, sweat, rotting sandbags, and human waste drifted straight through the trenches, clinging to clothes and blankets. Combined with poor water and cramped conditions, these unsanitary setups helped spread diarrhea, dysentery, and stomach illnesses almost as reliably as enemy fire.

29. Rations in the Trenches

Food was issued with military precision and rarely changed. A typical British daily ration included about 1 pound (450 grams) of bread or hard biscuits, 12–16 ounces (340–450 grams) of meat when available, plus small portions of cheese or jam and, above all, tea. Fresh food almost never reached the front, so meals usually meant tinned stew, salted beef, or thick soup heated over tiny trench stoves. Sugar was rationed carefully and treated like treasure, often saved for tea rather than eaten outright. Anything from home (chocolate, butter, sausage, or a loaf of real soft bread) felt like a luxury beyond imagination. Soldiers quickly learned to eat whenever food appeared, because the next delivery might be delayed for days by mud, broken supply lines, or shellfire cutting the roads behind them.

30. The Drink That Held British Troops Together

Tea became almost sacred to British troops, less a simple drink than a daily ritual that structured life in the trenches. Whenever there was a pause in shelling, men immediately set about boiling water in dented metal mess tins or blackened kettles balanced over tiny fires made from scraps of wood, coal, or solid fuel tablets. The brew was strong black tea leaves carried in ration sacks, usually mixed with condensed milk and as much sugar as a soldier could spare. A mug marked the rhythm of the day: one at dawn after "stand-to," another after long marches or repair work, another before night sentry duty. In the cold, wet trenches, that hot sweetness cut through mud, smoke, and exhaustion better than any medicine.

The habit became so universal that it occasionally created problems. Small cooking fires sent thin columns of smoke into the air, and enemy observers sometimes spotted these "tea smokes" rising from the lines, revealing occupied positions. Officers repeatedly ordered men not to light fires during daylight, but the rules were widely ignored. Soldiers joked that they would sooner miss a meal than miss their tea. Commanders eventually realized that banning it hurt morale more than it helped security, so instead they adapted, issuing safer trench stoves, braziers (a small metal container filled with coals used as a portable stove or heater), and insulated water cans so hot water could be prepared more discreetly.

Over time, tea became shorthand for comfort itself. Men shared mugs during quiet moments, traded sugar for favors, and used tea breaks as excuses to talk, complain, or simply feel human again. Veterans later wrote that a single hot drink could steady nerves after bombardment better than any speech from an officer. The dependence grew so ingrained that British military planners eventually designed vehicles with built-in boiling equipment so crews could heat water without leaving cover.

31. The Postal System That Reached the Front

Letters and parcels from home became lifelines that connected the trenches to normal life, and armies built surprisingly efficient postal systems to keep them moving. At the height of the war, the scale was staggering, with an estimated 12 million letters delivered to the Western Front every single week, turning the military post into one of the largest logistical operations of the conflict. Soldiers could usually send letters for free, marking them 'On Active Service,' while the government covered the postage. They were handed to unit runners who carried sacks of mail back through the lines to field post offices, where trains and ships carried them across the Channel. A note written in France might reach England in as little as two or three days during quiet periods, though heavy fighting could stretch delivery to weeks. Parcels followed more slowly and unpredictably. Families packed tins of biscuits, chocolate, tea, tobacco, socks, scarves, or even small cakes, hoping the contents survived the journey. Some boxes arrived crushed, moldy, or raided along the way, but when one made it through intact, it felt like a holiday. Men often shared the contents with their whole dugout, turning a single bar of chocolate or a pair of dry socks into an event everyone remembered. In a world of mud and rations, a letter in familiar handwriting or a package smelling faintly of home could lift morale more than any order or speech.

32. When Private Messages Became Military Secrets

Every letter leaving the trenches passed through human censors before it ever reached home, and that meant officers physically reading thousands of private messages by hand. At the company or battalion level, junior officers or sergeants sat at rough tables with piles of envelopes, opening each one and scanning for anything that revealed locations, unit names, casualties, or upcoming plans. If a soldier wrote "We're near Ypres" or "we attack tomorrow," the censor simply struck the line through with ink, cut it out with scissors, or blacked it over entirely before stamping the page "Passed by Censor." The work was slow and tedious, sometimes hundreds of letters in a single evening, and many officers disliked the job, calling it punishment duty. Yet commanders insisted on it, knowing that one careless sentence intercepted by the enemy could expose an entire sector of the front. As a result, most letters home arrived with awkward gaps or missing lines, quiet reminders that even personal words were part of the war.

33. Smoking, Drinking, and Surviving the War

Tobacco and alcohol became two of the most common comforts in the trenches, woven so deeply into daily life that many soldiers later said the war had turned them into lifelong smokers and drinkers. Cigarettes were everywhere. Armies issued them in rations, families packed them into parcels, and they quickly became a form of currency traded for food, favors, or information. By some estimates, more than three-quarters of British troops smoked regularly, and countless young men who had never touched tobacco before the war picked up the habit simply to calm their nerves or pass the endless hours of waiting. A shared smoke meant conversation, warmth, and a brief moment of normalcy. Alcohol was treated more cautiously but still common. British soldiers sometimes received small rum rations before cold nights or attacks, French troops were often issued wine, and beer or spirits appeared more freely in rest areas behind the lines. Drinking dulled fear and helped men sleep, though drunkenness near the front was punished strictly. Stories later exaggerated the idea of soldiers seeking stronger highs, but in reality most relied on nothing more exotic than nicotine, strong tea, and occasional rum.

34. Games and Small Escapes in the Trenches

Long stretches of waiting filled far more hours than fighting, and soldiers quickly invented small rituals and games to keep boredom from becoming unbearable. Card games like poker, pontoon (blackjack), and brag were played on overturned ammunition crates or flattened ration boxes, with cigarettes, chocolate, or extra sugar used as makeshift currency instead of money. Dice rattled in mess tins, coins were flipped, and arguments over rules broke up the monotony of damp afternoons. In reserve areas behind the lines, men kicked footballs through muddy fields, staged impromptu boxing matches, or tested their strength in wrestling contests, cheering loudly for anyone who could momentarily forget the war.

Others filled the quiet hours more gently. Some carved chess sets or dominoes from scrap wood and shell crates, whittled pipes, or etched souvenirs from spent bullets. Newspapers and dog-eared novels were passed from hand to hand until they fell apart, read so many times that men memorized entire articles. As night fell, dugouts often came alive with sound: harmonicas, mouth organs, fiddles, or battered guitars playing popular tunes while voices joined in softly. For a few minutes, laughter and music replaced artillery and orders.

35. The Creatures That Thrived in the War

The trenches weren't just filled with soldiers. They were alive with rats, and not the small city kind people imagined back home, but fat, bold, well-fed creatures that grew shockingly large on a constant diet of spilled rations and unburied bodies. Corpses often lay half-buried in the mud for days or weeks between the lines, and rats fed freely, growing sleek and heavy. Many soldiers swore some were "the size of cats," with thick bodies, long tails, and shining eyes that reflected lantern light at night. Men woke to the feeling of something crawling across their chest or face, only to find a rat scrambling away. Others reported the animals gnawing boots, uniforms, bread, and even the fingers of sleeping or dead soldiers.

Their numbers exploded because trench conditions were perfect for breeding. A single female rat can produce 6–10 litters a year, each with 6–12 pups, meaning one pair can theoretically multiply into hundreds within months. With thousands of tons of food waste, human refuse, and bodies scattered along a front that stretched for miles, populations soared into the millions. Some historians estimate that the Western Front may have hosted tens of millions of rats at peak periods. In crowded sectors, soldiers joked that there were more rats than men. Dugouts sometimes seemed to move with them at night, scratching inside walls and burrowing beneath floors.

Attempts to control them rarely worked. Men shot them for sport, clubbed them with shovels, set traps, or kept cats and terriers specifically to hunt them. Entire "rat hunts" were organized during quiet hours, yet by the next night they were back just as thick as before. Beyond the disgust, rats spread disease, contaminated food, and destroyed supplies, chewing through sacks and even electrical or telephone wires.

36. The Creatures That Comforted Soldiers

Animals quietly became part of trench life, and many units adopted unofficial "pets" that offered comfort in a place otherwise stripped of normal affection. Stray dogs wandered into the lines and were quickly fed scraps, given names, and treated like members of the platoon, sleeping beside sentries or following marching columns from trench to trench. Cats were especially valued for hunting the rats that swarmed dugouts and chewed through food and uniforms at night, and soldiers joked that a good trench cat was worth more than an extra ration. Pigeons were treated with near reverence, carefully protected because they often carried the only reliable messages during heavy fighting. One American pigeon, Cher Ami, became famous after being shot through the chest and losing a leg yet still delivering a message that saved nearly two hundred trapped soldiers, earning a medal for bravery. In quieter sectors, men even kept goats, chickens, or ducks taken from nearby farms for eggs, milk, or simply companionship. Units painted mascots on trench signs and dugout doors (bulldogs, goats, horses, or cartoon rats) and posed proudly for photographs beside their animals. In a landscape dominated by mud, wire, and artillery, caring for something small and alive gave soldiers a rare reminder of home, responsibility, and tenderness.

37. When War Messages Flew on Wings

Messenger pigeons became so important to the war that armies treated them almost like another branch of the signal corps. By some estimates, more than 500,000 pigeons were used across the Western Front, housed in mobile lofts, trucks, and wooden coops behind the lines. When telephone wires were cut by shellfire and runners were shot crossing open ground, these birds often became the fastest and most reliable way to send coordinates, artillery requests, or pleas for rescue. Small message slips were tucked into metal capsules attached to their legs, and the pigeons, trained to return instinctively to their home lofts, flew low and fast over trenches and smoke. Their value quickly made them targets. German units reportedly trained hawks and falcons to intercept carrier pigeons midair, turning parts of the sky into strange, silent dogfights between birds. Soldiers sometimes watched helplessly as a message disappeared in a sudden burst of feathers. In a war dominated by machines and artillery, it was often these fragile animals, beating their wings over no man's land, that carried the information that kept entire units alive.

38. A Simple Trick to Detect Deadly Gas

Animals were sometimes used in even stranger ways when it came to surviving chemical warfare. After poison gas attacks, soldiers had to clean and refill their gas masks carefully, but contaminated water could leave invisible traces of chlorine or other toxins that were still deadly to breathe. In some sectors, units kept small goldfish in jars or tins as crude living detectors. Before using a batch of water to wash masks or equipment, they would drop a fish inside and wait. If the fish quickly died or floated to the surface, the water was considered unsafe. If it survived, the water was likely clean enough to use. It was a simple, improvised test that required no instruments or chemicals, just a fragile creature reacting faster than any human could.

39. How War Dogs Delivered Critical Orders

Some trench dogs were more than mascots, they were trained messengers that carried information across the battlefield faster and more safely than most human runners. Signal units selected intelligent, athletic breeds like collies, sheepdogs, or Airedales and trained them to shuttle between two specific handlers rather than roam freely. Each dog bonded with both men, learning their scents and locations, then practiced running back and forth repeatedly for food rewards until the route became instinct. When needed, a small metal tube or leather pouch containing written messages was clipped to the dog's collar, and the animal was released. Staying low to the ground and moving quickly through shell holes, mud, and broken wire, the dogs were far less visible targets than soldiers standing upright. Unlike pigeons, they could run both directions, carrying replies back just as easily. In battles where telephone wires were constantly cut and human runners were often shot, these quiet four-legged couriers sometimes proved the most reliable link between isolated units.

40. War Dogs Searching for Injured Soldiers

Some trench dogs served an even more lifesaving role as so-called "casualty dogs," trained not just to carry messages but to help the wounded. Instead of message tubes, these dogs wore small saddlebags or pouches filled with bandages, water, and basic medical supplies. During or after attacks, they were sent out across shell holes and broken wire to search for injured soldiers lying between the lines. Moving low to the ground and harder to spot than human stretcher-bearers, the dogs could reach places too dangerous for medics under fire. A wounded man might suddenly hear panting in the mud beside him and find a dog carrying the first bandage or drink he'd had in hours. Some animals were trained to stay with the injured and bark or return to guide stretcher teams back to their location.

41. Capturing Small Moments in the Trenches

Cameras were surprisingly rare in the trenches, and most of the photographs people see today were taken not by ordinary soldiers but by official military photographers or newspaper correspondents. Armies tightly controlled photography, fearing that images of defenses, casualties, or troop locations could help the enemy or damage morale at home. Large, fragile cameras were expensive and awkward to carry, and many units banned them near the front lines altogether. A few officers or wealthier soldiers owned small pocket cameras, sometimes smuggling them into the trenches despite regulations, but getting caught could mean confiscation. As a result, most personal photos were taken during quieter moments behind the lines: groups of friends posing beside dugouts, men grinning with trench pets, homemade signs nailed to walls, or muddy "souvenirs" held up like trophies. Combat itself was rarely captured. Instead, the surviving pictures show laughter, boredom, and ordinary faces, small frozen moments of normal life in the middle of an extraordinary war.

42. The Constant Itch of Trench Life

Hygiene in the trenches was a constant losing battle, and lice quickly became one of the most universal enemies soldiers faced. The insects thrived in damp uniforms, crowded dugouts, and weeks without proper washing, hiding in seams and multiplying faster than men could remove them. Soldiers called them "chats," and the daily ritual of picking them out of clothing became known simply as "chatting." Men sat in small groups during quiet moments, turning their shirts inside out and crushing lice between their thumbnails with soft popping sounds, sometimes joking about it like a routine chore. Baths were rare near the front, often limited to a quick splash from a helmet or a shared bucket of cold water, and uniforms might not be properly cleaned for weeks. When units rotated to rest areas, clothes were sometimes passed through improvised steam disinfectors or "delousing stations," but reinfestation happened almost immediately back in the trenches. The itching could be relentless, keeping men awake at night and leaving red welts across their bodies. Many veterans later joked that the lice were the only army that truly occupied the trenches full time.

43. Broken Sleep in a World of Shellfire

Sleep in the trenches was shallow, fragmented, and rarely lasted more than a few hours at a time. Most units rotated through a rough cycle to prevent complete exhaustion: about four to eight days in the front line, several days in support trenches just behind it, and then a week or more in reserve or rest areas before returning forward again. Even so, "rest" was relative. In the front line, men usually slept fully dressed in cramped dugouts or against trench walls, boots on, rifles within arm's reach, ready to move instantly. Dawn and dusk "stand-to" alerts meant everyone was awake before sunrise and again at sunset, while sentry duty required soldiers to take turns watching the parapet in one or two hour shifts through the night. Shellfire, rats, lice, and cold water dripping from trench roofs regularly interrupted whatever sleep they managed. A good night might mean four broken hours; a bad one meant none at all. Only when rotated far to the rear could men finally stretch out on real beds or barn floors and sleep deeply, sometimes for half a day straight, as their bodies tried to repay weeks of accumulated exhaustion.

44. Inside the Giant Trench System

The scale of the trench system itself was almost impossible to imagine. By the later years of the war, the Western Front contained an estimated 25,000 miles of trenches, enough to stretch completely around the Earth. These weren't just single ditches but tangled networks of front lines, support trenches, reserve lines, and communication trenches branching like roots across fields and forests. Some sectors resembled underground towns, with dugouts, kitchens, aid posts, and supply stores carved into the walls. Maps often looked less like battle plans and more like subway diagrams. Maintaining this vast maze required constant labor, with soldiers digging, reinforcing, draining, and rebuilding day and night as rain, shellfire, and collapse destroyed sections faster than they could be repaired.

45. Life Behind the Front Line

Within that vast network, life was organized in layers rather than a single trench. Behind the front line, the battlefield unfolded in layers rather than a single trench. The support trench usually sat about 100–300 yards (90–275 meters) behind the firing line and looked similar but slightly less exposed. It was connected by narrow communication trenches and held reserve troops, ammunition stores, and medical aid posts. Shelling still reached it regularly, but it was somewhat safer and deeper, with more dugouts where men could sleep briefly or wait for orders. Farther back lay the reserve area, often 1–3 miles (1.5–5 kilometers) from the front. Here, trenches gave way to ruined villages, barns, tents, or makeshift camps where soldiers could wash, drill, receive mail, or rest more fully. Although called "rest," these zones were still within artillery range during major offensives and were crowded, noisy, and tense. Only beyond this, sometimes 5–10 miles (8–16 kilometers) behind the lines, did true rear areas exist, where men might sleep indoors, bathe properly, and feel briefly removed from the war. For most soldiers, life moved constantly back and forth through these layers, never far from danger, but always hoping the next step backward would last just a little longer.

46. Laughing at War in Trench Papers

When units rotated into quieter support or reserve areas, some soldiers even created their own homemade "trench newspapers," handwritten or typed sheets passed around like underground magazines to entertain bored troops. Using scavenged paper, pencils, or battered typewriters, men filled the pages with jokes, cartoons, fake advertisements, sports scores, and sarcastic articles about daily life. Headlines might mock rations, complain about the weather, or tease officers with tongue-in-cheek reports like "Mud Expected to Continue Indefinitely" or "General Promises Dry Trenches by 1925." Regular features included poetry, gossip, letters from readers, and humorous advice columns. Some units gave their papers grand names like *The Wipers Times*, *The Mud Lark*, or *The Listening Post*, parodying real newspapers back home. Copies were read aloud in dugouts or shared until they fell apart, giving soldiers something to laugh about in a place where laughter was rare. In the middle of a mechanized war, these fragile, hand-made papers became small acts of creativity and rebellion, proof that humor could survive even in the trenches.

47. Cleanliness as Survival in the Trenches

Staying clean in the trenches required constant improvisation, because proper washing facilities were almost nonexistent near the front. Most soldiers went days or even weeks without a real bath, relying instead on helmets or mess tins filled with cold water scooped from barrels or rain puddles to splash their faces and hands. Shaving, however, was often treated as a necessity rather than a luxury. After poison gas attacks became common, armies learned that gas masks only worked if the rubber seal pressed directly against bare skin, and even a short beard or heavy stubble could let deadly fumes leak inside. For that reason, many men were expected to remain clean-shaven, scraping their faces daily with dull razors, sometimes dry or with only a thin smear of soap, using small mirrors hung from trench walls or the reflection in a bayonet blade. Officers occasionally inspected for stubble, knowing that a missed shave could cost lives. Between washes, soldiers knocked mud from uniforms by beating them against sandbags, dried socks over candles or braziers, and picked out lice from seams by hand. When units finally rotated to the rear, makeshift bathhouses sometimes appeared (rows of tubs, hoses, or steam boilers where dozens of men washed quickly while their clothes were sent through hot "delousing" ovens to kill insects). The process was rushed and rarely comfortable, but even five minutes of warm water, a clean shirt, and a fresh shave could feel transformative. In a world of mud, sweat, and smoke, small acts of cleanliness weren't vanity, they were morale, health, and sometimes survival.

48. Souvenirs Forged From Shell Casings

Even in the middle of destruction, soldiers found ways to create small pieces of art, turning the debris of war into personal souvenirs. Empty shell casings, bullet cartridges, and scrap metal were hammered, carved, or polished into keepsakes during quiet hours. Men engraved names, dates, hometowns, or unit badges into brass artillery shells, shaping them into vases, cups, or decorative ornaments to send home. Others carved pipes, walking sticks, or chess pieces from broken wood crates, or etched designs into spent bullets and bayonets. Some stitched patches from old uniforms into makeshift flags or painted trench signs to mark their dugouts with nicknames and mascots. These handmade objects became tokens of survival, proof that they had endured something unimaginable. Many were mailed back to families or carried home in kit bags after the war, sitting later on mantelpieces or shelves as silent reminders that even surrounded by mud and machinery, soldiers still felt the urge to build something with their hands rather than destroy.

49. Improvising to Survive in the Trenches

Life in the trenches constantly forced soldiers to become inventors, and many small, improvised tools made the difference between misery and survival. Because raising your head above the parapet could mean a sniper's bullet, men built simple periscopes from scraps of wood, wire, and shaving mirrors, allowing them to look over the top safely without exposing themselves. Flooded trenches turned the ground into knee-deep mud, so units laid wooden "duckboards" (narrow slatted walkways) along the bottom to keep boots out of standing water and reduce cases of trench foot. Empty ration tins became stoves, cut and punched with holes to hold small fires or solid fuel tablets for heating tea or soup. Broken bayonets doubled as knives or tools, shell crates were turned into shelves and furniture, and sandbags stuffed with straw became crude mattresses. Communication trenches were reinforced with scavenged doors and beams from ruined houses, while old wire, metal scraps, and anything not nailed down found a second life as hooks, braces, or repairs. In a landscape where official supplies rarely solved everyday problems, soldiers learned to fix, build, and improvise constantly, turning the wreckage of war into the small inventions that kept them alive.

FOUR

Weapons, Machines & Battlefield Weirdness

World War I was a time of incredible and often terrifying invention. As the stalemate in the trenches dragged on, both sides raced to create new technologies that could break the deadlock. This led to the birth of massive machines, strange new weapons, and experimental tools that had never been seen on a battlefield before. This chapter looks at the reality of these inventions, from the first clumsy tanks and early airplanes to the unusual and often surprising ways that soldiers used technology to try and gain an advantage. It was a period where the traditional ways of fighting were replaced by a new kind of industrial and scientific warfare.

50. The Longest-Range Gun of World War I

In the spring of 1918, the people of Paris began hearing explosions that made no sense. The sky was clear. No enemy aircraft were visible. No artillery batteries were anywhere near the city. Yet, without warning, shells kept crashing into streets and rooftops, killing civilians at random. At first, many believed spies or hidden saboteurs were responsible. Others thought bombs were being dropped from invisible high-altitude planes. The truth turned out to be stranger and more unsettling.

More than 75 miles (120 kilometers) away, hidden deep inside a forest, German engineers had built an enormous supergun so large it required special railway tracks just to position it. The barrel stretched over 100 feet long, longer than a blue whale, and fired shells so fast and so high that they briefly entered the upper atmosphere before curving back down toward Paris. For a few seconds after firing, there was no sound at all. Only later would a faint rumble arrive, followed by a sudden explosion. The delay made the shells feel as if they were falling from nowhere. Each shot required precise calculations for wind, rotation of the Earth, and air pressure, making it one of the most advanced artillery experiments of the entire war.

The weapon, later nicknamed the "Paris Gun," was powerful but wildly impractical. Its barrel wore out quickly and had to be replaced after only a few dozen shots, accuracy was poor, and the shells caused more psychological fear than military damage. Still, the effect on the population was enormous. A city that believed itself safely behind the front lines suddenly realized nowhere was truly out of reach. Even hundreds of miles away, the war could still find you.

51. The Chaotic Birth of Tank Warfare

When tanks first appeared on the battlefield in 1916, many soldiers expected them to be unstoppable metal monsters that would roll straight through enemy lines. On paper, they looked revolutionary: armored, armed with cannons and machine guns, able to crush barbed wire and cross trenches that trapped ordinary infantry. But the reality was far messier. Early tanks were slow, unreliable machines that broke down almost as often as they fought. Engines overheated within minutes, tracks snapped in mud, gears jammed, and some vehicles simply stalled before even reaching the front. During their first major use at the Battle of the Somme, many never made it out of their starting positions. Others crawled forward at walking speed, sometimes barely 3 or 4 miles per hour (5–6 kilometers per hour), easy targets for artillery.

Inside, conditions were miserable. Crews worked in deafening noise, choking fumes, and extreme heat that could climb above 120°F (50°C). The air filled with smoke, oil vapor, and cordite from their own guns. There was no suspension, so every shell hole slammed the men against the metal walls. Drivers steered half-blind through tiny slits while mechanics constantly hammered at failing engines mid-battle. Some tanks became stuck in mud so deep that crews simply abandoned them and walked back. Others accidentally drove into shell craters or broke through weak ground and tipped sideways like stranded ships.

Yet even when they barely functioned, their psychological effect was enormous. Enemy troops who had never seen anything like them sometimes fled at the sight of these lumbering steel boxes creeping through the fog. Over time the technology improved, but the first tanks were less sleek war machines and more experimental tractors bolted together under pressure. They represented the awkward birth of modern armored warfare, powerful in theory but, at first, just as likely to defeat themselves as the enemy.

52. A Weapon of Fire and Fear

While engineers experimented with giant superguns and unreliable tanks, the Germans also introduced a far more primitive and terrifying weapon for close combat: the flamethrower. First deployed in 1915, it looked less like advanced technology and more like something from a nightmare. Operators carried heavy metal fuel tanks strapped to their backs, weighing 45–65 pounds (20–30 kilograms), connected by hoses to a long nozzle that blasted a jet of burning fuel when ignited. But the weapon's power came with limits. Most early flamethrowers only held enough fuel for about 10 to 20 seconds of continuous fire. That meant each burst had to count. A few seconds of flame, then silence. Then either the trench was cleared, or the operator was dangerously exposed.

In the tight, narrow spaces of trench warfare, those few seconds could be devastating. Fire curled over sandbags, poured into dugouts, and set wooden supports ablaze almost instantly. Smoke swallowed the air. Men had nowhere to run. Even seasoned troops sometimes fled at the mere sight of a flamethrower team advancing. The psychological effect was enormous. The hiss of pressurized fuel followed by a sudden wall of fire often caused panic long before the flames reached anyone.

Yet carrying one was among the most dangerous jobs on the battlefield. The large fuel tank made the operator an obvious target, and a single bullet could rupture the pack and turn the soldier into an explosion of fire. Because of this, flamethrowers were never common weapons. They were issued only to small specialist assault teams, often volunteers or carefully chosen troops known for their nerve. Many saw it as either an elite role or a near-suicidal one. Used sparingly during raids or breakthroughs, they were designed less for sustained fighting and more for shock and terror. Though rare compared to rifles or artillery, the flamethrower earned an outsized reputation, becoming one of the most feared sights of the entire war.

53. The Deadly Evolution of Gas Warfare

Not every invention tested in World War I was a breakthrough. In fact, many were borderline absurd. Desperate to cross no man's land without being cut down by machine guns, some soldiers were issued heavy armored shields mounted on small wheels, meant to be pushed forward as portable cover. On paper they looked like mobile walls of steel. In reality they were slow, clumsy, and rattled loudly over broken ground, snagging on wire and sinking into mud until the men behind them were left struggling and exposed, easy targets for enemy fire. Other units experimented with early "land torpedoes," small tracked machines packed with explosives that crawled toward enemy trenches by remote control or long wires. Many flipped over in shell holes, got tangled, or exploded too soon, sometimes killing the very soldiers who launched them.

Elsewhere, engineers tried all sorts of desperate contraptions that sounded clever in workshops but fell apart the moment they touched the battlefield. Some units experimented with crude trench catapults, wooden or metal frames with springs or counterweights designed to hurl grenades or bundles of explosives farther than a man could throw. In theory they would let soldiers bombard enemy trenches safely from cover. In practice they were slow to reload, wildly inaccurate, and often snapped or jammed after a few shots, sometimes sending explosives tumbling backward into their own lines.

Others built mechanical digging machines, squat metal devices fitted with blades or rotating scoops that were supposed to carve new trenches automatically while shielding the operator. On paper they promised to save hours of backbreaking labor. But the engines clogged with mud, the gears jammed with stones, and the machines frequently stalled or broke down under shellfire. Soldiers quickly discovered it was faster and safer to use an ordinary shovel.

Personal protection experiments were just as awkward. Some troops were issued improvised body armor made from steel plates sewn into vests or strapped to their chests and backs. The armor could sometimes stop shrapnel or a glancing bullet, but it weighed around 60–70 pounds (27–32 kilograms) and trapped heat against the body. After a few minutes of climbing out of trenches or running across open ground, men were gasping for breath and shedding the plates just to move properly. Protection meant nothing if you couldn't run.

Strange wheeled machines, oversized shields, and homemade devices appeared briefly along the front lines like mechanical curiosities, only to vanish just as quickly. Axles snapped, engines overheated, wheels sank axle-deep into mud, and anything heavier than a man quickly became dead weight.

54. The Poison Gas Arms Race

As the war dragged on, poison gas didn't remain a single terrifying experiment but evolved into a grim chemical arms race. After the first chlorine clouds rolled across the trenches in 1915, both sides began racing to develop new substances that were deadlier, harder to detect, and more difficult to defend against. Phosgene soon replaced chlorine as the primary killer. It was almost invisible and smelled faintly of hay or freshly cut grass, harmless enough that many soldiers removed their masks too early, only to collapse hours later as their lungs slowly filled with fluid. Later came mustard gas, which attacked not just the lungs but the skin and eyes, seeping into clothing and lingering in mud for days. Men who thought they had escaped an attack sometimes woke covered in painful yellow blisters, temporarily blinded or burned raw from the inside out. Unlike earlier gases, mustard didn't always kill quickly, but it filled hospitals with thousands of long-term casualties, overwhelming medical systems and keeping soldiers out of the fight for weeks or months.

Delivery methods grew just as sophisticated. Early attacks relied on large cylinders opened when the wind blew in the right direction, but this was unreliable and sometimes blew gas back onto the attackers themselves. Soon armies switched to artillery shells filled with chemicals, allowing gas to be fired directly onto enemy positions with precision, day or night, regardless of wind. Mortars, rockets, and special projectors spread clouds suddenly and without warning, mixing gas shells with normal high explosives so soldiers never knew what was coming next. Some bombardments layered different chemicals together, forcing troops to keep masks on for hours until exhaustion set in. By the later years of the war, entire barrages were designed not to kill outright but to contaminate trenches, roads, and supply routes, turning the environment itself hostile. The battlefield no longer felt like just mud and wire. The air, the ground, and even the rain could burn or suffocate. Chemistry had become as much a weapon as bullets or shells, and every breath carried uncertainty.

55. Turning Night into Day on the Battlefield

To counter or conceal movement, armies also created artificial weather. Smoke shells and canisters poured thick white or gray clouds across the battlefield, hiding advancing troops, masking retreats, or blinding enemy machine gunners. Entire attacks unfolded inside rolling walls of smoke, where men could barely see a few yards ahead and often stumbled into shell holes or even their own barbed wire.

At night, communication often depended on signal flares and "Very lights," small pistol-like launchers that fired colored stars high above the trenches. These bursts weren't meant to illuminate the battlefield so much as to send urgent messages when telephones were cut and runners couldn't get through. Every unit memorized a simple code. A red flare might mean "enemy attack" or "send help immediately," green could signal "objective taken" or "lift the barrage," (which meant stop firing on friendly positions) and other combinations marked positions, called for reinforcements, or warned of gas. Officers kept flare pistols tucked into their belts like sidearms, ready to fire a message skyward in seconds.

Because so much depended on these signals, mistakes could be deadly. Smoke, stress, or poor timing sometimes led to the wrong color going up, or two flares being mistaken for three. Artillery batteries miles away might respond instantly, shells landing on the wrong trench simply because a signal was misread. Entire attacks occasionally stalled or advanced based on one brief flash of color. Over time, soldiers grew used to glancing upward automatically whenever a flare hissed into the air, reading the sky the way others read a map. In a war where wires were constantly cut and radios unreliable, these tiny sparks became the army's emergency language, quick, crude, and sometimes the only thing keeping chaos from taking over. Soldiers joked that the front never truly slept, because the sky was always flickering with color.

56. Turning Night into Day on the Battlefield

Night fighting was so dangerous and confusing that armies tried to cheat the darkness itself. One of the simplest but most dramatic inventions was the parachute flare. Fired high into the sky from special pistols or mortars, the flare burst open with a sharp crack and released a burning magnesium light suspended beneath a small silk parachute. Instead of falling quickly, it drifted slowly downward, flooding the battlefield with an eerie white glow that could last nearly a minute. For those seconds, no man's land looked like midday. Every crater, strand of barbed wire, and moving figure became sharply visible. Soldiers caught advancing across open ground suddenly found themselves frozen in bright light, their shadows stretching long behind them like targets painted on the earth. Night raids that depended on stealth could collapse instantly when a single flare hissed overhead. Men learned to dive flat and stay perfectly still, praying the light would drift past without revealing them. What had begun as darkness for protection became a stage spotlight, and the sky itself turned into a weapon.

57. Smoke, Flares, and the Battlefield Sky

Long before radar existed, armies tried to hunt enemies in the sky and darkness with pure light. Massive electric searchlights, some more than 3 feet (1 meter) wide across the lens, were mounted on trucks or concrete platforms behind the lines and powered by noisy generators. At night, crews swung their beams slowly across the sky, sweeping back and forth like enormous white fingers. When the light caught something, a Zeppelin, a bomber, or even drifting smoke, the beam locked onto it and tracked it relentlessly. Other lights joined in, crossing their rays until the target was trapped inside a glowing cage of light. From the ground, the sky looked like a theater stage, crisscrossed with bright columns. For the aircraft crews above, it was terrifying. One moment they were hidden in darkness, the next they were fully exposed, every wing and rivet visible, anti-aircraft guns immediately opening fire. Some pilots said being caught in a searchlight felt like being pinned by a spotlight with the whole world shooting at you. The same lights were sometimes turned toward no man's land to illuminate night patrols or expected attacks, transforming muddy fields into harsh, ghostly landscapes where nothing could hide.

58. Listening for the Enemy Before Radar

Before radar could see the enemy, armies tried to hear them first. Along quiet stretches of the front, strange metal horns, wooden funnels, and giant concrete "ears" appeared, looking more like oversized musical instruments than weapons. These listening devices were built to capture the faintest distant sounds: the rumble of trucks, the clank of tanks, the buzz of aircraft engines, or the deep thud of enemy artillery firing miles away. Operators wearing headphones sat perfectly still, turning the horns slowly like telescopes for the ears, trying to pinpoint direction by sound alone. Some horns were small enough to carry; others were enormous, fixed structures several feet wide. On the British coast, huge curved concrete walls called acoustic mirrors were even constructed to reflect the noise of approaching

Zeppelins and bombers toward microphones, giving defenders a few extra minutes of warning.

At the front, a related system called "sound ranging" became surprisingly scientific. Microphones were spread out along the line and connected by cables. When an enemy gun fired, the boom reached each microphone at slightly different times. By measuring those tiny differences, sometimes fractions of a second, technicians could triangulate the exact position of the gun and relay coordinates to their own artillery for counterfire. Entire batteries were located and destroyed this way without ever being seen. It felt almost magical to soldiers: guns hidden behind hills suddenly shelled with uncanny accuracy.

59. An Unusual Vehicle of the War

Not every soldier moved by truck or horse. In many sectors, especially early in the war, armies experimented with bicycle infantry, troops who could travel faster than marching men but far more quietly and cheaply than motor vehicles. Soldiers rode sturdy military bicycles reinforced with thicker frames, tool kits, and racks for rifles and packs, sometimes even fitted with folding designs so they could be carried over obstacles or slung across the back. On paved roads or firm ground, a cyclist could cover two or three times the distance of a marching column while using far less energy, arriving less exhausted and ready to fight. Units used them for scouting, message carrying, rapid reinforcements, and quick flanking movements where surprise mattered more than firepower.

Bicycles were nearly silent compared to engines, making them ideal for night movement or slipping along tree-lined roads without alerting the enemy. Whole platoons could glide forward with only the faint crunch of tires on gravel. But the advantages vanished the moment the terrain turned to mud. Shell holes, barbed wire, churned fields, and shattered forests quickly made riding impossible, forcing men to push or carry the heavy machines instead. Many soldiers joked that their "iron horses" were useful only until the first rainstorm. As the war became more static and the front lines more cratered, bicycles grew less practical, yet they never disappeared entirely. In quieter sectors and rear areas, columns of riflemen pedaling past ruined villages remained a strange sight, half modern and half improvised, proof that even in an industrial war, something as simple as a bicycle could still be a useful piece of military technology.

60. The Daredevils Who Carried the War's Messages

Before radios became reliable, getting a message from one headquarters to another often depended on a single man and a fast engine. Motorcycle dispatch riders became the nervous system of the army, carrying orders, maps, and reports between units when telephone wires were cut by shellfire and runners on foot were too slow or too exposed. Riding lightweight, stripped-down bikes built for rough ground, they sped along muddy roads, through shattered villages, and across open fields under fire, sometimes with leather satchels strapped to their chests or handlebars containing documents that entire battles depended on. A rider might deliver a new attack time, an artillery correction, or a warning that enemy troops were breaking through. If he failed to arrive, hundreds or thousands of men might move at the wrong moment.

The job was notoriously dangerous. Roads near the front were prime targets for artillery, snipers, and aircraft, and dispatch riders often rode alone with no protection. Headlights were dimmed or covered at night to avoid detection, forcing them to navigate by moonlight or memory while dodging shell holes and wrecked wagons. Many bikes skidded in mud or broke down under constant strain, and riders sometimes had to abandon the machine and run the last stretch on foot. Casualty rates were high enough that the role earned a grim reputation, yet volunteers kept stepping forward, drawn by the speed and independence of the work. Soldiers joked that dispatch riders lived fast and died young, but they also knew these lone motorcyclists were often the difference between chaos and coordination.

61. Motorcycle Machine-Gun Teams

As armies searched for ways to add speed and firepower to a battlefield that was mostly mud and trenches, some experimented with an odd hybrid between cavalry and early mechanized warfare: motorcycles fitted with sidecars carrying machine guns. These three-wheeled machines looked almost improvised, a roaring bike with a metal tub bolted to the side, but inside the sidecar sat a gunner crouched behind a mounted weapon, often a Lewis gun or Maxim, ready to fire while the driver steered. The idea was simple: move fast, hit hard, and relocate before the enemy could respond. On firm roads or open countryside, these units could race ahead of infantry columns, escort convoys, chase retreating troops, or quickly reinforce weak points.

In theory, they combined the mobility of a motorcycle with the firepower of a machine-gun team. In practice, they were temperamental and risky. The extra weight made steering awkward, especially over ruts or shell holes, and sharp turns could flip the entire machine. Mud clogged wheels, engines overheated, and a single bullet could disable both rider and gunner at once. Once the fighting moved off roads and into cratered no man's land, the sidecars often bogged down completely, becoming little more than expensive targets. Still, in rear areas, deserts, or less damaged sectors, they proved useful for patrols and quick raids, and some armies kept them throughout the war. To soldiers watching them bounce past in clouds of dust, they looked like something from the future, a glimpse of the fast, mechanized warfare that would dominate the next global conflict.

62. The Steel Traps of the Western Front

Long before tanks or flamethrowers changed the battlefield, one of the most effective and feared weapons of World War I was something far simpler: barbed wire. Originally designed for fencing cattle, it became a deadly military tool that shaped almost every trench system on the Western Front. Engineers didn't just string up a few lines. They built vast, tangled belts of wire sometimes 20–50 yards (18–45 meters) deep, layered in overlapping coils, stakes, and spirals known as "concertina" wire. From a distance it looked like messy metal brush. Up close it was a maze of razor-sharp barbs waiting to snag clothing, packs, rifles, or flesh. At night or in fog, soldiers often didn't see it until they were already trapped inside.

These barriers weren't random obstacles but carefully planned killing zones. Machine-gun crews positioned their guns to fire directly over the wire, knowing any attacking soldier slowed down or stuck would become an easy target. Artillery shells frequently failed to cut the thicker strands, leaving gaps too small to crawl through. Men carried heavy wire cutters or special explosives called Bangalore torpedoes, long pipes filled with explosives that were shoved under the wire and detonated to blast a narrow path. Even then, clearing lanes took precious minutes under fire. Many assaults collapsed not because defenders shot everyone immediately, but because attacking waves piled up helplessly in the wire, tangled together while bullets and shells rained down. Survivors described hearing the awful metallic scraping of men struggling to free themselves and the cries of the wounded caught fast.

Maintaining these barriers became constant labor. Patrols repaired damaged sections every night, hammering in new stakes and weaving fresh coils under cover of darkness. By the later years of the war, millions of miles of wire crisscrossed the front, enough to fence entire countries many times over. Some sectors looked less like farmland and more like twisted steel forests. For soldiers, wire became almost as terrifying as artillery itself. You could hide from shells and dodge bullets, but once the wire grabbed you, there was nowhere left to run.

63. The Close-Range Terror of Trench Mortars

Not all artillery fired from miles away. Some of the most feared weapons on the Western Front were squat, ugly tubes that sat only a few hundred yards from the enemy. These were trench mortars, known to the Germans as *minenwerfers* or "mine throwers," short-range weapons designed specifically for the tight, cramped geometry of trench warfare. Instead of long barrels and flat trajectories like traditional guns, they looked like oversized stovepipes or metal drainpipes bolted to a baseplate, angled steeply upward to lob enormous shells high into the air. From a distance they almost looked homemade, like plumbing parts stuck in the mud, but the damage they caused was anything but crude.

Their ammunition was shockingly large for such small weapons. Some shells were the size of a bucket or small barrel, weighing 20–100 pounds (9–45 kilograms) or more, packed with explosives and scrap metal. Because the mortars fired at a steep arc, the bombs dropped almost straight down into trenches, dugouts, and strongpoints that normal artillery often missed. Soldiers quickly learned to fear the sound. Unlike the long whistle of distant artillery, mortar bombs made a dull, slow "plop" or hollow *thunk* as they left the tube, followed by a few seconds of dreadful silence while the shell hung invisibly overhead. Then came a sudden, earth-shaking blast that collapsed trench walls, buried men alive, or blew sandbags and timber into splinters. Veterans said that quiet pause between launch and impact was worse than the explosion itself, giving just enough time to realize something terrible was about to land nearby.

Mortars also had a brutal psychological effect. Because the mortars were positioned so close to the front, crews could often see their targets directly and adjust the angle after each shot, making them far more accurate than distant artillery. After only a few rounds, shells could be dropped almost exactly into a chosen trench bay or dugout entrance, which made the weapon feel personal as well as deadly. Entire sections could disappear in one hit. In response, both sides built their own mortar units, leading to constant back-and-forth bombardments at ranges sometimes shorter than a football field. Crude, heavy, and ugly, trench mortars perfectly matched the nature of the war itself: close, dirty, and devastating.

64. Floating Watchtowers Above the Front

Long before fighter planes ruled the sky, the most important eyes on the battlefield were not aircraft at all but giant hydrogen-filled observation balloons that hovered silently above the trenches like strange gray sea creatures. These were not hot-air balloons with flames, and not true blimps with engines, but tethered "kite balloons," fat sausage-shaped gas bags anchored to the ground by a thick steel cable and raised or lowered by a winch truck. Once inflated with hydrogen, they could climb 3,000–5,000 feet (900–1,500 meters) into the air and remain almost perfectly still for hours, acting like floating watchtowers. From that height, an observer with binoculars could see miles beyond the front lines: gun flashes, moving columns, supply trains, trenches being dug, even men gathering for an attack. What looked hidden from the mud below was completely exposed from above.

Inside the small wicker basket, one or two officers worked like calm air-traffic controllers of destruction. Most communicated through a field telephone line that ran down the tether cable, essentially a wired phone stretching from the sky to the artillery batteries below. Others tapped out Morse code on early wireless radios powered by heavy batteries and generators.

They didn't speak dramatically or shout orders. They simply made tiny corrections: "Left fifty… drop one hundred… fire again." Artillery rarely hit perfectly on the first shot, so each adjustment moved the next shell a little closer, the explosions creeping step by step across the ground. Soldiers called this "walking" the fire, because the blasts seemed to march forward like footsteps in the mud, one impact after another, until they landed directly on a trench, road, or gun position. From above, the observer could literally watch the shells advance toward their target and guide them in with calm, almost casual instructions. Within minutes, guns miles away could zero in with frightening precision. For the first time in history, artillery stopped being blind and became accurate, turning distant cannons into something closer to guided weapons than guesswork.

Because of that deadly precision, balloon crews became some of the most hunted men in the war. Infantry hated seeing an enemy balloon overhead, knowing it meant artillery would soon follow. Snipers couldn't reach them at that height, but artillery targeted the winch trucks and ground crews, and fighter pilots were given special "balloon busting" missions. These attacks were among the most dangerous jobs in the air. Pilots had to dive low through heavy anti-aircraft fire and shoot incendiary bullets into the hydrogen bag. These were special rounds filled with flammable chemicals like phosphorus that ignited on impact, designed not just to pierce fabric but to start fires. Ordinary bullets would only punch small holes and let the gas leak slowly, but incendiaries sparked and burned the instant they struck. When hit, the balloon didn't sag or slowly deflate. It erupted almost instantly into a towering fireball, sometimes hundreds of feet high, the explosion visible for miles across the front.

For that reason, balloon observers were among the first soldiers in the war to routinely carry parachutes. While many fighter pilots early in the war had none at all, balloon crews wore static-line silk chutes packed beside the basket. If flames appeared, they had only seconds to jump. When they did, the parachute snapped open automatically, and men drifted slowly down while their balloon burned above them like a falling sun. The parachutes were surprisingly reliable, often saving lives, but timing mattered. Jump too late, and the silk could catch fire or the blast could flip the basket before escape.

By 1918, hundreds of these balloons dotted the Western Front. In some sectors, they formed entire "balloon lines," rising and lowering throughout the day like mechanical suns. Soldiers learned to glance upward instinctively. If the sky held a gray shape watching them, nowhere felt safe. Even miles behind the trenches, you could still be seen. Many veterans later said the balloons felt worse than airplanes, not because they moved, but because they didn't. They simply hung there, silent and patient, like unblinking eyes tethered to the sky, proving that in modern war, even the clouds were watching.

65. Fooling the Enemy From the Air

As aircraft and observation balloons began watching the front from above, the battlefield became a strange game of deception where looking real could be just as dangerous as being real. Armies quickly learned that anything visible from the sky, guns, roads, supply dumps, even kitchens, could draw artillery within minutes. So soldiers started hiding everything. Nets woven with strips of cloth and burlap were draped over trenches and vehicles to break up their outlines. Mud, branches, and scraps of vegetation were piled onto helmets and guns to make them blend into the ground.

Artillery pieces were painted in blotchy greens and browns or covered with patterned canvas so they looked like patches of earth instead of metal. From the air, a well-camouflaged battery could vanish completely.

But hiding wasn't enough. Soon both sides began building things that were deliberately fake. Dummy cannons made from wood or painted canvas were set up to attract enemy fire away from real guns. Fake horses and supply wagons stood in open fields to suggest troop movements that didn't exist. Engineers dug entire dummy trench systems, complete with sandbags, duckboards, and even smoke from fake cook fires, hoping enemy pilots would photograph and shell empty ground. Some sectors built canvas "tanks" or plywood vehicles that looked convincing from a few thousand feet up but collapsed if touched. In a few cases, fake villages and roads were constructed behind the lines to mislead bombers, complete with painted rooftops and carefully arranged lights at night.

The goal wasn't just concealment but confusion. If the enemy couldn't tell what was real, they wasted shells, time, and aircraft on ghosts. From above, the front sometimes resembled a theatrical stage set, part reality and part illusion.

FIVE

The Hidden War

Beyond the visible battlefields of mud and wire, another kind of conflict was being fought in the shadows. This was a war of secrets, where information was as valuable as ammunition and a single intercepted message could change the fate of an entire army. This chapter looks at the reality of espionage and intelligence, from the daring work of spies and codebreakers to the clever ways that nations tried to hide their plans from the enemy. It was a silent and dangerous struggle that took place in quiet offices, behind enemy lines, and even in the air, proving that some of the most important battles of World War I were the ones that no one ever saw.

66. Spies and Secret Intelligence

Every army built networks of spies, codebreakers, and informants, trying to learn enemy plans while hiding their own. Civilians, shopkeepers, waiters, and railway workers were quietly recruited to watch troop movements or listen for rumors. Letters were intercepted, telegrams copied, and telephone lines tapped. Entire departments existed solely to open mail with steam, read it, reseal it, and send it on without the sender ever knowing. Suspicion spread everywhere. A stranger with a camera, an accent, or a notebook could be arrested on the spot.

Professional spies operated under false names and forged papers, slipping across borders to steal maps or count trains. Some carried invisible ink or hid microfilm inside buttons, shoes, or hollow coins. Others posed as nurses, businessmen, or journalists while secretly passing information at night. Intelligence officers studied aerial photographs, decoded radio signals, and pieced together clues like detectives solving a crime. A single intercepted message could reveal an entire offensive and save thousands of lives. By the end of the war, espionage had grown into a vast, organized system, laying the foundations for the modern intelligence agencies that still operate today.

67. Disguised Observation Posts of the War

Along the Western Front, even the trees could be spies. In some sectors where the ground was too flat or exposed for safe observation, both sides built fake trees that doubled as hidden lookout posts. Engineers studied real, dead tree trunks in no man's land, then carefully removed them at night and replaced them with hollow steel replicas shaped and painted to look identical, complete with fake bark, knots, and broken branches. Inside, just enough space existed for one soldier to climb up and stand with binoculars or a periscope, peering through tiny concealed slits. From a distance, it looked like nothing more than another shattered stump left by shellfire. By day, the observer quietly mapped enemy trenches, counted troop movements, and reported artillery positions. By night, messages were carried back through communication trenches. The job was terrifying. If the enemy noticed movement or suspected the deception, the entire "tree" could be blasted apart by artillery or snipers, trapping the man inside. Yet these disguised posts provided some of the most valuable intelligence on the battlefield, proving that sometimes survival depended less on firepower and more on looking like part of the landscape itself.

68. The Decoy City of Paris

As German bombers began targeting Paris at night, the French came up with a solution that sounded more like stage magic than warfare: they built a fake city to trick enemy pilots. On the outskirts of the real capital, engineers constructed an elaborate decoy "Paris" made from wood, canvas, and painted fabric, complete with imitation streets, rail yards, factories, and even a mock version of the Seine River. At night, hundreds of carefully arranged lights flickered on to mimic neighborhoods, train stations, and moving traffic. Some buildings were only empty frames covered with cloth, just convincing enough from the air to look real. Fake railway lines were built with glowing lamps that simulated trains arriving and departing, while rotating lights copied the patterns of factories working late into the night. From thousands of feet above, through darkness and haze, the illusion was good enough to fool pilots navigating by sight. The hope was simple: bombs dropped on the fake city meant fewer falling on the real one. Although the war ended before the decoy was fully completed and heavily tested, the project remains one of the strangest defensive ideas of the conflict.

69. The Psychological War of Propaganda Leaflets

As the war dragged into its third and fourth years, armies discovered that breaking a soldier's mind could be easier than breaking a trench. Both sides began printing thousands, then millions, of small paper leaflets in the enemy's language and scattering them across the front like artificial snow. Special artillery shells were designed to burst open midair and release clouds of paper instead of shrapnel. Mortars, observation balloons, and even aircraft dropped bundles that fluttered down into trenches and dugouts. The messages were simple and tempting: surrender and you will be fed, kept warm, treated for wounds, and sent safely to a prison camp. Some leaflets showed staged photographs of smiling prisoners of war eating bread, smoking cigarettes, or playing football behind the lines, making captivity look almost comfortable compared to mud and shellfire. Others included "safe conduct passes" that soldiers could carry in their pockets and hold up when approaching enemy lines. Many exaggerated enemy defeats or claimed the war was already lost, quietly planting the idea that further fighting was pointless.

At first, men joked about them or used them as toilet paper, but by 1917–1918, after years of hunger, cold, and failed offensives, the leaflets began to work. Captured soldiers were sometimes found with the passes folded carefully in their tunics. Entire groups surrendered together, stepping out with hands raised rather than die in another assault. In some sectors during the final months, dozens or even hundreds of exhausted German troops gave themselves up in a single day. For many, prison camps meant regular meals, dry beds, and safety from artillery, conditions that could feel better than the front line. Commanders hated the leaflets not because they were laughable, but because they quietly eroded morale and made surrender seem reasonable. It became one of the earliest and most effective forms of large-scale psychological warfare, proving that sometimes a piece of paper could succeed where bullets could not.

70. The Dangerous Power of Battlefield Rumors

In the trenches, information was often scarcer than food. There were no radios, no live reports, and no reliable way for ordinary soldiers to know what was happening even a few miles away, let alone across the front. Newspapers arrived days or weeks late, letters were delayed or censored, and officers rarely shared plans with the ranks. Into that silence poured rumor. News traveled mouth to mouth faster than any official message. A man might hear from a runner that the neighboring regiment had been wiped out, from a letter that the war would end by Christmas, or from a cook that relief was coming tomorrow. By nightfall the story had changed three times. Hopeful rumors spread just as quickly as frightening ones: "We're being pulled out at dawn," "the enemy is retreating," "a breakthrough happened up north," or "fresh Americans are arriving." Others crushed morale overnight: exaggerated casualty lists, claims that an entire brigade had vanished, whispers of unstoppable gas or new super-weapons. Sometimes the gossip turned out to be half-true or even accurate, which made it feel trustworthy; soldiers occasionally heard about real offensives, shortages, or collapses days before official confirmation. Censorship made things worse. Missing details created speculation, and speculation bred wild stories. Men began to believe almost anything: spies everywhere, cursed trenches, lucky charms, even angels protecting the lines. Officers tried to fight the chaos with daily briefings and posted bulletins, but fear and boredom were stronger than facts.

71. The Spy Who Became a Legend

Among the many shadowy figures accused of espionage during the war, none became more famous than Mata Hari, the glamorous dancer who transformed into one of history's most legendary spies. Born Margaretha Zelle in the Netherlands, she reinvented herself in Paris before the war as an exotic performer, adopting the stage name "Mata Hari," meaning "eye of the day" in Malay. Draped in silk and jewels, she captivated wealthy officers, diplomats, and politicians, moving easily through elite circles across Europe. When war broke out, those connections suddenly made her valuable, and dangerous. Traveling between neutral and enemy countries, she accepted money from both French and German intelligence, claiming she was merely gathering gossip, not secrets.

But as the war dragged on and France suffered devastating losses, the government desperately needed someone to blame for military failures. Mata Hari's independence, foreign status, and reputation for seducing officers made her an easy target. Arrested in 1917, she was accused of causing the deaths of thousands of soldiers by passing information to Germany, though historians later found little real evidence that she had ever provided anything important. Her trial was brief and sensational. Newspapers painted her as a deadly femme fatale, a beautiful traitor who used romance as a weapon.

At dawn on October 15, 1917, she faced a firing squad outside Paris. Refusing a blindfold, she reportedly stood straight, dressed elegantly, and blew a final kiss to the soldiers before the shots rang out. Whether master spy or convenient scapegoat, her execution turned her into a symbol of the hidden war.

72. Inside the Hidden World of Wartime Cryptography

While popular imagination pictured spies slipping through shadows with forged passports and secret meetings, much of the real intelligence war happened in quiet rooms filled with desks, maps, and exhausted clerks. Across Europe, armies built entire codebreaking centers where intercepted telegrams and radio signals were sorted, copied, and studied line by line. Operators tapped out enemy messages in Morse code, then teams of linguists, mathematicians, and puzzle-solvers tried to turn the scrambled letters back into meaning. Walls filled with pinned notes, string connections, and half-solved ciphers. The work was slow, repetitive, and maddening, sometimes taking days to decode a single message.

In Britain, a secret unit known as Room 40 intercepted and decrypted thousands of German naval signals, quietly tracking submarine movements and fleet positions. One intercepted telegram, later called the Zimmermann Telegram, revealed Germany's attempt to persuade Mexico to attack the United States, helping push America into the war. No guns were fired, no trenches stormed, yet a few sheets of decoded paper changed the course of history. The people doing this work rarely left their desks and never received medals, but their victories could save more lives than entire divisions.

SIX

Medicine & Survival

The massive scale of World War I forced a revolution in how doctors and nurses cared for the wounded and the sick. On a battlefield where industrial weapons caused injuries never seen before, the struggle to save lives became a race against time and infection. This chapter looks at the reality of medical care during the conflict, from the development of life-saving new techniques to the incredible resilience of those who worked in the shadow of the front lines. It was a time of rapid discovery and immense bravery, where the goal was not just to fight the war, but to survive the devastating toll it took on the human body and mind.

73. The Birth of Modern Battlefield Triage

The chaos of industrial warfare also forced doctors to rethink a brutal question: who should be treated first when hundreds of wounded men arrive at once? Earlier wars often treated soldiers in the order they appeared or by rank, but World War I made that impossible. After major offensives, stretcher-bearers might carry in thousands of casualties within hours, far more than any medical team could handle. Treating everyone equally meant many would die waiting. So military doctors developed a new system called "triage," from the French word trier, meaning "to sort." Instead of first come, first served, the wounded were rapidly divided into categories: those who would survive without help, those too badly injured to save, and those who could live if treated immediately. Resources went to the last group first. It was a cold, mathematical approach to survival, sometimes forcing medics to walk past dying men to reach someone with better odds. Yet the system dramatically increased survival rates, saving thousands who might otherwise have been lost. The method proved so effective that it became standard practice in modern emergency rooms, ambulances, and disaster zones. Every time doctors today prioritize patients after an accident or earthquake, they are using a system forged in the overcrowded field hospitals of World War I.

74. Speed Becomes a Weapon Against Death

Speed often meant the difference between life and death, yet at the start of the war most wounded soldiers were still hauled away in horse-drawn carts little different from those used a century earlier. After battles, stretcher-bearers struggled through mud and shell holes carrying men for miles to reach aid posts, then loaded them onto slow wagons that jolted painfully over rough roads. The journey could take hours. Many soldiers who survived the initial wound simply bled to death before ever reaching a surgeon. As the scale of casualties exploded, armies began replacing horses with motorized ambulances, small petrol-powered vehicles that could weave through damaged roads and reach hospitals far faster than animal teams. For the first time, wounded men could be transported lying flat instead of stacked upright, reducing shock and further injury. Drivers often raced through artillery fire at night with headlights dimmed, knowing every minute counted. Combined with triage and better surgery, these faster evacuations dramatically increased survival rates.

75. A Medical Breakthrough That Saved Thousands

Before World War I, blood transfusions were chaotic and dangerously improvised. If a wounded soldier needed blood, a donor often had to lie beside him while doctors transferred blood directly from one arm to another through rubber tubes. There was no way to store it, no organized supply, and no guarantee the donor's blood type would match. Thousands of men who might have survived simply bled to death because fresh blood wasn't available in time. In 1917, a U.S. Army doctor named Captain Oswald Robertson changed that by creating what is considered the world's first true blood bank. Working near the front lines in France, he collected blood from donors, mixed it with sodium citrate to prevent clotting, and stored it in bottles packed in ice so it could last for days instead of minutes. For the first time, blood could be stockpiled, labeled by type, transported by truck, and given exactly when needed. Robertson's small refrigerated crates followed the fighting like mobile lifelines, supplying surgeons during major battles and saving countless wounded soldiers who would previously have died on the operating table.

76. The Fight Against Deadly Infection

For much of the early war, surviving a bullet or shell wound did not mean surviving the hospital. Infection killed almost as many soldiers as the weapons themselves. Trench mud was thick with manure, bacteria, and rotting debris, and when shrapnel tore through flesh it carried that contamination deep into the body. Even small wounds could turn deadly within days. Limbs swelled, skin blackened, and a sweet, foul smell signaled the arrival of gangrene or blood poisoning. Surgeons often had no choice but to amputate quickly or watch the infection spread. Entire wards filled with men dying not from their injuries, but from what grew inside them afterward. The scale of the problem forced doctors to rethink battlefield hygiene completely. Medical teams began aggressively cleaning and cutting away contaminated tissue, flushing wounds with antiseptic solutions like carbolic acid or diluted bleach, and sterilizing instruments between operations. New methods such as the Carrel-Dakin system continuously dripped disinfectant into deep wounds to kill bacteria before they multiplied. Field hospitals improved handwashing, boiling of bandages, and separation of infected patients. These practices sound basic today, but at the time they were revolutionary. Death rates from infected wounds dropped dramatically, and survival rates soared.

77. When Doctors Could Finally See Inside Wounds

Finding bullets and shrapnel inside the human body used to be a grim guessing game. Surgeons often had to probe blindly with their fingers or knives, searching for metal fragments they couldn't see, sometimes causing more damage than the wound itself. World War I changed that with the introduction of mobile X-ray units, many of them organized by the famous scientist Marie Curie. Realizing that wounded soldiers were dying simply because doctors couldn't locate internal injuries quickly enough, Curie helped design small, portable radiology labs built inside cars and trucks. These vehicles carried X-ray machines, generators, and photographic equipment, allowing doctors to drive directly to field hospitals near the front. Nicknamed "Little Curies," the units glowed faintly in darkened tents as technicians developed images showing bones, bullets, and shrapnel clearly for the first time. Surgeons could suddenly see exactly where to cut instead of guessing, dramatically reducing surgery time and saving countless lives. Curie personally trained dozens of women as radiology operators and even drove some of the vehicles herself. By the end of the war, hundreds of thousands of soldiers had been examined using these mobile X-rays, turning a laboratory discovery into a battlefield lifesaver and laying the groundwork for modern medical imaging used in hospitals today.

78. The Birth of Modern Plastic Surgery

Modern plastic surgery was born not in beauty clinics, but in the shattered trenches of World War I. The nature of trench fighting meant soldiers often exposed only their heads above the parapet, and when artillery shells or sniper bullets struck, they frequently destroyed faces rather than bodies. Thousands of men survived wounds that would have killed them in earlier wars, but they returned with missing jaws, shattered cheekbones, torn noses, or entire sections of their faces blown away. Doctors suddenly faced a problem medicine had never seen on this scale: how to rebuild a human face. At hospitals in Britain and France, surgeons like Harold Gillies began experimenting with revolutionary techniques, grafting skin from a patient's chest or forehead, shaping new noses from cartilage, and inventing the "tube pedicle," a method of moving living skin across the body without cutting off its blood supply. Some soldiers underwent dozens of operations over months or years. Artists even sculpted painted metal or leather masks to cover disfigurements while reconstruction continued. The results were crude by modern standards but miraculous for the time, allowing men to eat, speak, and walk in public again without hiding their faces.

79. Pain and Anesthesia in Field Hospitals

Saving a life did not mean sparing a soldier pain. Field hospitals during World War I were places of relentless suffering, where men arrived with shattered limbs, torn flesh, and faces burned or broken beyond recognition. Surgery was often performed quickly and repeatedly, sometimes with only basic anesthesia, and recovery could be agony. To cope, doctors relied heavily on morphine, chloroform, and ether, powerful drugs that dulled pain but carried their own risks. Small glass morphine syrettes were injected before operations or given to wounded men lying on stretchers, the drug bringing a heavy, floating calm that many described as the only relief they felt for days. For surgeons, morphine felt like a miracle when it was available. Small glass syrettes were injected before operations or given to men lying on stretchers, bringing a heavy, floating calm that dulled the worst of the pain. But supplies were never guaranteed. During major battles, when hundreds or thousands arrived at once, drugs ran short and doses were rationed carefully. Some men went into surgery sedated; others endured procedures with only chloroform, ether, or nothing stronger than a leather strap to bite down on. In overcrowded wards lit by lanterns and filled with groans, nurses sometimes had to hold patients still while surgeons worked as quickly as they could.

80. Learning to Walk Again After the War

Saving a soldier's life was only the first step. For tens of thousands of survivors, the war had taken an arm or a leg, and returning home meant learning how to live inside a permanently altered body. Before World War I, most prosthetic limbs were crude wooden pegs or simple hooks, heavy, uncomfortable, and more symbolic than useful. But the sheer number of amputees forced rapid innovation. Hospitals and workshops began designing lighter artificial legs with hinged knees and ankles, shaped sockets that fit the body more naturally, and straps that allowed men to walk with something close to a normal gait. Artificial arms evolved from stiff wooden blocks into mechanical hands with moving fingers, cables, and springs that could grip tools, hold cups, or even write. Entire rehabilitation centers were created where veterans practiced walking, climbing stairs, or relearning trades like carpentry and typing. For the first time, prosthetics weren't just replacements, they were engineered for function.

81. Fighting War With Toothache

Not every medical problem in the trenches came from bullets or shells. Sometimes the most disabling enemy was a simple toothache. Soldiers lived on hard biscuits, tough salted meat, sugary tea, and constant tobacco, rarely brushing and almost never seeing a dentist. Cavities, abscesses, and broken teeth became common, and without treatment the pain could be unbearable. A man might be unable to sleep, eat, or even hold a rifle steady, effectively removing him from duty as surely as a wound. Early in the war, thousands of soldiers were evacuated from the front for dental problems alone, clogging hospitals with cases that had nothing to do with combat. Armies soon realized they were losing more manpower to teeth than to some minor battles. In response, they created mobile field dentistry units, small tents or trucks where dentists worked near the front lines extracting teeth, filling cavities, and fitting crude dentures. The solution was often blunt and fast: if a tooth hurt, it came out. Rows of men sometimes lined up outside aid posts waiting their turn, gripping chairs while dentists pulled teeth in minutes before sending them straight back to duty. It was painful and primitive, but effective. By the end of the war, organized military dentistry had become standard, laying the foundation for modern army dental corps.

82. Nurses on the Front Lines of Medicine

While new technologies like blood banks, X-rays, and ambulances transformed battlefield medicine, much of the real work of saving lives fell to exhausted nurses working in fragile hospitals just behind the front. These were rarely solid buildings. Most were canvas tents, wooden huts, or barns hastily converted into wards, their floors muddy, their roofs leaking, and their walls rattling whenever artillery boomed nearby. Inside, rows of stretchers lay shoulder to shoulder, often so tightly packed that staff had to turn sideways just to squeeze between them. Lanterns or weak electric bulbs cast a yellow glow over makeshift operating tables built from wooden doors balanced on crates. The air smelled of blood, antiseptic, wet wool, and smoke. Boots never fully dried, and everything felt permanently damp.

When major offensives began, the wounded arrived in waves that didn't stop for days. Ambulances and stretcher-bearers unloaded men faster than beds could be cleared. Nurses cleaned mud and lice from uniforms, cut away clothing stiff with blood, washed wounds, held down screaming patients during surgery, and carried buckets of water back and forth until their arms shook. Shifts stretched to 18 or even 20 hours at a time, with only minutes to sit or eat. Many learned to nap standing against a wall between cases. Some wrote final letters home for dying soldiers who could no longer hold a pen, or simply sat beside them so they wouldn't be alone. For countless men, the first gentle voice they heard after being hit belonged not to a doctor, but to a nurse offering water or calling them "love."

These hospitals were not safe havens. They were often still within artillery range, and shells sometimes landed close enough to shatter windows or collapse tents. Nurses were killed or wounded while tending patients, yet many refused to move farther back, knowing every extra mile of transport meant more soldiers dying before reaching care. In a war dominated by machinery, steel, and mass destruction, their work was intensely personal: hands bandaging, hands lifting, hands comforting. Long after the war, veterans remembered the faces of the nurses who treated them more clearly than the generals who commanded them.

SEVEN

Prisoners of War

For many soldiers, the war did not end on the battlefield, but in the hands of the enemy. Being captured was a sudden and life-changing event that turned a fighter into a prisoner, often for years at a time. This chapter looks at the reality of life behind the wire, from the initial shock of being taken to the daily struggle of living in crowded camps. It was a unique and difficult experience where survival depended on patience, resilience, and the hope of one day returning home to a world that was changing without them.

83. Surrender and Survival in the Trenches

Most prisoners of war were not captured in dramatic last-stand battles but during the quieter, more chaotic moments when units broke, got lost, or were simply surrounded. In trench warfare, entire sections of line could collapse in minutes. A failed attack might leave survivors stranded in shell holes with no officers and no ammunition. When artillery cut telephone wires and smoke covered the battlefield, men often had no idea where friendly lines even were. Some wandered straight into enemy trenches by mistake. Others were cut off when flanking units retreated. During large offensives, thousands surrendered at once when resistance became pointless. Machine-gun crews out of bullets, stretcher-bearers caught in the open, and exhausted soldiers trapped behind new enemy positions often raised their hands rather than die needlessly.

The scale was enormous. By the end of the war, roughly 8 to 9 million soldiers worldwide had become prisoners. Germany alone held about 2.5 to 3 million captives, many of them Russians. Russia captured roughly 2 to 2.5 million Austro-Hungarian and German troops. Austria-Hungary held around 1 to 1.5 million, mostly Russians and Italians. Britain and France together held hundreds of thousands more, including Ottoman and German soldiers. Some single battles produced staggering numbers. At Tannenberg in 1914, tens of thousands of Russians were captured in days. During the final Allied offensives of 1918, entire German units surrendered by the thousands as morale collapsed. For many men, becoming a prisoner wasn't a heroic last moment but a simple calculation: wounded, hungry, and surrounded, captivity meant survival.

84. Life Outside the Prison Camps

Many prisoners were assigned to labor detachments rather than kept inside main camps. Captives were sent out in small groups to farms, mines, factories, and rail yards, where they worked under guard but often interacted directly with civilians. In agricultural regions especially, prisoners sometimes lived in barns or village quarters instead of fenced compounds. For farmers facing labor shortages, these men became essential workers, blurring the line between enemy soldier and temporary employee.

85. Hunger and Hope in Prison Camps

Food quickly became the central obsession of prisoner-of-war camp life, because rations were designed only to keep men barely alive, not healthy. A typical daily issue in many German camps might be thin turnip or cabbage soup, a chunk of coarse black bread weighing about half a pound (225 grams), and sometimes a small portion of potatoes or barley. Meat was rare, often just scraps of fat or gristle floating in broth. Coffee was usually a bitter substitute made from roasted acorns or chicory. Many prisoners consumed fewer than 1,000–1,400 calories a day, far below what a working adult needed, and weight loss was constant. Men grew hollow-cheeked and weak, and conversations revolved endlessly around food: what they missed, what they would eat first at home, or imaginary recipes made from memory.

Because official rations were so poor, parcels from home became lifesavers rather than luxuries. Families, charities, and organizations like the Red Cross shipped millions of packages containing real bread, tinned beef, jam, chocolate, condensed milk, tea, sugar, butter, sausages, or biscuits. A single

Red Cross parcel could provide several days' worth of proper calories. Camps often allowed one parcel per man per week if transport lines were functioning. Prisoners guarded these boxes fiercely, trading items like currency or pooling ingredients to cook shared meals on small improvised stoves. Entire barracks might celebrate the arrival of one intact parcel, turning a tin of jam or slab of chocolate into an event that lifted morale more than any speech.

Letters followed a similar path. Mail was censored but usually permitted under the Geneva Convention. Prisoners wrote home on thin, preprinted cards with limited space and strict rules about what they could say. Messages traveled through camp post offices, then by rail and ship through neutral countries before reaching families. Delivery could take weeks or months, but even a short note in familiar handwriting was priceless. Men reread letters until the paper wore thin, memorizing every line. In a world of barbed wire and hunger, food parcels fed the body, but letters fed something just as important; the stubborn hope that life still existed beyond the fence.

86. Escape Attempts from Prison Camps

Escape attempts ranged from impulsive sprints toward nearby woods to carefully planned operations that took months to prepare. Prisoners dug tunnels beneath fences, forged documents, disguised themselves as laborers, or slipped away during work details. Most attempts failed, often ending with recapture within days. Yet the idea of escape mattered psychologically, giving prisoners a sense of agency in a situation otherwise defined by powerlessness.

87. Trade and Barter Behind Barbed Wire

Camps developed their own internal economies. Cigarettes, bread, soap, and chocolate functioned as currency, traded for favors or extra food. Skilled prisoners repaired boots, cut hair, or carved small crafts in exchange for supplies. Bartering created a fragile marketplace inside the wire, where survival often depended on negotiation rather than strength. In some camps, this informal economy became more organized than the official ration system.

88. Culture and Learning Behind Barbed Wire

Cultural life persisted even in confinement. Prisoners staged plays using makeshift costumes, formed choirs and bands, and organized lectures on history, mathematics, or languages. Former teachers held classes, determined that captivity would not steal years of learning. These activities were not luxuries but survival tools, helping men maintain routine and purpose when the future felt suspended indefinitely.

89. Discipline and Punishment in POW Camps

Discipline inside camps was usually strict but inconsistent. Minor rule-breaking could result in extra labor, confinement, or reduced rations, while serious offenses led to solitary cells or transfer to harsher facilities. Yet enforcement varied widely depending on guards and local commanders. Some camps were rigid and punitive, while others operated with surprising flexibility, reflecting how individual personalities often mattered more than official regulations.

90. Friendships Across Enemy Lines

Language barriers created unexpected challenges and alliances. Prisoners from different nations were sometimes housed together, forced to communicate through gestures, shared slang, or improvised mixtures of words. Over time, friendships formed across national lines as men discovered that captivity made former enemies share the same daily struggles. The war's divisions blurred inside the wire, replaced by a common identity as prisoners.

91. Improvised Medicine in Prison Camps

Medical care in camps was uneven but often improvised. Doctors who were themselves prisoners treated the sick using limited supplies, converting barracks into makeshift hospitals. Disease spread easily in crowded conditions, especially influenza and dysentery, yet professional skill sometimes made the difference between life and death. In some cases, enemy medical staff cooperated quietly to prevent outbreaks that could devastate both prisoners and guards.

92. The Psychological Burden of Waiting

Time passed strangely in captivity. Without battle rhythms or clear progress, days blended together into long stretches of waiting. Some prisoners scratched calendars into wood or walls to track the date, refusing to let months disappear unnoticed. Others stopped counting altogether, finding it easier not to measure how much of their lives had slipped away. The psychological weight of lost time became one of captivity's heaviest burdens.

93. The Long Journey Home After Captivity

When the war finally ended, release was rarely immediate or orderly. Transportation networks were damaged, governments disorganized, and millions of men needed to be moved across continents. Prisoners sometimes waited months after the armistice before trains or ships arrived. For many, freedom came slowly, in stages, marked not by celebration but by confusion and exhaustion as they tried to rebuild lives paused years earlier.

94. The Quiet Scars of Prisoner Life

For some former prisoners, captivity left deeper memories than combat itself. Years spent behind wire, separated from home and stripped of control, reshaped how they viewed authority and national loyalty. The war they remembered most clearly was not the charge across no man's land, but the long, quiet struggle to remain human in a place designed to hold them still.

EIGHT

Heroes, Legends & Life at the Front

While the history of the World War I is often told through the dates of battles and the names of generals, the true story lives in the remarkable experiences of the people who were there. This chapter looks at the human side of the conflict, from the famous figures who served in the mud before they became world leaders or legendary authors to the extraordinary bravery of units like the Harlem Hellfighters and the Lost Battalion. It also explores the smaller, everyday parts of life at the front, including the songs the soldiers sang, and the strange superstitions they relied on to get through each day. These are the legends and personal stories that show how, even in the middle of a global catastrophe, the human spirit found ways to endure, laugh, and hope.

95. The Lost Battalion in the Argonne Forest

In October 1918, deep in the tangled woods of France's Argonne Forest, more than 500 American soldiers advanced farther than anyone realized and accidentally marched straight into a trap. Thick trees, smoke, and confusion hid the enemy's movements, and by the time officers understood their position, German troops had already slipped around both flanks and sealed the gap behind them. The unit, made up mostly of the 77th Division from New York, suddenly found itself completely surrounded, cut off from supplies, reinforcements, and even its own army. Phone lines were severed by shellfire, runners sent for help were shot or captured, and food quickly ran out. The men dug shallow foxholes among the roots and rocks and prepared to hold their ground.

For nearly a week they endured constant attacks from every direction. Snipers fired from the trees. Artillery pounded their small pocket of forest day and night. Water grew scarce, rations dwindled to almost nothing, and the wounded piled up faster than medics could treat them. At one point, American artillery, unaware of their exact position, began shelling their own trapped troops. With no other way to communicate, the soldiers turned to carrier pigeons. One desperate note read, "Our artillery is dropping a barrage directly on us. For heaven's sake stop it." The message was tied to a pigeon named Cher Ami. Shot through the chest and losing a leg, the bird still flew miles through the gunfire and delivered the note, saving the survivors from being destroyed by friendly fire.

By the time relief forces finally broke through, nearly two-thirds of the battalion were dead, wounded, or missing. The men who staggered out of the forest looked skeletal, filthy, and half-starved, having survived for days on almost nothing while fighting off repeated assaults. Newspapers later called them "The Lost Battalion," turning their ordeal into a symbol of stubborn endurance.

96. From the Trenches to the Birth of Jazz in Europe

Among the American troops who arrived in France was the 369th Infantry Regiment, an all-Black unit from New York that would later earn the nickname "The Harlem Hellfighters." Because of segregation in the U.S. Army, they were often assigned labor duties instead of combat and were initially treated as second-class soldiers. But they brought something no other unit did: a full regimental band led by composer and conductor James Reese Europe. Packed with brass horns, clarinets, drums, and banjos, the band played a fast, syncopated style of music that many Europeans had never heard before, early jazz.

When the Hellfighters performed in French towns and behind the lines, crowds gathered instantly. Their music was louder, livelier, and freer than traditional military marches. Instead of stiff parades, people danced. Soldiers who had just come off the front forgot the war for a few minutes, clapping and laughing in muddy boots. The band toured constantly, sometimes playing for thousands at a time, introducing jazz to villages, cities, and even Parisian theaters. Many historians later credited them with helping spark Europe's first real exposure to jazz music.

The regiment itself also saw heavy combat, spending more days in the trenches than almost any other American unit and earning high praise from the French army, which awarded many of them the Croix de Guerre for bravery. Yet their cultural impact may have lasted even longer than their battlefield record. Long after the guns fell silent, the rhythms they carried overseas kept spreading.

97. A Pacifist Who Became a War Hero

Not every extraordinary moment of the war involved massive machines or entire divisions. Sometimes it came down to one exhausted soldier with a rifle. In October 1918, during the Meuse-Argonne Offensive, a quiet Tennessee farm boy named Alvin York found himself leading a small group of American troops through thick woods when they suddenly walked into a nest of German machine guns. The first burst of fire dropped most of the Americans instantly. Officers were killed, men scattered, and York, now one of the few still standing, suddenly found himself in charge.

Before the war, York had been a deeply religious pacifist who didn't even want to fight. He believed killing was wrong and had tried to claim conscientious objector status. Only after long conversations with his pastor did he reluctantly agree that defending others might be justified. Now, under fire, that decision was being tested. Instead of retreating, York crawled forward alone. Using a rifle and his skill as a hunter, he began picking off German gunners one by one with calm, careful shots. When a group charged him with bayonets, he switched to his pistol and dropped them at close range. The sudden, precise fire convinced many Germans that they were facing a much larger force. Confused and intimidated, dozens began surrendering.

By the end of the fight, York and a handful of surviving Americans had captured 132 German soldiers and silenced more than thirty machine guns almost single-handedly. What began as an ambush turned into one of the most unlikely reversals of the war. York later received the Medal of Honor and returned home to national fame, though he always downplayed the story, insisting he had simply done what he had to do.

98. The Attack of the Dead Men at Osowiec Fortress

One of the strangest and most nightmarish battles of the entire war took place at the Russian-held Osowiec Fortress in 1915, during a German gas attack so horrific that it later sounded more like legend than history. Before dawn, German artillery fired shells filled with chlorine gas, releasing a thick, greenish cloud that rolled slowly toward the Russian trenches like fog. Chlorine reacted with moisture in the lungs to form acid, burning throats and eyes, blistering skin, and drowning men from the inside as their lungs filled with fluid. Soldiers choked, vomited blood, and collapsed where they stood. Vegetation blackened, birds fell from the sky, and even metal equipment corroded in the fumes. From a distance, the fortress looked silent and dead. Convinced that no one could have survived, German infantry advanced confidently to occupy the position.

Then shapes began moving in the haze. Out of the drifting gas stumbled dozens of Russian survivors, barely alive but still armed. Their faces were wrapped in blood-soaked rags, uniforms torn and burned by chemicals, coughing up blood and pieces of lung tissue as they staggered forward. Some could barely stand. Others leaned on rifles like walking sticks. Yet instead of retreating, they charged. Witnesses later said the men looked like corpses clawing their way out of graves. Terrified by the sight of these half-blinded, half-suffocated figures screaming and advancing through the smoke, the German troops broke formation and fled in panic. The fortress held. The clash became known as "The Attack of the Dead Men," a moment when shock and fear proved stronger than gas or artillery, and when soldiers who should have been dead somehow kept fighting anyway.

99. The Hidden War Beneath the Trenches

Some soldiers didn't just live underground, they fought there. Along parts of the Western Front, specialist tunnelling units spent months digging secret passageways beneath enemy trenches, turning the war into a silent, suffocating world beneath the battlefield. Recruited mainly from coal miners, engineers, and railway workers who already knew how to work in tight spaces, these men carved tunnels by hand with picks and short shovels, scraping through clay and chalk while lying almost flat on their stomachs. Many shafts were barely three or four feet (about one meter) high, forcing men to crawl or crouch the entire time. The earth pressed in from all sides. Timber supports creaked constantly. Every few minutes, dirt trickled down from the ceiling like slow rain.

Light was scarce. Candles, oil lamps, or small carbide lamps gave off weak yellow glows and filled the air with smoke. Sometimes the flame would suddenly gutter out, a terrifying sign that oxygen was running low or gas had built up. The air smelled of damp soil, sweat, and stale breath. Ventilation was poor, and some tunnels grew so hot and stuffy that men struggled to breathe. There were no proper toilets, only buckets or tins shoved into corners, quickly turning the cramped passages foul. After hours underground, clothes were soaked with mud and grime, faces streaked black like coal miners.

Silence was everything. Even a dropped tool might give away their position. Many worked barefoot or in socks to muffle sound, stopping constantly to press their ears or stethoscopes against the walls to listen for enemy digging only feet away. If they broke through into an opposing tunnel, the fighting became desperate and primitive. There was no space to swing rifles, so men used pistols, bayonets, knives, clubs, or even sharpened entrenching tools in near-total darkness, grappling at arm's length in choking dust. The real objective was explosives. Tunnellers packed chambers with tons of ammonal beneath enemy lines, then retreated and detonated the charges, blowing entire trenches into the air like volcanoes. Some explosions were so massive they were heard dozens of miles away.

The work was so claustrophobic and nerve-racking that many veterans later said they feared the underground more than open combat. This hidden war beneath the trenches inspired modern portrayals like Thomas Shelby in *Peaky Blinders*, whose tunnelling scenes closely mirror the real experiences of these men. For them, the front line wasn't above ground at all, but in the dark earth itself, fighting an unseen enemy through inches of soil.

100. When Horses Beat Machine Guns

While most of World War I was fought from muddy trenches in Europe, one of its most dramatic battles took place thousands of miles away in the desert. After the failure of Gallipoli, Australian and New Zealand troops were redeployed to Egypt and the Middle East to protect the Suez Canal and fight the Ottoman Empire in what became the Sinai and Palestine Campaign. There, wide open terrain made horses useful again, and the Australian Light Horse became fast-moving desert fighters instead of trench soldiers.

On October 31, 1917, near the town of Beersheba, the Allies faced a desperate problem: water. Without capturing the town's wells before nightfall, thousands of men and horses risked collapsing from dehydration. With time running out, commanders ordered something almost unthinkable in modern warfare, a full cavalry charge straight at entrenched defenders.

Just before sunset, nearly 800 riders formed up in long ranks. Bayonets were held in their hands like makeshift swords, since they carried no traditional sabers. Then the order came. The horses surged forward at a trot, then a gallop, hooves thundering across the hard desert floor. Dust clouds rose behind them as Turkish artillery and machine guns opened fire. Shells burst overhead, bullets kicked up sand, but the riders kept coming, faster and faster.

The speed saved them. Enemy gunners had trouble lowering their sights quickly enough to hit targets moving so fast. Within minutes, the Australians were crashing over the trenches, leaping obstacles, and fighting hand-to-hand among stunned defenders who had expected an infantry assault, not a wall of charging horses. By nightfall, Beersheba was captured, along with its precious wells, and the advance continued.

The charge cost dozens of lives, but it succeeded where slower tactics might have failed. For many Australians and New Zealanders, it became a symbol of daring, improvisation, and "mateship" under pressure. Photographs of mounted troops racing across open desert stand in sharp contrast to the barbed wire and mud of the Western Front.

101. Marks Left in the Trenches

The walls of trenches, dugouts, and ruined buildings slowly filled with graffiti as soldiers carved their presence into the war wherever they could. Men scratched their names, hometowns, and dates into wooden beams and chalky stone, leaving behind simple lines like "Tom, Manchester, 1916" or "Still here somehow." Others posted dark jokes and warnings, painting signs that read "If you're reading this, you're too tall" near sniper zones or "Keep your head down" above exposed corners. Directions were mocked with arrows pointing "This way to Berlin," while miserable sectors earned sarcastic welcomes such as "Hotel Somme" or "Paradise Alley." Rotating units left messages for the next group: "Good luck lads" or "Watch the rats at night," turning the trenches into a kind of passing conversation between strangers. Long after the fighting stopped, archaeologists and hikers would still find these carvings preserved in concrete and wood, small handwritten proof that frightened young men had once stood there, trying to leave some trace that they had existed at all.

102. The Dark Humor of Trench Songs

Songs became one of the fastest ways trench slang, complaints, and dark humor spread across the front, with soldiers constantly rewriting familiar tunes to match their reality. Cheerful prewar music hall songs were often sung with heavy irony, like *"Pack Up Your Troubles in Your Old Kit-Bag, and smile, smile, smile,"* belted out while men marched through rain and mud with anything but smiles. Others were openly sarcastic, such as the endlessly repeated chant set to *Auld Lang Syne*: *"We're here because we're here, because we're here, because we're here,"* a deliberately pointless lyric that joked about the senselessness of their situation. Some songs mocked officers directly, especially in the popular trench parody *"Hanging on the Old Barbed Wire,"* where verses complained, *"If you want to find the general, I know where he is… he's hanging on the old barbed wire,"* a biting joke about leaders staying safely behind the lines. Men sang while marching, digging, or waiting for rations, passing verses from unit to unit until entire battalions knew the same choruses. In a world of shellfire and orders, these songs became a shared language of sarcasm and survival, turning fear and frustration into something you could shout together in the dark.

103. Code Words Soldiers Used for War

Soldiers also developed a quiet system of code words and euphemisms that allowed them to talk about danger without ever naming it directly. Instead of saying an attack, they might casually mention "going over for a stroll" or "doing a bit of work tonight," while a hazardous repair mission became a harmless-sounding "working party." Dawn and dusk alerts were simply "stand-to," and a supposedly safe stretch of line was labeled a "quiet sector," a phrase veterans learned to distrust immediately. Death itself was softened into phrases like "lost," "missing," or "not coming back," and being sent away sick or injured was described as "getting a ticket out." Officers wrote reports filled with bland wording such as "slight losses" or "enemy activity," language that hid the chaos underneath. Over time, this understatement became second nature, turning catastrophe into routine vocabulary. By shrinking terrifying events into mild phrases, soldiers protected themselves emotionally, speaking about the worst moments of their lives as if they were nothing more than minor inconveniences.

104. From Trenches to Everyday Speech

World War I didn't just redraw maps and topple empires. It quietly rewired everyday language. Words that had once belonged strictly to generals and field reports slipped into kitchens, classrooms, and shop floors. Civilians reading newspapers suddenly spoke of the "front line," "mobilizing," "casualties," and "barrages" as casually as weather forecasts. War vocabulary became normal vocabulary. Conflict, urgency, and even business problems were described using the language of battle, as if the entire world had begun thinking like an army.

At the same time, the men actually living in the trenches invented a private dialect to survive mentally as much as physically. The front was too miserable to describe plainly, so everything was renamed with dry humor. A tiny dirt shelter scraped into a wall became a "funk hole." Wooden planks over the mud were "duckboards." Tins of corned beef were "bully beef," hard crackers "dog biscuits," and lice "chats," leading to the daily ritual of "chatting" for hours while picking them out of seams. Big shells were "whizz-bangs" or "Jack Johnsons," nicknamed after the heavyweight boxer because they hit with a crushing punch. A safer posting was "cushy." Dawn and dusk alerts were simply "stand-to." The vocabulary made chaos sound domestic, almost ordinary, as if renaming danger could shrink it.

Humor went further. Shellfire was described as "a bit lively." Flooded trenches became "the seaside." Rats were "trench terriers." Death itself softened into phrases like "gone west." Even letters home were coded. Because officers might read every line, soldiers learned to understate everything. A bombardment became "busy today." A coming assault was "going for a walk." A miserable, rat-infested hole was "comfortable enough." Families learned that cheerful phrases usually meant the opposite. This habit of understatement followed many veterans home, shaping a restrained, guarded way of speaking long after the guns fell silent.

The trenches were also linguistic melting pots. British troops longed for "Blighty," their slang for home, and called a lucky wound a "Blighty one" if it meant evacuation. Australians spoke of their "mates" and cursed foolish officers as "drongos." Canadians mixed British and American expressions like "buddy" and "okay." Indian soldiers shared words like "pukka" for something genuine and "dekko" for a quick look. African troops contributed terms such as "askari" and "safari." In crowded dugouts and marching columns, these phrases spread from unit to unit, turning the front into an accidental classroom where words traveled faster than any official language ever could.

Even the need for speed changed speech. Expressions like "AWOL" (absent without leave) and "SNAFU" (situation normal, all fouled up) grew from the need to convey complex situations quickly under stress. Wartime communication favored short, efficient language that later influenced everything from offices to government paperwork.

When the war ended, the vocabulary didn't stay behind. Veterans carried it into civilian life, and soon factories launched "campaigns," politicians planned "offensives," newspapers covered elections like "battles," and workers complained about being "in the trenches." Sports teams "attacked" and "defended." Without realizing it, society kept speaking the language of war. The mud and barbed wire were gone, but the words remained, shaping how an entire generation described effort, struggle, and loss. In that sense, World War I never fully ended. It lived on every time someone said they were holding the line.

105. Brilliant Minds in the Shadow of War

Not everyone who shaped the twentieth century carried a rifle the same way, and the war pulled brilliant minds into it from every direction, some into uniform, others into open protest. In Britain, philosopher Bertrand Russell refused to fight at all. While patriotic crowds cheered enlistment, Russell publicly condemned the war as a tragic mistake driven by nationalism, pride, and political ego. He gave speeches against conscription, wrote essays attacking the government, and urged young men not to sacrifice themselves for what he believed was pointless slaughter. Authorities treated dissent almost like treason. He lost his lectureship at Cambridge, was fined, banned from certain cities, and in 1918 was jailed for months. From his prison cell he continued writing about peace, free speech, and civil liberties, becoming one of the most famous antiwar voices of the era. Simply questioning the war could cost a man his job, reputation, and freedom.

At the same time, millions of other young men who would later become household names were quietly serving in the mud like everyone else. J.R.R. Tolkien worked as a signals officer at the Somme, watching most of his closest friends die, experiences that later echoed in the bleak landscapes, loyal friendships, and sense of loss that filled The Lord of the Rings. Adolf Hitler served as a German messenger, running through shellfire with dispatches and earning medals for bravery, wounds and defeat feeding the bitterness and nationalism that later defined his politics. Future U.S. President Harry Truman commanded an artillery battery in France and learned leadership under fire. Ernest Hemingway drove ambulances for the Red Cross, was badly wounded by mortar fire, and later turned those memories into A Farewell to Arms. Walt Disney, still underage, lied about his age to enlist as an ambulance driver and decorated his vehicle with cartoons to amuse wounded soldiers. Even A. A. Milne, creator of Winnie-the-Pooh, first wore a British officer's uniform in the trenches.

106. Christmas in the Trenches

Even in the middle of war, the calendar still turned, and Christmas became one of the few moments when the trenches briefly felt human again. In December, parcels from home increased, stuffed with fruitcake, chocolate, socks, scarves, tobacco, and small gifts that were saved carefully for the day itself. Units decorated dugouts with scraps of greenery, empty shell casings, or candles stuck into bottles to resemble makeshift trees. Cooks improvised special meals when supplies allowed, adding extra meat, jam, or pudding to rations, and tea or rum was issued more generously than usual. Men sang carols softly at night, shared food between platoons, and wrote longer letters home describing the strange mix of celebration and homesickness. In quieter sectors, football matches, concerts, or small church services were organized behind the lines.

The most famous Christmas came in 1914, when parts of the Western Front fell unexpectedly silent in what became known as the Christmas Truce. It was not ordered by generals or planned by politicians but began spontaneously when German soldiers placed small Christmas trees and candles along their parapets and started singing carols like *Stille Nacht (Silent Night)* across the darkness. British troops answered with songs of their own, and soon voices replaced rifle fire. Curious men cautiously climbed out of their trenches, meeting halfway in no man's land with raised hands and nervous smiles. They shook hands, exchanged cigarettes, chocolate, buttons, and caps, and helped one another bury bodies that had been lying between the lines for weeks. In some places they posed for photographs together or kicked footballs back and forth in the mud. The truce lasted only hours in some sectors and a day or two in others before officers ordered everyone back to their positions and the shooting slowly resumed. Still, for a brief moment, the war loosened its grip, and enemies saw each other not as targets but as ordinary young men far from home, sharing the same cold and longing for peace.

107. The Rituals Soldiers Used to Cheat Fate

In a war where death often felt random and unpredictable, many soldiers clung to small superstitions and lucky charms, believing that tiny rituals might somehow tilt fate in their favor. Coins, lockets, photographs, or scraps of ribbon from sweethearts were tucked into breast pockets like protective talismans. Some men carried rabbit's feet, church medals, or bits of hometown soil sewn into their uniforms. Others refused to change "lucky" socks, wore the same scarf on every patrol, or insisted on stepping into the trench with the same foot first each morning. Dice, playing cards, and carved trinkets became pocket charms rubbed before going over the top. Entire units developed shared rituals, avoiding certain dugouts considered unlucky or repeating the same jokes and phrases before attacks. Even hardened veterans who claimed not to believe often followed these habits quietly, reasoning that it was safer not to tempt fate. In a world ruled by artillery and chance, these small objects and routines offered something the war rarely did, the comforting illusion of control.

NINE

The War at Home

World War I was not just fought on distant battlefields; it was a conflict that reached into every home, factory, and street across the globe. As the struggle dragged on, the line between the soldier and the civilian began to disappear, and the people left behind were called upon to support the war effort in ways never seen before. This chapter looks at the reality of life on the home front, from the massive social changes that saw women entering the industrial workforce to the clever and often intense ways that governments used propaganda and rationing to keep their nations focused on the fight. It was a time of shared sacrifice and immense pressure, where the endurance of those at home became just as vital to the final outcome as the strength of the armies at the front.

108. The Birth of Total War

When the war erupted in 1914, almost everyone believed it would be short. Politicians spoke confidently of being "home by Christmas." Generals expected a few decisive battles followed by peace talks. Factories continued making consumer goods, shops stayed open, and most civilians assumed the fighting would be handled by professional soldiers far away. But within months, the reality shattered those expectations. The front lines barely moved, casualties climbed into the hundreds of thousands, and armies burned through ammunition, food, uniforms, and fuel at a pace no peacetime economy had ever imagined. The war wasn't ending. It was expanding.

Governments quickly realized something alarming: the battlefield wasn't just short of men, it was short of everything. Guns needed shells. Soldiers needed boots. Railways needed coal. Hospitals needed bandages. Every day the front consumed mountains of supplies that had to be replaced immediately or entire offensives would stall. Victory no longer depended only on bravery or tactics. It depended on production. So states did something unprecedented. They stepped in and took control.

Factories that had once competed freely were reorganized like military units. Car plants stopped making cars and began building trucks, ambulances, and aircraft parts. Piano makers produced shell casings. Bicycle shops machined rifle components. Textile mills churned out uniforms and bandages instead of clothing. Steelworks forged artillery barrels around the clock. Governments created powerful ministries (like Britain's Ministry of Munitions) that told businesses exactly what to produce and how much. Quotas replaced profits. Output charts replaced sales targets. Whistles and sirens marked shifts like bugles marked drills.

Civilians were mobilized almost like soldiers. Millions of men left farms and offices for the trenches, and women filled their places in factories and transport jobs. Children collected scrap metal. Families planted vegetable gardens to stretch food supplies. Coal, rubber, and bread were rationed. Railways prioritized troop trains over passengers.

By 1915, it was clear this was no longer a conflict between armies. It was a contest between whole societies. One side's strength came not just from its generals, but from how many shells its factories could produce, how much food its farms could grow, and how long its civilians could endure shortages and long shifts. The war had spread far beyond the trenches. It had reached into workshops, kitchens, and city streets, turning entire nations into vast, coordinated war machines. For the first time in history, everyone was part of the front line.

109. The Women Who Powered the War

When millions of men marched off to war, their places at the machines could not stay empty. By 1915–16, governments realized that winning battles depended just as much on shells and bullets as on soldiers. So the gates of heavy industry swung open to women for the first time. Across Britain, France, Germany, and beyond, women poured into shipyards, steel mills, and especially munitions factories, trading aprons and classrooms for overalls, gloves, and steel presses. In Britain alone, more than a million women entered munitions work, and by the middle of the war women made up the majority of workers producing shells, cartridges, and explosives.

The work was exhausting and relentless. Shifts often lasted 10–12 hours, sometimes longer during offensives when armies demanded millions of extra rounds. Factories ran day and night under bright electric lamps, machines pounding without pause. Women stood for hours filling shells with TNT, screwing in fuses, polishing brass casings, hauling crates, or operating heavy lathes and presses that shook the floor. Supervisors treated output like a battlefield objective. Every delay meant fewer shells at the front.

But the real danger wasn't just fatigue. It was the chemicals. TNT dust soaked into hair, clothes, and skin. Over time it stained workers a sickly yellow color and irritated their eyes and lungs. Their faces, hands, and even the whites of their eyes could turn mustard-yellow, earning them the nickname "canary girls." Some suffered headaches, nausea, liver damage, or poisoning. A few collapsed at their benches. Yet many kept working because the pay, though still unequal, was often better than anything they had earned before.

Explosions were an ever-present fear. Entire buildings could vanish in a second if sparks hit loose powder. In several disasters, factories detonated with the force of small earthquakes, killing dozens or even hundreds at once. Windows shattered miles away. Roofs lifted into the sky. Rescue crews sometimes found nothing but craters where workshops had stood. Unlike the trenches, there were no medals or parades here, yet these women were dying in what many quietly called the "factory front line."

Still, for many, the job brought something new and unexpected: independence. Regular wages meant their own money, their own choices. Some rented rooms, bought bicycles, went to cinemas, or supported families without relying on husbands or fathers. For the first time, women handled heavy machinery, worked in teams, joined unions, and proved they could do jobs once declared impossible for them.

When the war ended, many were pushed back out of these roles to make space for returning men. But the change couldn't be fully undone. The experience had cracked open old assumptions. Women had built the shells, forged the steel, and kept the war running. After proving they could power an entire industrial nation, it was much harder to argue they belonged only in kitchens and parlors. The factories had quietly reshaped society as surely as the trenches had reshaped the battlefield.

110. Wages, Coins, and Independence

Money itself felt different during the war, partly because the old British currency system sounded like a code. Instead of simple dollars and cents, pay was counted in pounds, shillings, and pence. One pound (£1) equaled 20 shillings, and one shilling equaled 12 pence, meaning there were 240 pence in a pound. A few coins could still buy everyday necessities. A loaf of bread might cost 1–2 pence, a tram ride a penny, and weekly rent for a small room perhaps 5–8 shillings. A cinema ticket was often just 3–6 pence, cheap enough for an evening out after work. A sturdy pair of leather boots might cost 6–10 shillings, a winter coat around a pound, and a second-hand bicycle, one of the most desired symbols of independence, could be bought for £3–£5, letting a woman travel miles without relying on trams or escorts. Small luxuries suddenly felt possible: tea in a café, a new hat, a gramophone record, or a few shillings sent home to family each week. Motorcars technically existed, but they were still luxury items costing £150 or more, far beyond a factory worker's reach and mostly owned by doctors, businessmen, or the wealthy. For most women, the bicycle, not the car, was the true vehicle of freedom, turning wages into mobility and independence in a way earlier generations had never experienced. So even what looks like a small number on paper could stretch surprisingly far.

Before the war, many working-class women earned very little actual cash. Domestic servants, shop girls, laundresses, or farm hands often made only 10–15 shillings a week. Some were partly paid in food and lodging rather than wages. In modern terms, that might equal roughly $80–$120 a week today, barely enough for independence. Many handed their pay straight to parents or husbands and kept almost nothing themselves.

War industry changed their earning power dramatically. Women in munitions and engineering plants commonly earned 30–40 shillings a week, and with overtime or skilled tasks some reached 50–60 shillings. That was double or triple their old income. Converted to today's money, this might look like about $250–$350 a week, or roughly $1,000–$1,400 a month. By modern standards that sounds modest, but at 1916 prices it could cover rent, food, coal for heating, clothes, and still leave savings. For many women, it was the first time they had steady disposable income at all.

Payday became a small ceremony. Wages were often handed out in envelopes of coins and notes on Friday afternoons. Women counted their money right there on the factory floor, comparing totals, planning purchases, sending a few shillings home, or saving for boots, a bicycle, or a cinema ticket. Diaries mention the quiet pride of buying things without asking permission from anyone.

111. Factories Ordered to War

As the war dragged on and casualties mounted, governments realized that victory would depend not just on soldiers, but on production. In 1915 Britain created the Ministry of Munitions, a powerful new department that effectively took control of large parts of the economy and began running industry like an army. Private businesses no longer chose what they made or how much. Instead, telegrams and official orders arrived with exact instructions: convert your workshop, retool your machines, produce this many shells by this date. Car factories that once built touring cars were ordered to manufacture artillery shells and engines. Piano makers, skilled at bending wood and shaping metal frames, were reassigned to make shell casings. Bicycle shops began producing gun parts and ball bearings. Even small family workshops found themselves suddenly making fuses, detonators, or rifle components.

Production targets were strict and mathematical. A plant might be told to deliver 10,000 shells per week, 50 machine guns per month, or thousands of rifles by a fixed deadline. Inspectors checked output constantly. If a factory fell short, managers could be fined, removed, or even threatened with government takeover. Workers were sometimes forbidden to leave their jobs, and strikes in key industries were restricted or temporarily banned under wartime laws. Yet these were not unpaid demands. The government issued formal contracts and paid companies directly, often guaranteeing profits to keep production flowing, turning war work into a massive state-funded enterprise.

For the first time in modern history, an entire industrial nation functioned under centralized command. Schedules, quotas, and supply chains were treated like military orders. Steel, coal, and labor were allocated the way generals allocated troops. Factories became regiments, foremen acted like officers, and output numbers were measured almost like battlefield victories.

112. When the Guns Ran Out of Ammunition

By 1915, the First World War had already revealed a brutal truth: modern war consumed ammunition faster than any nation on earth could manufacture it. Prewar planners had imagined short campaigns lasting weeks. Instead, guns fired for months without pause. On some days, a single British artillery battery might fire more shells in an hour than entire armies had used in previous wars. During major offensives, thousands of guns firing together could burn through hundreds of thousands of shells in a single day. Entire hillsides shook continuously, and ammunition trains struggled to keep up. Then, suddenly, the impossible happened: the shells ran out.

This shortage became known as the "Shell Crisis" of 1915–16. British units preparing for attacks discovered their guns had only a few days' supply left. Some batteries were ordered to fire sparingly, rationing shots as if counting food. Infantry assaults went forward without proper bombardments, costing thousands of lives because enemy barbed wire and machine-gun nests remained intact. Newspapers exploded with anger, blaming the government for sending men into battle without bullets. It was one of the first moments civilians realized the war wasn't just fought by soldiers, but by factories.

The solution required something unprecedented: entire economies were reorganized for total war. Governments seized control of industry, creating ministries of munitions and converting anything that could hold a lathe (a machine tool that shapes metal by spinning the material very fast while a cutting blade shaves pieces off) into a weapons factory. Car plants, sewing machine workshops, piano makers, and bicycle companies suddenly found themselves producing rifles, shells, and machine-gun parts. Women flooded into these factories by the hundreds of thousands, operating presses and packing explosives around the clock. In Britain alone, shell production jumped from roughly 13,000 shells per day in 1914 to over 1.5 million per day by 1916. By the end of the war, millions of shells were being produced every single week.

Making a single artillery shell wasn't simple. Steel had to be forged and machined precisely, packed with high explosives, fitted with fuses, painted, inspected, and transported. A heavy shell could take hours of labor across multiple factories before it ever reached the front. Rifles required dozens of parts milled to tight tolerances. Tanks, still new and experimental, took weeks to assemble, involving engines, armor plates, tracks, and crews of specialized workers. Costs soared into billions. A single artillery shell might equal hundreds of dollars in modern money. Multiply that by millions fired each month, and the scale became staggering.

By 1917–18, the war had become less a contest of generals and more a contest of production lines. Victory depended not only on courage, but on which nation could manufacture more steel, more explosives, and more bullets faster than the other side. In the trenches, soldiers experienced war one shot at a time. Behind the lines, entire cities roared day and night to keep those shots coming, proving that modern warfare wasn't just fought at the front, but hammered, welded, and packed in factories miles away.

113. Turning Junk into Weapons

As the war dragged on and artillery consumed steel faster than mines and factories could replace it, governments began asking civilians for something unexpected: their junk. Old metal suddenly became as valuable as ammunition. Towns across Britain, France, Germany, and the United States organized massive scrap metal drives, urging families to donate anything made of iron, brass, copper, or steel so it could be melted down and turned into shells, rifles, rails, and machine parts.

Posters declared that "Every pound of metal is a bullet" or "Your old pot could save a soldier." Schoolchildren collected nails and hinges. Housewives gave up kettles, pans, and broken stoves. Churches donated cracked bells. Parks lost their decorative railings. Iron fences, gates, bed frames, farm tools, plumbing pipes, and even statues disappeared onto carts headed for foundries. In some cities, entire lampposts and tram tracks were removed and replaced with cheaper wood or concrete.

The numbers were staggering. Single cities sometimes gathered thousands of tons in a few weeks, enough metal to produce millions of artillery shells. Trains hauled scrap to giant steelworks where it was sorted, melted in roaring furnaces, and poured into molds for new weapons. Yesterday's frying pan might return to the front as a shell casing within days.

For civilians, it made the war feel uncomfortably close. Streets literally changed shape. Homes grew barer. Everyday life looked stripped and temporary. Children grew up playing in parks without fences because the metal had gone to the front.

114. When Every Meal Was Measured

As the war tightened its grip on shipping and farmland, food quietly became another battlefield. German submarines sank merchant ships faster than Britain could replace them, and by 1917 the country was importing barely half the grain and meat it normally relied on. Store shelves thinned, queues stretched around corners, and panic buying emptied shops within hours. To prevent hunger and riots, the government stepped in and began regulating what every household could eat.

By the later years of the war, many adults lived on strict weekly rations that sounded small even on paper: about 1 pound (450 grams) of meat, 8 ounces (225 grams) of sugar, 4 ounces (115 grams) of butter or margarine, 4 ounces (115 grams) of bacon or ham, and just 2 ounces (55 grams) of tea. Bread was sometimes limited or stretched with cheaper flours. Those amounts weren't daily allowances, they were for an entire week. A pound of meat had to last seven days. Sugar worked out to barely two spoonfuls a day. Butter became something you scraped thinly, not spread. Eggs were scarce luxuries. Milk was prioritized for children and the sick. Coal, needed for cooking and heating, was also rationed, meaning families often had to choose between a hot meal or a warm room.

Prices were tightly controlled to stop profiteering. Bread, milk, and coal were capped at fixed costs so the poor wouldn't be priced out of survival. Shopkeepers who overcharged could be fined or shut down. Even so, people grew used to substitutes and stretching meals. Margarine replaced butter. Turnips and potatoes bulked out stews. Bones were boiled repeatedly for soup. Tea leaves were reused until they turned pale.

To fill the gap, civilians were urged to grow their own food. Parks, schoolyards, and back gardens were turned into "victory gardens," rows of cabbages, carrots, and beans planted wherever there was soil. Children kept chickens. Office workers dug potatoes after work. Posters urged people to "Dig for Victory" and waste nothing. Saving leftovers became patriotic, almost like conserving ammunition.

By the end of the war, the average dinner table looked very different from the one people remembered in 1914. Meals were smaller, plainer, and carefully measured.

115. When the Fields Replaced the Classroom

As millions of adult men left farms for the army, the countryside suddenly faced a different kind of emergency: there was no one left to grow food. Crops still needed planting, harvesting, and hauling, but the strongest workers were now in uniform somewhere in France. To keep the nation fed, governments quietly turned to the people who were still available; women, the elderly, and children. Across Britain and much of Europe, schoolboys and girls as young as twelve or thirteen were pulled from classrooms and sent into the fields to replace missing laborers.

At first it was presented as patriotic volunteer work, but it quickly became organized and semi-compulsory. Schools shortened terms or closed entirely during harvest seasons. Teachers marched groups of children out to farms where they weeded rows, picked potatoes, milked cows, scared birds from grain, and hauled heavy sacks that sometimes weighed nearly as much as they did. Some worked ten-hour days in mud and rain for only a few pennies. Others lived temporarily on farms in rough dormitories, sleeping in barns or sheds. Blisters, backaches, and exhaustion became normal parts of childhood.

Britain even created official programs like the School Harvest Camps and later the Women's Land Army, where teenagers often worked alongside adult women, driving horses, operating tools, and performing jobs once considered strictly "men's work." Posters framed it as service equal to soldiering: "Food is Ammunition - Don't Waste It." Growing wheat or digging potatoes was treated almost like loading shells.

For many children, the war years meant fewer lessons and more labor. Some missed months of schooling. Others never fully returned. Yet their work mattered. Without those extra hands, cities already strained by submarine blockades and rationing might have faced real famine.

116. How World War I Shifted the Clock

One of the strangest "weapons" introduced during the war wasn't a gun or a shell, but the clock itself. By 1916, coal shortages were becoming serious across Europe. Coal powered everything: trains, factories, ships, electric lights, and home heating. Every extra hour of artificial light burned more fuel the war desperately needed for munitions and transport. So governments looked for a simple solution that cost nothing and saved millions of tons of energy. Their answer was to change time.

In the spring of 1916, Germany became the first country to introduce daylight saving time, moving clocks forward one hour so people would wake earlier and make better use of natural daylight. Britain followed within weeks, along with France and many other nations. The idea was straightforward: if sunset came "later" on the clock, families would use fewer lamps at night, factories could run longer on daylight, and less coal would be burned for lighting and heating.

The savings added up quickly. Officials estimated that Britain alone conserved hundreds of thousands of tons of coal per year, simply by shifting the clock. For a nation running railways, shipyards, and shell factories nonstop, that fuel meant more trains moving troops, more steel smelted, and more shells produced.

But the change felt strange at first. Farmers complained their animals didn't understand the new time. Children walked to school in darker mornings. Factory whistles blew "earlier" than they ever had. Newspapers printed guides explaining how to reset watches and clocks. Some people even feared it was government overreach, tampering with something as natural as time itself.

Still, the system worked well enough that it stuck. What began as an emergency wartime fuel-saving measure eventually became permanent policy in many countries. More than a century later, millions of people still change their clocks every spring and autumn, rarely realizing the habit started not for convenience, but because World War I turned even daylight into a resource to be rationed.

117. How Air Raids Changed City Nights

For the first time in history, civilians learned that war could arrive from the sky. Beginning in 1915, huge German Zeppelins (hydrogen-filled airships hundreds of feet long) drifted silently over the North Sea and dropped bombs on British towns and cities at night. They weren't very accurate, but accuracy didn't matter. From thousands of feet up, crews simply released explosives and incendiaries onto the glow of streetlights below. Entire neighborhoods suddenly realized that light itself had become a target.

The solution was something completely new: blackouts. When air raid warnings sounded, cities went dark within minutes. Streetlamps were switched off. Shop signs went black. Trams stopped running. Homes covered windows with thick curtains, blankets, or painted glass so no light leaked outside. Even a thin crack of yellow glow could attract bombs.

Police and volunteer wardens patrolled streets shouting at anyone who showed a candle or cigarette near a window.

Nighttime cities became eerie and silent. People stumbled through pitch-black streets, bumping into curbs and lampposts. Carriages and early cars crept forward without headlights or used tiny slits of light pointed downward. The sky overhead, once dotted with lamps and cafés, turned completely black except for searchlights and anti-aircraft flashes.

Factories and rail yards (prime targets) were especially strict. Workers sometimes finished shifts in total darkness to avoid revealing their position. The psychological effect was enormous. Children slept in basements. Families kept bags packed in case of evacuation.

Though later wars would perfect the system, World War I created the first true "lights out" cities, where millions of people learned that survival sometimes meant simply disappearing into the night.

118. The Strikes on the Factory Front

As the war dragged into its second and third years, the factories that fed the front began to resemble battlefields of their own. Munitions plants ran day and night under glaring lamps, machines clattering without pause, air thick with metal dust and chemical fumes. Shifts regularly stretched to ten, twelve, even fourteen hours, six or seven days a week. Overtime became normal. Sleep became rare. Many workers, especially women in shell and explosive plants, stood for hours at heavy presses or handled toxic chemicals that stained skin yellow and burned their lungs. Exhaustion built quietly, then snapped.

Despite patriotic posters urging everyone to "work as soldiers of industry," strikes still broke out. Workers walked off the job over low pay, unsafe conditions, food shortages, or simply sheer fatigue. In Britain alone, hundreds of small stoppages erupted between 1915 and 1918. Some lasted hours, others days. Entire factories sometimes shut down when thousands refused to clock in. It shocked the government: the same factories producing the shells and bullets needed at the front were suddenly silent.

The state reacted quickly and harshly. Under laws like the Munitions of War Act (1915), strikes were technically illegal. Workers were forbidden to leave their jobs without permission, wages were tightly controlled, and disputes were sent to compulsory arbitration. Skilled workers couldn't even change employers freely. In extreme cases, men who stopped work could be fined, arrested, or threatened with conscription into the army. Soldiers were occasionally stationed outside plants to keep order, a reminder that these "civilian" workplaces were now treated almost like military bases.

Yet the strikes never fully disappeared. Many were short "down tools" protests rather than full rebellions, brief acts of defiance to demand better hours or safer conditions. Sometimes they worked. Pay was raised. Shifts shortened slightly. Safety rules improved. The government realized that pushing workers too hard could stop production entirely.

The irony was unavoidable. While soldiers collapsed from shellfire at the front, workers collapsed from exhaustion at the machines behind it. Both were fighting the same war, just in different uniforms.

119. The Deadly Risks of Making Shells

Working in a munitions factory could be almost as dangerous as serving in the trenches. Explosives like TNT, cordite, and picric acid were packed, pressed, and poured by hand in huge quantities, often inside crowded wooden buildings designed for speed rather than safety. Floors were swept constantly to prevent sparks. Workers wore soft shoes with no nails. Metal tools were banned. Even a dropped hammer, a static shock, or a grain of dust in the wrong place could trigger a chain reaction. Everyone knew the rule: one mistake could erase the entire building. And sometimes it did.

On January 19, 1917, the Silvertown explosion in East London proved just how fragile these factories were. A plant refining TNT caught fire and then detonated with the force of a small earthquake. The blast was so powerful it shattered windows up to 10 miles (16 km) away and was heard across the city. Entire streets collapsed. Houses lifted off their foundations. Nearly 70,000 buildings were damaged, and the shockwave felt like an air raid. About 70 people were killed and hundreds injured, many of them ordinary civilians who had nothing to do with the factory but simply lived nearby. Survivors described a black cloud rising over London like a volcano.

Silvertown wasn't unique. Smaller explosions happened regularly across Britain, France, Germany, and the United States. Shell-filling plants sometimes erupted without warning, killing dozens or even hundreds in seconds. Newspapers occasionally downplayed the disasters to avoid hurting morale, but workers knew the risks. Some joked grimly that every shift might be their last.

Inside the plants, accidents were often sudden and invisible. A tray of unstable shells could detonate and set off the entire room. A spark in a cordite-drying shed could blow apart the roof. TNT dust in the air could ignite like gunpowder. When it happened, there was usually no escape. Entire sections simply vanished in flame.

Yet production rarely stopped for long. Debris was cleared, new sheds built, and workers returned within days. Replacement crews filled the gaps. The war demanded shells faster than safety improvements could keep up.

120. How War Bonds Funded the Fighting

World War I wasn't just fought with rifles and shells. It was fought with savings accounts. Modern industrial war cost so much money that taxes alone couldn't pay for it, so governments turned to their own citizens and essentially asked them to bankroll the fighting. Instead of forcing the money outright, they sold "War Bonds," loans from ordinary families to the state. Posters covered walls and train stations with slogans like "Lend Your Savings to Win the War," "Your Money Fights," and "Buy a Bond, Save a Soldier." Schoolchildren collected coins. Bank clerks encouraged customers to invest. Employers deducted bond payments directly from wages. The message was simple: even if you couldn't fight, your money could.

In Britain, the most famous was the 5% War Loan, which paid 5% interest each year. That meant if you lent the government £100, you earned £5 annually in return, a strong rate for the time. The bonds were marketed as both patriotic and practical, safe investments backed by the government itself. Families poured in life savings, shopkeepers invested profits, and entire communities subscribed together. By the end of the war, millions of citizens had become creditors to their own country.

The sums were staggering. Britain raised billions of pounds through bond drives, equivalent to hundreds of billions today. The war was literally financed by bakers, factory girls, teachers, and clerks. In some households, the bond certificate was treated like a family treasure, tucked into drawers beside birth certificates and wills.

But there was a catch: the money wasn't returned quickly. Some bonds weren't fully repaid for decades. In fact, portions of Britain's World War I debt weren't finally paid off until the 21st century. A grandmother's wartime investment could still be earning interest long after the trenches were gone.

For many civilians, buying a bond felt like sending a piece of themselves to the front. If their son couldn't be there, their savings would be. In that sense, the war didn't just mobilize soldiers and factories. It mobilized wallets. Entire nations were fighting not only with blood, but with borrowed money.

121. The Images That Drove the War Effort

Before the war, advertising sold soap and cigarettes. During the war, it sold survival. Governments plastered every wall, train station, and shop window with posters designed to tug at pride, fear, guilt, and duty. Bright colors, bold fonts, and simple slogans turned the entire country into one giant message board. Propaganda wasn't subtle. It pointed fingers, shamed hesitation, and reminded people daily that the war depended on them personally.

One of the most famous images showed Britain's war secretary, Lord Kitchener, staring straight at the viewer with his finger extended: "Your Country Needs YOU." The design was so powerful it was copied worldwide, including America's Uncle Sam poster. Another showed women and children waving goodbye under the words "Women of Britain Say — GO!", implying that real men enlisted and that families expected it. Some posters went further, showing little girls asking their fathers, "Daddy, what did YOU do in the Great War?" quietly threatening future shame for anyone who stayed home.

Factories displayed signs reading "Every Shell Saves Lives" or "Speed Means Victory." Newspapers printed stories of enemy "atrocities," sometimes exaggerated or invented, to keep anger high and doubt low. Germans were often portrayed as monsters or apes, making the conflict feel moral as well as military.

Politicians reinforced it with speeches. British Prime Minister David Lloyd George spoke of fighting "a war to end war" and insisted the nation must mobilize "every man and every woman, every shilling and every resource." The language made factories sound like battlefields and workers sound like soldiers. Even children collected scrap metal and knitted socks because they were told they were part of the fight. By 1918, propaganda shaped daily life so completely that it was hard to separate reality from messaging. It filled streets, classrooms, pay packets, and newspapers.

TEN

A Global Conflict

World War I is often remembered through the lens of the Western Front, but the reality is that the conflict stretched across every continent and ocean on the planet. From the deserts of the Middle East to the jungles of Africa and the islands of the Pacific, millions of people who had no say in the decisions of European leaders were drawn into the fighting. This chapter looks at the truly global nature of the war, including the vast contributions of colonial troops, the forgotten battles fought far from the trenches of France, and the lasting impact the conflict had on the borders and politics of the wider world. It was a war that reshaped not just Europe, but the entire globe in ways that are still being felt today.

122. A Different Kind of War in Africa

Fighting in Africa looked nothing like the trench warfare of Europe. There were no endless belts of barbed wire or miles of zigzag trenches carved into the mud. In many places, there were no real "front lines" at all. Instead of sitting for months in fortified positions, soldiers were almost constantly on the move, marching across deserts, open savannas, and dense jungle where the map often showed little more than blank space. The war became less about holding ground and more about simply surviving the distance.

Campaigns stretched across enormous areas. Units might trek 200–300 miles (320–480 km) in a single month, sometimes covering more ground in one expedition than Western Front troops advanced in years. There were few roads and almost no railways, so columns hacked paths through brush with machetes, dragged artillery through mud, and hauled supplies over rocky ridges under a relentless sun. Boots rotted, uniforms tore, and rifles rusted from sweat and humidity long before an enemy was even sighted. Men grew exhausted not from battle, but from walking.

Even the landscape fought back. Rivers had to be crossed constantly for drinking water, washing, and moving supplies, yet many were murky, slow-moving channels teeming with wildlife. Crocodiles lurked just below the surface, perfectly camouflaged, sometimes snatching livestock (and occasionally men) who stepped too close to the banks. Soldiers wrote about porters vanishing midstream or being dragged under without warning, the water closing as if nothing had happened. Hippos, often mistaken for lazy and harmless, were in some ways even more dangerous. Highly territorial and weighing up to 3,000–4,000 pounds (1,400–1,800 kilograms), they could charge faster than a human could run, smash small boats, or overturn supply canoes with a single lunge. Nighttime crossings were especially tense, with splashes and grunts echoing through the dark. Beyond the rivers, the bush held its own hazards: venomous snakes hidden in tall grass, swarms of biting insects, and mosquitoes thick enough to darken the air at dusk. Animal attacks were rare compared to disease and exhaustion, but they added a constant edge of fear. In Africa, even something as simple as fetching water could feel like stepping into enemy territory.

When fighting finally came, it was rarely the massive, scheduled offensives seen in France. Instead, it felt like a chase. One force would appear briefly, fire a few shots, then vanish back into the bush, forcing the other side to pursue. Days or weeks might pass without contact, then suddenly erupt into a short, chaotic clash before the enemy slipped away again. Small patrols, ambushes, and skirmishes replaced the giant battles of the Western Front. Thick vegetation limited visibility to just a few yards, so soldiers often heard enemies moving before they saw them.

Mobility mattered more than fortifications. Speed, endurance, and knowledge of the terrain often decided survival. In Africa, the war wasn't about digging in and defending a trench. It was about who could keep marching the longest, who could navigate the wilderness, and who could outlast both the enemy and the environment itself.

123. The Enemy That Wasn't an Army

Disease proved deadlier than bullets for many forces operating in Africa. In some campaigns, sickness crippled armies long before they ever saw the enemy. Malaria, dysentery, sleeping sickness, typhoid, and heatstroke spread through camps with frightening speed, turning entire units weak and feverish within days. Mosquitoes rose in thick clouds at dusk, contaminating every bite with malaria parasites, while polluted rivers and stagnant water carried bacteria that caused violent stomach illnesses. A single drink could leave a soldier bedridden for weeks.

European troops, trained for cold European winters, were completely unprepared for tropical heat that regularly climbed above 100°F (38–40°C). Heavy wool uniforms trapped sweat, boots rotted in the humidity, and dehydration set in quickly during long marches. Men collapsed by the roadside with heat exhaustion, sometimes dying without ever firing a shot. Quinine, the main treatment for malaria, was often in short supply, and field hospitals were little more than tents with stretchers. Once sickness spread, there was often nowhere to evacuate the wounded.

The numbers were stark. In some African expeditions, more than half of a unit could be listed as "sick" at any given time, and for every man wounded in combat, several others were lost to disease.

124. The Carrier Corps and the Hidden Cost of War

Because railways and proper roads barely existed across much of Africa, armies could not rely on trains or trucks to move supplies. Instead, they depended on human muscle. Hundreds of thousands of local civilians were recruited or simply forced into service as porters. These men were not professional soldiers. Most were farmers, fishermen, laborers, and even teenage boys pulled from their villages with little warning. In British territory this system became known as the Carrier Corps.

Colonial officers often refused to arm large numbers of Africans, fearing rebellion and believing European troops should do the fighting. But the armies still needed food, ammunition, tents, rifles, and medical gear carried across hundreds of miles of bush and savanna. The solution was simple and brutal: use people instead of machines. In many areas, it took three to five porters just to keep one combat soldier supplied. A single battalion might require thousands of carriers trailing behind it like a moving supply line.

Each porter hauled loads weighing 45–65 pounds (20–30 kilograms), sometimes more, marching day after day through heat, mud, and disease with little rest and almost no medical care. Many went barefoot. Pay was low or nonexistent. Food was often worse than what the soldiers received.

The scale was enormous. In British East Africa alone, historians estimate that around one million porters were recruited during the war, compared to only a few hundred thousand fighting troops. And the death toll was staggering. Disease, exhaustion, and starvation killed an estimated 90,000 to 120,000 or more carriers, likely more than the number of soldiers lost in combat. Many deaths were never recorded at all. Entire villages lost their strongest workers, leaving fields untended and families without support.

125. Fighting Through the Bush of East Africa

The fighting itself was chaotic and intensely personal. In thick bush and jungle, visibility sometimes shrank to just a few yards. Tall grass swallowed entire patrols. Branches snapped underfoot. Gunfire could erupt suddenly from unseen positions, and soldiers often heard the enemy moving before they ever caught a glimpse of them. Battles were rarely grand formations clashing in open fields. They were short, sharp ambushes. A burst of rifle fire, a scramble for cover, then silence as one side melted back into the landscape.

No commander embodied this style of warfare more than German officer Paul von Lettow-Vorbeck. With a force that rarely exceeded 12,000–15,000 men (many of them African askari troops) he tied down Allied armies that sometimes numbered more than 100,000 across the region. Instead of defending territory, he focused on movement. Railways were sabotaged. Bridges were destroyed. Supply depots were raided. When pressed, he simply retreated deeper into remote terrain, forcing the Allies to chase him across thousands of miles over four years. His campaign stretched from German East Africa into modern-day Tanzania, Mozambique, and Zambia, continuing even after other fronts in Europe had collapsed.

For civilians, this kind of war was devastating. Villages might serve as temporary headquarters or supply depots one week and be abandoned or stripped bare the next. Armies seized grain stores, slaughtered livestock, and confiscated tools. Fields went untended as men were recruited or forced into service. In some regions, famine followed in the wake of marching columns. The war did not always arrive as artillery or gunfire. Sometimes it arrived as empty granaries and missing workers.

Communication across these vast territories was painfully slow. Messages traveled by runner, horse, or telegraph lines that could be cut or sabotaged. Units sometimes operated for days without clear instructions. When the Armistice was signed in Europe on November 11, 1918, news did not instantly ripple across Africa. Some forces continued moving and fighting for days before official confirmation reached them. Lettow-Vorbeck himself only agreed to cease hostilities after receiving verified news of Germany's surrender.

126. A Distant Country in a Global War

Even nations far from Europe were drawn into the conflict, sometimes for reasons that had little to do with the trenches themselves. In 1917, Siam (modern-day Thailand) declared war on Germany and Austria-Hungary, not because it was directly threatened, but as a calculated political move. Although never formally colonized, Siam had long been pressured by Western powers into "unequal treaties" that limited its trade, courts, and sovereignty. By joining the Allies, the king hoped to prove Siam was a modern nation worthy of equal treatment at the peace table. The country seized German ships and businesses at home and sent about 1,200–1,300 volunteers (including pilots, mechanics, and drivers) to Europe, where some trained with French forces and served on the Western Front. Their numbers were small compared to the great powers, but their presence was symbolic. Siamese troops even marched in the Paris Victory Parade in 1919, one of the few Asian nations represented. When the war ended, Siam successfully used its contribution to renegotiate those unequal treaties and reclaim greater independence, showing how even a limited role in a global war could reshape a country's future.

127. Where the ANZAC Story Began

For Australia and New Zealand, the First World War did not truly begin in the muddy trenches of France but on the rocky beaches of Gallipoli, thousands of miles from home. Before dawn on April 25, 1915, thousands of young soldiers from the newly formed Australian and New Zealand Army Corps, many of them teenagers who had never left their hometowns before boarding a ship, climbed down rope ladders into small boats and rowed toward the dark Turkish coastline. Navigation errors carried them to the wrong stretch of shore, where steep cliffs rose sharply above the water instead of the flat beaches planners had expected. As the first men stumbled onto the stones, Turkish defenders opened fire from the heights. Soldiers slipped on loose gravel, tangled in wire, and scrambled uphill under bullets, units mixing together in confusion as officers were killed within minutes. Many fought their first battle before even learning the names of the men beside them.

The campaign was meant to be a quick strike to knock the Ottoman Empire out of the war and open a supply route to Russia, but instead it dragged into eight months of stalemate that looked eerily like the Western Front. Both sides dug trenches only yards apart, trading sniper fire, grenades, flies, disease, and heat that spoiled food within hours. In summer, the smell of unburied bodies drifted across no man's land; in winter, freezing rain flooded dugouts and turned the ground to mud. By the end, more than 8,000 Australians were dead, a staggering loss for a country of fewer than five million people, meaning almost every town knew someone who never came home.

Ironically, the most successful part of the campaign came at the end. During the evacuation in late 1915, soldiers built clever self-firing rifles using dripping water tins to pull triggers automatically, left fires burning, and arranged supplies to make the trenches appear occupied. Under cover of darkness, tens of thousands slipped away silently to the beaches. When Turkish troops finally attacked, they found only empty trenches and cold tea mugs, the enemy gone without a sound.

Though Gallipoli was a military failure, it became something else entirely: a defining moment in national memory. Letters home spoke of "mateship," stubborn humor, and loyalty under impossible conditions, and the word "Anzac" slowly transformed from an acronym into a symbol of courage and endurance. More than a century later, Australians and New Zealanders still gather before sunrise each April 25 for Anzac Day services, standing quietly in the dark as bugles play the Last Post at the exact hour those first boats reached the shore. In a war fought on the other side of the world, Gallipoli remains deeply personal, a story of sacrifice that helped shape how two nations see themselves.

128. The Coin Game That Became an ANZAC Tradition

Australian soldiers carried their favorite gambling game with them wherever they went, and nowhere did it thrive more than the vast training camps of Egypt before Gallipoli. In 1914 and early 1915, tens of thousands of young "diggers" were stationed near Cairo and the pyramids, living for months in endless rows of canvas tents pitched in hot, windblown desert sand. Training filled the mornings, but afternoons and evenings brought long stretches of boredom, regular army pay, and little supervision. With nothing to spend money on except cheap food, beer, and cigarettes, gambling quickly became the main entertainment. Their game of choice was "two-up," played with two pennies and a small wooden paddle called a "kip." One man flipped the coins high into the air while a ring of soldiers crowded around shouting bets, calling "heads!" or "tails!" and waving notes and cigarettes. When the coins smacked down onto the wood, cheers or groans erupted instantly. Fortunes could change in seconds. Some men lost an entire week's wages in a single throw, while others walked away rich enough to buy drinks for half the camp.

The games grew loud and chaotic, with dust clouds, laughter, arguments, and coins clacking late into the night. Gambling was officially illegal, and military police occasionally stormed through the tents to break up what they called "two-up schools," scattering players in every direction. But officers often tolerated it because it kept morale high and burned off restless energy. The game followed Australians from Egypt to Gallipoli and later to the trenches of France, becoming as much a part of their identity as their slang and their reputation for irreverence. More than a century later, that tradition still survives: two-up remains illegal across Australia on every day of the year except one, Anzac Day, when coins are legally tossed in pubs and veterans' halls in memory of the soldiers who once played it between battles under the desert sun and distant pyramids.

129. The Hundred Days That Ended the War

For nearly four years the Western Front had barely moved. Men died by the hundreds of thousands for gains measured in yards. Verdun, the Somme, Passchendaele, each offensive followed the same pattern: weeks of artillery, then soldiers climbing out of trenches into machine guns, only to end up almost exactly where they started. It felt like the war might last forever. Then, in the late summer of 1918, something changed. Historians call it the Hundred Days Offensive, not a separate war but the final, relentless stretch of fighting that finally shattered Germany's ability to continue. It began on August 8, 1918, at the Battle of Amiens, and ended with the Armistice on November 11, roughly ninety-five to one hundred days later. In that short span, the most static war in modern history suddenly became fluid.

Instead of launching one giant, suicidal assault, the Allies changed tactics completely. Attacks were shorter, sharper, and better coordinated. Tanks rolled forward in waves to crush barbed wire. Aircraft spotted targets and strafed roads. Artillery fired creeping barrages that moved like a curtain of explosions just ahead of advancing troops. Infantry followed close behind rather than charging blindly. And most importantly, fresh American divisions were arriving by the tens of thousands, adding manpower the exhausted European armies no longer had. Rather than waiting months between battles, the Allies attacked again and again, hammering different points along the line so the Germans never had time to rest or rebuild.

Germany simply couldn't keep up. Years of blockade had left the country hungry. Supplies were short. Horses were dying. Ammunition stocks were thin. Reinforcements were scarce. Morale was cracking, and mutinies were already simmering. Against this, the Allies suddenly had new trucks, new shells, new food, and seemingly endless American replacements. The balance flipped almost overnight.

The shock came immediately. On the first day at Amiens, Allied forces advanced 10–12 kilometers, an almost unimaginable distance in a war where a few hundred meters had once cost thousands of lives. Tens of thousands of German soldiers surrendered in a single day. Entire units simply gave up rather than fight. German General Erich Ludendorff later called it "the black day of the German Army." From that moment on, Germany mostly retreated instead of attacking.

Over the next three months, the Allies smashed through the supposedly impregnable Hindenburg Line, retook huge areas of France and Belgium, and captured hundreds of thousands of prisoners. Railways collapsed. Supply lines failed. German soldiers marched backward faster than they had ever advanced. At home, food riots spread. Sailors mutinied. Workers struck. The government itself began to crumble. It became painfully clear that the war was no longer about victory but survival.

130. How the War Moved Power from London to New York

By the time American soldiers finally stepped into the trenches in 1918, the United States had already been fighting the war for years in a quieter but equally decisive way, with money. When the war began in 1914, London was the undisputed financial capital of the world. Britain controlled global trade routes, insured most of the world's shipping, lent money to other nations, and backed its powerful currency with vast gold reserves. The United States was wealthy but still secondary, an industrial giant that had not yet replaced Europe as the center of global finance. Four years later, that balance had completely flipped.

At first, Britain and France simply paid cash for American supplies. Then they paid in gold. Ship after ship crossed the Atlantic not with troops but with bullion, crates of gold bars hauled from European vaults and stacked into the holds of steamers bound for New York. The metal was used to buy American wheat, beef, coal, boots, rifles, trucks, and millions of artillery shells. By 1915 and 1916, so much gold had flowed west that Britain's reserves were nearly exhausted. The empire that had once financed half the planet was literally running out of metal. When the gold ran dry, they began borrowing.

The first lifeline came from Wall Street. In 1915, American bankers led by J.P. Morgan & Co. arranged what was then the largest foreign loan in history: a $500 million Anglo-French bond issue sold to American investors at 5 percent interest, repayable over about five years. It was only the beginning. As the war dragged on and costs exploded, the Allies kept ordering more supplies on credit. By early 1917, billions of dollars' worth of American goods were crossing the ocean every month, all paid for with borrowed money.

Then the United States entered the war in April 1917, and lending became official government policy. Washington began selling "Liberty Bonds" to its own citizens, encouraging ordinary Americans to invest their savings "to win the war." The money raised didn't stay at home. It was immediately lent to Britain and France. In effect, American families financed the Allied war effort directly. The sums were staggering. By the end of the conflict, the U.S. government had loaned the Allies roughly $10 billion in total. Britain alone owed about $4.6 billion to the United States government, on top of earlier private loans. France owed several billion more. At the time, those figures were almost unimaginable. In modern terms, Britain's debt alone would equal roughly $80–90+ billion today.

The terms were relatively soft but still heavy. Interest ran around 4 to 5 percent, sometimes deferred during the war itself. Afterward, formal agreements stretched payments over decades. Britain's 1923 settlement spread repayment across 62 years at reduced interest, requiring annual payments of around $160–170 million a year, the equivalent of billions annually today. In theory, Britain would still be paying into the late twentieth century. In practice, the strain was enormous. When the Great Depression hit in 1929, trade collapsed, unemployment soared, and government tax revenue shrank dramatically, making those yearly payments feel crushing. Britain struggled to meet installments, payments faltered or were temporarily suspended, and debts were repeatedly renegotiated. Then, before the old loans were even settled, the world slid into another catastrophe. World War II forced Britain to borrow vast sums from the United States all over again just to survive, layering fresh debts on top of the old ones. The result was a financial burden that stretched across generations. Astonishingly, Britain did not fully finish repaying its combined World War I and World War II debts to the United States until 2006, nearly ninety years after the first loans were taken out.

While Europe drained its gold and mortgaged its future, American industry boomed. Factories that once made consumer goods switched to rifles, trucks, engines, and shells. Steel mills poured out rails and artillery. Farms shipped mountains of grain and meat overseas. Shipyards launched freighters faster than German submarines could sink them. And because the American homeland was never bombed or invaded, none of this infrastructure was destroyed. While Europe's factories burned and fields became battlefields, American production only grew.

By 1918, the United States held close to half of the world's gold supply. The global financial center quietly shifted from London to New York. Before the war, nations borrowed from Britain. After the war, they borrowed from America. The change was permanent. Britain emerged victorious but financially crippled, weighed down by debt and reconstruction costs. The United States emerged richer, stronger, and suddenly the world's largest creditor. Power had crossed the Atlantic without a single shot being fired.

So when fresh American troops finally marched into France in 1918, they weren't just bringing rifles and uniforms. Behind them stood the full weight of a booming economy that could outproduce entire continents. In many ways, the war wasn't only won in the trenches. It was won in factories, banks, and shipyards thousands of miles away. And when the guns finally fell silent, the twentieth century no longer belonged to Europe. It belonged to America.

ELEVEN

The End & The Long Shadow

131. The Collapse of Germany

By the autumn of 1918, Germany was no longer losing the war in dramatic last stands or heroic defeats. It was simply coming apart. After four years of grinding conflict, the army that had once marched confidently across Europe now retreated day after day, step by step, across ground it had sworn never to surrender. Railways were shattered by artillery and air raids. Supply depots burned. Horses starved. Reinforcements barely existed. Units that had once numbered in the thousands sometimes mustered only a few hundred exhausted men. The illusion of stalemate that had defined the Western Front for years suddenly vanished, replaced by a steady, unstoppable backward drift.

The arrival of fresh American forces made the imbalance impossible to ignore. Every week brought new Allied divisions, new trucks, new tanks, new artillery. Germany, by contrast, had nothing left to replace its losses. Its soldiers knew the math. For every man they lost, the enemy seemed to gain two more. Rumors spread through the trenches about endless American arrivals, about factories across the Atlantic working day and night. The war no longer felt winnable. It felt infinite. Surrenders increased. Patrols hesitated. Entire groups gave up rather than die for ground that would be abandoned tomorrow anyway. German General Erich Ludendorff later called August 8, 1918, the opening of the Allied breakthrough at Amiens, "the black day of the German Army." From that moment on, retreat became routine.

But the collapse was not only military. It was psychological. After years of sacrifice, hunger, and grief, belief itself began to crumble. Orders still came down the chain of command, but they carried less and less weight. Officers could demand obedience, yet could no longer promise victory. Men who had survived Verdun and the Somme now asked a simple question: why keep fighting?

Behind the front lines, civilian Germany was unraveling just as quickly. The British naval blockade had strangled imports for years, leaving shelves empty and diets thin. By 1918, food shortages were severe. Bread was stretched with fillers. Meat was rare. Coal ran short in winter. Families queued for hours for basic rations that sometimes never arrived. Inflation eroded wages. Children grew malnourished. What had begun as patriotic endurance turned into quiet anger. Strikes spread through factories and shipyards, not as ideology at first, but as desperation. The home front that had once supported the war effort simply ran out of strength.

Then the breaking point came from below. In late 1918, sailors ordered to launch one final, suicidal attack against the British fleet refused. Mutinies erupted in the ports. Workers joined them. Protests spread from city to city with startling speed. Red flags appeared over town halls. Local councils replaced imperial officials. Authority dissolved almost overnight. It wasn't a carefully planned revolution. It was exhaustion made visible. After four years of total war, ordinary people simply stopped obeying.

Faced with an army that could no longer advance, a navy that would not sail, and civilians who would not sacrifice more, Germany's leaders confronted an unavoidable truth. Continuing the war would not save the nation, it would destroy it completely. There were no reserves left, no miracle weapons, no hidden strength waiting to be unleashed. The only option remaining was to ask for the fighting to stop.

So the request for an armistice went out, not as a bargaining move, but as an admission of reality. Germany had not been knocked down in a single blow. It had been worn out, militarily, economically, and emotionally. The empire that had entered the war confident and united now ended it hungry, fractured, and leaderless. Before the guns even fell silent, the old order had already collapsed. What remained was not defeat in one last battle, but the slow, unmistakable realization that the war had taken everything, and there was nothing left to give.

132. The Silence of the Armistice

When the end finally came, it did not look like victory parades or cheering crowds. It looked like paperwork, exhaustion, and surrender dressed up as negotiation. By November 1918, Germany had no real leverage left. Its armies were retreating, its navy mutinying, and its cities sliding into unrest. Continuing the war meant collapse or invasion. So German representatives were sent through the lines under a white flag to request an armistice, not to bargain as equals, but to accept whatever terms the Allies chose to impose.

The meeting took place far from any grand capital or ceremonial hall, deep inside the Forest of Compiègne in northern France. There, in a quiet railway clearing, stood a single railcar belonging to French Marshal Ferdinand Foch, the Supreme Allied Commander. The setting was deliberate. Isolated, controlled, and symbolic, it emphasized who held power and who did not. Inside the carriage, the German delegation was handed a list of demands and given little room to argue. The terms were not a compromise. They were instructions.

Germany was required to stop fighting immediately, withdraw from all occupied territories, and retreat behind the Rhine. Vast quantities of weapons had to be surrendered, including thousands of artillery guns, machine guns, aircraft, trucks, and railway engines. Much of the fleet was to be handed over. Allied prisoners of war were to be released at once, while German prisoners would remain in captivity. Perhaps most crushing of all, the Allied naval blockade would continue even after the shooting stopped, meaning food shortages at home would not immediately end. The message was clear. The war was over, but Germany would not dictate how.

The agreement was signed in the early hours of November 11, 1918. Yet the ceasefire was not set to begin immediately. It would take effect at 11 a.m., several hours later, to allow orders to reach armies stretched across hundreds of miles of front lines. The timing created a strange and tragic countdown. Fighting continued through the morning. Artillery still fired. Patrols still advanced. Men were still killed, some only minutes before the deadline, fully aware that the war was about to end. For them, peace came too late.

Then the moment arrived. The eleventh hour of the eleventh day of the eleventh month. After more than four years of constant gunfire, shell bursts, and engines, the noise simply stopped. No grand signal announced it. The cannons fell quiet one by one. Machine guns ceased. The air, which had trembled with explosions for years, settled into an unfamiliar stillness.

Many soldiers did not cheer. Some stood cautiously, unsure if it was real. Others sat down where they were, too tired to react. A few wept quietly. After living so long under the expectation of sudden death, silence itself felt unnatural. The landscape around them remained cratered and broken, littered with wire, mud, and graves. Nothing looked like victory. It looked like survival.

World War I did not end with celebration. It ended with relief, disbelief, and a quiet that felt heavier than the guns had ever sounded.

133. The Difficult Journey Home

When the guns fell silent, millions of soldiers faced a new and unexpected challenge: going home. Ending the war on paper was far simpler than dismantling armies that had grown to unprecedented size. Entire divisions needed to be processed, transported, documented, and discharged. Rail networks were damaged or overwhelmed. Camps overflowed with men waiting for orders that arrived slowly or not at all. Some soldiers waited weeks or even months before being officially released, stuck in a strange limbo between war and peace, unsure what came next.

For those who finally boarded trains and ships, the journey home carried a mix of anticipation and unease. Families imagined joyful reunions. Towns prepared celebrations. But the men returning were not the same ones who had left in 1914 or 1915. They stepped off trains thinner, older in the face, often quieter than expected. Many carried visible reminders of the war. Hundreds of thousands had lost limbs, eyesight, or mobility. Artificial legs and arms were fitted as best as technology allowed, but prosthetics were crude and uncomfortable. Veterans missing hands or legs had to relearn basic tasks in societies unprepared to provide long-term support. Governments struggled to supply pensions, rehabilitation, or meaningful employment for such vast numbers of disabled men.

Even for those without obvious wounds, reintegration proved difficult. Cities had changed. Jobs had disappeared or been filled. Prices had risen sharply. Inflation eroded savings. Industries that had boomed during wartime contracts slowed abruptly. Some returning soldiers found that the skills that had kept them alive in trenches and bombardments meant little in civilian life. The discipline of military structure vanished overnight, replaced by uncertainty.

Emotionally, the distance between veterans and civilians often felt just as large as the physical distance they had crossed. Families wanted stories of bravery and closure. Many soldiers had only confusion, grief, or silence to offer. Experiences of mud, bombardment, and constant death did not translate easily into conversation at a kitchen table. When they did speak, civilians often struggled to understand. When they stayed silent, misunderstandings grew. Shared experience created tight bonds among veterans, while separating them from those who had remained at home.

Years of following orders, watching friends die, and enduring promises of eventual victory had reshaped how many men viewed authority. Patriotic slogans sounded hollow after so much loss. Political speeches felt detached from reality. In defeated nations, resentment simmered. In victorious ones, triumph felt muted by the scale of sacrifice. Across Europe, returning soldiers carried not celebration, but skepticism.

The war had demanded everything from them. When they returned, they found that peace offered no simple reward. For millions, coming home was not a return to the world they remembered, but the beginning of a different struggle to understand what the war had taken and what, if anything, it had given back.

134. The Invisible Wounds of War

Not all wounds bled. As the war dragged on, armies began encountering a different kind of injury that confused and unsettled everyone who witnessed it. Soldiers who had survived months or years of combat sometimes broke down without warning. Strong, experienced men who had endured artillery barrages and machine gun fire suddenly trembled uncontrollably, stared into space, or collapsed in tears. Some lost the ability to speak. Others could not stop shaking. A few became frozen and unresponsive, unable to follow even the simplest orders. There were no visible cuts or broken bones, yet these men were as incapacitated as if they had been physically struck.

At first, doctors assumed the condition must be caused by exploding shells physically damaging the brain. The term "shell shock" reflected this early theory. But cases soon appeared in soldiers who had never been near a blast. It became clear that something else was happening. Weeks of sleepless nights, constant bombardment, the sight of friends killed without warning, and the unrelenting fear of sudden death pushed the human nervous system past its limits. The mind, like the body, could simply give out.

Military authorities struggled to understand what they were seeing. Some doctors argued that these men were suffering genuine psychological trauma and needed rest, safety, and time away from the front. Others saw the symptoms as weakness, cowardice, or even deliberate avoidance of duty. Because the injury left no visible scar, it was easy to doubt. In an army built on discipline and obedience, an invisible wound was often treated as a moral failure rather than a medical one.

The results could be cruel. Instead of compassion, some soldiers were punished or shamed. A few were threatened with court-martial. Others were subjected to harsh "treatments" meant to shock them back into reality, including electric currents, shouting, or forced drills. The message was clear. The body could be injured, but the mind was expected to endure indefinitely.

For those who survived and returned home, the symptoms rarely vanished with the armistice. Nightmares replayed bombardments long after the guns fell silent. Sudden noises triggered panic. Crowds felt overwhelming. Some veterans avoided sleep altogether. Others became withdrawn, irritable, or emotionally numb, unable to reconnect with families who remembered a different person. Loved ones often watched in confusion as husbands, sons, or brothers seemed changed in ways they could not explain.

Society had few answers. The language to describe psychological trauma barely existed, and long-term support was limited or nonexistent. Many veterans simply carried their suffering quietly for decades. Only years later would doctors begin to understand that what they had witnessed was not cowardice or weakness, but a natural response to prolonged terror. The modern term post-traumatic stress disorder would not be coined until much later, yet its reality had already shaped millions of lives.

World War I proved that industrial warfare could wound the mind as deeply and permanently as the body. Even when the fighting ended, for many survivors the war continued in memories they could not escape, battles replayed each night in the dark long after the world around them had finally found peace.

135. Remembering the Unknown

When the fighting stopped, the dead did not neatly return home with the living. Across Europe, the battlefields remained littered with the aftermath of four years of industrial killing. Shell craters, collapsed trenches, and shattered forests concealed bodies that had never been recovered. In earlier wars, most families could bury their loved ones in local cemeteries. In World War I, that simple ritual became impossible for millions. Entire units had vanished under artillery fire. Men were buried where they fell, often quickly and without ceremony, sometimes by comrades working under gunfire, sometimes by exhausted burial parties ordered to clear the ground before disease spread.

The scale of death overwhelmed any system meant to track it. Graves were dug hastily and marked with rough wooden crosses that rotted or were blown away. Shelling churned the earth so violently that burial sites were disturbed again and again, mixing remains together or erasing locations entirely. Artillery blasts shattered bodies and destroyed identification tags. Uniforms disintegrated in mud and rain. When teams later returned to exhume and rebury the fallen properly, they often found bones from several men intertwined with no reliable way to separate them. What earlier generations would have mourned as individual deaths increasingly became anonymous losses.

For families waiting at home, uncertainty could be worse than confirmation. Letters stopped. Names appeared on lists marked "missing" rather than "killed." Weeks stretched into months, then years, with no answers. Mothers, wives, and siblings lived with the quiet hope that perhaps their soldier had been captured or stranded somewhere far away. For many, that hope never fully faded because there was no body to prove otherwise. Grief without a grave felt unfinished.

In response, societies searched for new ways to mourn losses too vast to comprehend. Towns and villages began erecting memorials in public squares and churchyards, not to celebrate victory, but simply to record absence. Long columns of names were carved into stone, sometimes so many that they covered entire walls. In small communities, the lists could include nearly every young man of fighting age. These monuments became gathering places for collective remembrance, spaces where private sorrow turned into shared silence.

Out of this grief grew one of the most powerful symbols of the war: the Unknown Soldier. Since so many bodies could not be identified, one unidentified set of remains was chosen to represent them all. Buried with full military honors in national ceremonies, this single grave stood in for thousands who would never come home. In France and the United Kingdom, tombs of the Unknown Soldier became sacred spaces, guarded, visited, and covered in flowers year after year. The strength of the symbol lay in its anonymity. Without a name, the soldier could belong to anyone. Every family could imagine that their missing son rested there.

Remembrance itself changed. Earlier wars had favored statues of generals and triumph. After World War I, memorials were quieter, heavier, more somber. Ceremonies emphasized stillness rather than celebration. Moments of silence replaced cheers. The war had cost too much to glorify. It had taken too many lives to frame as victory alone.

By the early 1920s, the land still gave up reminders of the scale of loss. Farmers plowing former battlefields uncovered bones and fragments of uniforms. Construction crews unearthed forgotten graves. Even decades later, remains continued to surface, small proofs that the war had never been fully cleared away. For countless families, there would never be a marked resting place, only a name on stone and an empty chair at home.

In the end, World War I did not leave behind tidy cemeteries and closure. It left gaps. Gaps in families, gaps in towns, gaps in memory. The monuments and the Unknown Soldier did not solve that absence, but they gave it shape, allowing entire nations to mourn together for the millions who were lost without a trace.

136. The War That Still Lies Underground

Even after the dead were buried and the monuments raised, the war refused to fully leave the landscape. During four years of industrialized fighting, armies fired an estimated one billion artillery shells across Europe. Not all of them exploded. Millions failed to detonate on impact, burying themselves deep in churned soil or sinking into cratered fields. When the guns fell silent in November 1918, the ground itself remained armed.

In northern France and Belgium, entire regions were so saturated with unexploded munitions that authorities declared parts of the countryside permanently unsafe. Some areas became known as the "red zones," land considered too contaminated with explosives, chemicals, and human remains to safely farm or inhabit. Yet over time, as people returned to rebuild their lives, fields once scarred by trenches were plowed again. With each turn of the soil, metal rose to the surface.

Farmers began calling it the "iron harvest." Every year, plows struck artillery shells buried for decades. Rusted cylinders containing high explosives or poison gas emerged from the earth like relics from another age. Many remained dangerously unstable despite lying underground for a century. Bomb disposal teams in France and Belgium still collect hundreds of tons of World War I munitions annually. Some shells contain mustard gas or other chemical agents that have slowly corroded their casings, leaking toxins into surrounding soil and groundwater.

Accidents continue to happen. Construction workers uncover buried ordnance while laying foundations. Road crews disturb shells while repairing highways. Occasionally, civilians handling what appears to be harmless scrap metal trigger explosions that kill or injure more than a hundred years after the war officially ended. In some areas, children are warned never to touch strange metal objects found in fields because they might still be live.

The persistence of unexploded shells is a stark reminder of how intensely the land was bombarded. During major offensives, artillery fire was so heavy that the ground itself seemed to boil. Shells landed faster than they could be counted, turning fields into mud and forests into splintered stumps. Unlike monuments carved in stone, these remnants do not symbolize sacrifice or memory. They remain active threats, hidden beneath crops and grass.

More than a century later, World War I still demands caution from those who live where it was fought. The war may have ended in silence on November 11, 1918, but beneath the surface, fragments of it remain armed, waiting. The battlefield was never entirely cleared. It was simply buried.

137. When Empires Fell

When the shooting stopped, the damage was not limited to shattered towns and cratered fields. Entire political systems collapsed alongside the armies that had defended them. World War I did not simply defeat countries. It erased empires that had ruled for centuries. Governments that once appeared permanent vanished in a matter of months, leaving behind vast regions with no clear authority and no agreed future.

The German Empire fell first. As defeat became unavoidable, the Kaiser abdicated and fled into exile, ending a monarchy that had dominated central Europe. Soon after, the Austro-Hungarian Empire, a sprawling state that had stitched together dozens of languages and ethnic groups under one crown, splintered almost overnight. What had once been a single political unit fractured into separate national movements, each demanding independence. At the same time, the Russian Empire had already collapsed into revolution and civil war, while the Ottoman Empire, which had ruled much of the Middle East for hundreds of years, disintegrated under military defeat and occupation. By 1919, four great empires that had shaped Europe and its neighbors for generations were simply gone.

In their place, diplomats gathered around conference tables and began drawing new borders across maps that only partially reflected reality on the ground. Nations such as Poland, Czechoslovakia, and Yugoslavia were created or restored, carved from former imperial territory. On paper, these new states promised self-determination and freedom. In practice, the lines were often compromises sketched by negotiators far from the people who actually lived there. Rivers, railways, and strategic concerns mattered as much as culture or language.

As a result, millions of people woke up to find themselves foreigners in their own homes. Germans now lived inside Poland. Hungarians found themselves outside Hungary. Ethnic and religious minorities were scattered across borders that did not match where communities actually existed. Old rivalries that had once been contained within empires suddenly hardened into international disputes. What looked tidy on a map felt messy and unstable on the ground.

The same pattern unfolded beyond Europe. In the former Ottoman lands, Allied powers divided territory into "mandates" administered by Britain and France, claiming the regions were not yet ready for independence. Borders were drawn with straight lines across deserts and mountains, grouping together communities that had rarely shared governance while separating others that had long been connected. Decisions made in distant conference rooms reshaped the Middle East without consulting many of the people who lived there, planting tensions that would echo for generations.

The collapse of empire also changed how people thought about power itself. For decades, European empires had seemed invincible, their authority backed by vast armies and global wealth. The war shattered that illusion.

Soldiers and civilians alike had watched supposedly permanent systems crumble in just a few years. Monarchies fell. Flags changed. Capitals shifted. The old world order that had defined the nineteenth century disappeared faster than anyone thought possible.

Peace, it turned out, was not simply the absence of fighting. It was the beginning of a new, uncertain map. Instead of restoring stability, the end of the war created dozens of fragile states, disputed borders, and unresolved grievances. The guns had stopped, but the political shockwaves were only beginning, reshaping Europe, the Middle East, and much of the modern world in ways that would continue to unfold long after 1918.

138. The Lost Generation

When the war ended, the damage was not measured only in borders or ruined cities. It lived inside the people who had survived it. Across Europe, an entire generation carried the weight of four years spent in trenches, bombardments, and mass death. These were the young men who had marched off in 1914 believing they were heading toward adventure or glory. By 1918, many returned home older than their years, quieter, and deeply skeptical of everything they had once been told. Later writers would call them the "Lost Generation," not because they had disappeared, but because the world they had expected to inherit no longer existed.

Before the war, many Europeans trusted their governments, their monarchies, and the idea that progress was inevitable. After the war, those beliefs felt hollow. Millions had followed orders faithfully, watched friends die for yards of mud, and endured years of sacrifice, only to come home to unemployment, inflation, and political chaos. The promises of honor and victory rang empty against the reality of broken bodies and crowded cemeteries. For many veterans, it seemed that the people who had sent them to fight had never truly understood what the fighting cost.

This disillusionment shaped daily life. Former soldiers often struggled to settle into routines that once felt normal. Civilian problems seemed small compared to what they had endured, yet the lack of purpose felt equally unsettling. Factories, offices, and farms offered little of the structure or intensity they had grown used to. Some drifted from job to job. Others gathered mainly with fellow veterans who shared the same memories and frustrations. Among themselves, they could speak openly. With everyone else, there was often silence.

Politically, the consequences were profound. Faith in gradual reform weakened. Compromise felt pointless after years of total war. Many people no longer trusted traditional parties or cautious leaders. Instead, they gravitated toward movements that promised simple answers, strong leadership, and national revival. In defeated countries especially, humiliation and hardship mixed with anger. Veterans who felt their sacrifices had been wasted became receptive to anyone who claimed to restore pride and meaning.

In Germany and other unstable regions, former soldiers formed paramilitary groups that offered exactly what civilian life lacked. These organizations provided camaraderie, discipline, uniforms, and a clear sense of belonging. Marching together, drilling together, and following commands again felt familiar. Violence, which had once been confined to battlefields, began spilling into politics. Street fights, uprisings, and armed demonstrations became common as extremist groups battled for influence. The habits of war proved difficult to leave behind.

Even in victorious nations, the mood was darker than expected. Celebrations were muted by the sheer scale of loss. Nearly every town had lost sons, brothers, and fathers. Instead of triumph, many people felt exhaustion. Art, literature, and culture reflected this shift. Writers and poets described a world stripped of innocence. Optimism gave way to cynicism. The belief that modern society was steadily improving had been shattered by the most destructive conflict humanity had ever seen.

World War I had not simply redrawn maps. It had reshaped how millions of people thought about authority, sacrifice, and the future. The generation that came of age in the trenches returned home less trusting, less patient, and far more willing to embrace radical change. The war had taught them that entire systems could collapse in months and that violence could transform history overnight. Those lessons would echo through the decades that followed, influencing revolutions, uprisings, and the rise of new, more extreme political movements.

The fighting had ended, but the mindset it created did not. In many ways, the war's most lasting legacy was not the destruction it left behind, but the hardened attitudes of the people who survived it, a generation shaped by loss and searching for certainty in a world that no longer felt stable.

139. A World Transformed

When World War I ended, the world did not return to what it had been in 1914. Too much had broken. Too many systems had collapsed. The war did more than destroy armies and cities. It quietly rearranged the balance of power across the entire planet, reshaping politics, economies, and societies in ways that still define the modern world.

Before the war, Europe had stood at the unquestioned center of global power. London was the financial capital of the world. Empires controlled vast colonies across Africa, Asia, and the Middle East. European governments dictated trade, borders, and diplomacy. By 1918, that dominance had cracked. Britain and France had technically won, but they emerged exhausted, indebted, and physically scarred. Their industries were damaged, their populations depleted, and their economies strained by years of borrowing. Victory had left them weaker, not stronger.

Across the Atlantic, a different story unfolded. The United States, largely untouched at home by the fighting, had supplied food, weapons, money, and fresh troops on a scale no European nation could match. While Europe burned, American factories expanded. While European treasuries emptied, American banks filled. By the end of the war, the United States held enormous gold reserves and had become the world's largest creditor. Financial power shifted from London to New York, marking the beginning of a new era in which global influence increasingly flowed westward. Without conquering territory, America had become the strongest economic force on Earth.

The war also weakened the idea that empires were permanent. Millions of colonial soldiers from Africa, Asia, and the Caribbean had fought and died for European powers. They had seen those supposedly invincible empires struggle, retreat, and bleed like anyone else. When these men returned home, they carried new expectations. They had traveled, trained, and fought overseas. They had witnessed both European strength and European vulnerability. Many began to question why they should accept foreign rule at all. In the decades that followed, independence movements grew louder and more organized, fueled in part by veterans who knew that imperial authority was not untouchable.

Technologically, the war accelerated humanity into a new and more dangerous age. Airplanes, tanks, submarines, machine guns, poison gas, and industrial artillery had transformed battlefields into factories of destruction. Warfare was no longer limited by courage or cavalry charges. It became mechanical, efficient, and impersonal. Entire landscapes could be erased in hours. Civilians could be starved by blockades or bombed from the sky. The conflict showed that modern industry could produce death on a scale previously unimaginable, setting the blueprint for every major war that followed.

Even daily life changed. Governments had expanded their control over economies, transportation, and information to manage total war. Propaganda, rationing, mass production, and centralized planning became normal tools of the state. After the war, many of these powers did not fully disappear. The relationship between citizens and governments had shifted permanently toward larger, more interventionist systems.

Most of all, the war altered how people saw the future. The confident optimism of the late nineteenth century, the belief that science and progress would steadily improve life, faded in the face of mechanized slaughter and mass graves. Societies became more cautious, more fractured, and in some places more radical. Borders drawn in haste created tensions that would spark new conflicts. Disillusioned veterans reshaped politics. Fragile peace settlements planted the seeds of future wars.

By the time the world reached the 1920s, it was clear that World War I had not simply been another European conflict. It had been a turning point for humanity. Old empires had fallen. New nations had risen. Power had shifted across oceans. Entire generations had been marked by loss. The map looked different. The balance of wealth looked different. The way wars were fought looked different.

The guns fell silent in 1918, but the world they left behind was not the one that had existed before. In countless visible and invisible ways, the modern age began in the shadow of the First World War.

TWELVE

Unusual Moments

Every war has its strange, surprising, and hard-to-believe moments that don't fit neatly into any single category. World War I was no different. This chapter is a collection of the facts that stood out on their own, from bizarre coincidences and record-breaking feats to the lesser-known stories that fell through the cracks of the bigger narrative. These are the moments that make you pause and think, proving that even in the middle of the most devastating conflict in history, the world still found ways to be unpredictable.

140. Tricking the Snipers

Snipers ruled the trenches, and simply lifting your head above the parapet for a second could mean instant death. To fight back, soldiers began building fake targets to trick enemy marksmen into revealing themselves. Using papier-mâché, sandbags, straw, and old uniforms, they crafted realistic dummy heads and torsos, sometimes painting faces, adding helmets, or even placing cigarettes in the mouths to make them look alive. These "soldiers" were slowly raised on sticks or propped along the trench edge like men on watch. Enemy snipers, thinking they had spotted a careless target, fired immediately. The crack of the shot or puff of muzzle smoke gave away their hidden position, and friendly snipers could then shoot back within seconds. Some units staged entire scenes, fake bodies slumped over sandbags, helmets set just high enough to tempt a shot, even mock horses or supply figures made from sacks and wood. It became a strange form of deadly theater, where both sides tried to outsmart each other with props and illusions.

141. Those Who Refused to Fight

Not every man called to fight picked up a rifle. In Britain alone, around 16,000 men registered as conscientious objectors, refusing military service on religious, moral, or political grounds. Some were Quakers (members of a Christian pacifist group who believed killing was always wrong), while others rejected the war entirely. They quickly became targets of public anger. Strangers sometimes pinned white feathers, the symbol of cowardice, onto their coats in the street, and newspapers mocked them as "conchies" nicknamed 'conchies,' a shortened, often mocking slang for conscientious objectors. Many were arrested, court-martialed, and imprisoned for months or even years, treated more like deserters than civilians. A few were sent to harsh labor camps or forced into noncombat roles such as farming, road building, or stretcher bearing, risking their lives to save the wounded without carrying weapons themselves. Yet a large number still agreed to serve in noncombat roles, becoming stretcher-bearers, medics, or farm laborers. Unarmed, they followed assaults into shellfire to carry wounded men back from no man's land, sometimes making trip after trip across open ground while bullets snapped overhead. Refusing to kill did not mean avoiding danger; it often meant risking their lives to save others. In a society that celebrated sacrifice and heroism, their quiet refusal stood out sharply, reminding the nation that not everyone believed the war was worth fighting.

142. America's War at Home

In the United States, fear of the enemy reached beyond the battlefield and into everyday life. German-Americans, who had long been one of the country's largest immigrant groups, suddenly faced suspicion and hostility. Schools stopped teaching German, orchestras renamed "German" music, and even foods were rebranded, with sauerkraut becoming "liberty cabbage" and hamburgers called "liberty steaks." Towns changed German street names, and some families avoided speaking their native language in public. A war fought across the ocean quietly reshaped culture at home, erasing traces of German identity almost overnight.

143. The Flower That Became a Symbol

One of the most enduring symbols of the war grew from a single moment of grief on the battlefield. In May 1915, after a brutal artillery bombardment near Ypres, Canadian army doctor John McCrae helped bury a close friend killed by a shell. The next morning, he noticed something strange and beautiful: bright red poppies blooming across the torn earth between fresh graves. The seeds had been stirred up by the digging and the explosions, turning the battlefield into a field of flowers. Sitting on the back of an ambulance, McCrae scribbled a poem beginning with the now-famous line, *"In Flanders fields the poppies blow, between the crosses, row on row."*

At first, he disliked the poem and reportedly tossed it away, but another officer rescued it and sent it to a magazine, where it spread rapidly through newspapers across the Allied world. Soldiers memorized it, families clipped it out, and the poppy quickly became a symbol of both sacrifice and remembrance. After the war, a teacher named Moina Michael began wearing a small red poppy in honor of the dead and started selling handmade versions to raise money for veterans. The idea spread internationally, and millions of paper poppies are still sold each year around November 11, with the money supporting former soldiers and their families.

144. Saving Lives Under Fire

Under the laws of war, doctors, nurses, and stretcher-bearers were not supposed to be targets at all. International agreements like the Geneva Conventions classified medical personnel as noncombatants, meaning they carried no weapons and were protected from deliberate attack. To mark their status, they wore white armbands with red crosses and worked under tents, wagons, and hospital roofs painted with the same symbol, a clear signal to enemy troops: do not fire. In theory, anyone treating the wounded was off-limits. In practice, the battlefield rarely respected theory. Artillery shells did not distinguish between soldiers and medics, air raids missed their marks, and stretcher-bearers often had to walk upright across open ground carrying heavy loads, making them easy targets. Casualty rates among medical teams could be shockingly high. The red cross offered legal protection, but not safety, and many of the men who came to save lives ended up losing their own.

145. The Villages That Never Returned

Entire towns simply disappeared because of the war. Across northern France and Belgium, villages that had existed for centuries were reduced to rubble so completely that they were never rebuilt. Constant shelling flattened houses, churches, schools, and roads until nothing remained but broken brick, twisted metal, and poisoned soil. Forests were shredded into splinters, wells filled with debris, and farmland churned so deeply by craters that it resembled the surface of the moon. In some places the destruction was so severe that governments declared the land permanently uninhabitable, marking it as part of the "Red Zone," where unexploded shells, chemicals, and buried bodies made rebuilding too dangerous. A few of these communities still exist only on maps and memorial signs, officially listed as villages that "died for France," with no residents but still recognized as towns out of respect for what was lost.

146. When the Battlefield Refuses to Disappear

In parts of France and Belgium, the First World War is still not entirely over. More than a century after the last shots were fired, farmers, construction crews, and road workers continue to dig up live artillery shells, grenades, and buried munitions left behind in the soil. During the war, millions of shells failed to explode on impact, sinking harmlessly into mud only to remain armed underground. Each year, an estimated hundreds of tons of unexploded ordnance are still recovered in what locals call the "iron harvest," as plows regularly strike rusted bombs the way earlier generations struck stones. Specialized bomb disposal teams travel from village to village collecting piles of old shells stacked at field edges like firewood before safely detonating them. Some still contain deadly gas or unstable explosives and can kill instantly if disturbed. Farmers are taught to leave anything metal untouched and call authorities instead. Entire areas of the former front, especially inside the old Red Zone, remain too dangerous to live on or farm properly.

147. Letters That Arrived a Century Late

Not everything left behind by the war was deadly. Sometimes, what the earth gives back is heartbreakingly human. Across former battlefields in France and Belgium, construction crews and farmers occasionally uncover bundles of old mail bags, sealed tins, or rusted boxes filled with letters that were never delivered. Some were dropped when trenches collapsed, others lost during retreats, or buried when shells destroyed field post offices. Decades later, mud preserves the paper surprisingly well. Inside are ordinary words frozen in time: sons telling mothers they're safe, husbands promising they'll be home by Christmas, soldiers describing muddy boots, bad food, or the hope that the war will end soon. Many of the writers were killed days or even hours after putting pen to paper, never knowing their final messages never arrived.

In some cases, archivists or volunteers still try to track down surviving relatives and deliver the letters a century late. For families, opening one can feel like hearing a voice from the past speaking directly across generations.

148. The Ghosts of Mons

After the Battle of Mons in August 1914, as exhausted British troops retreated under heavy German pressure, rumors began spreading of something impossible on the battlefield. Soldiers claimed that shadowy figures had appeared between the lines during the fighting, protecting them from enemy fire. Some described glowing shapes or silent men standing in the smoke. Others swore they saw medieval archers, like ghosts from England's past, firing invisible arrows into the advancing Germans. A few simply said "angels" had shielded them. The stories spread rapidly through the ranks and then back home through letters and newspapers, where they were repeated as miracles. Churches printed pamphlets celebrating divine protection for British troops.

The truth turned out to be stranger in a different way. Around the same time, a popular short story had been published in London describing phantom archers from the Battle of Agincourt returning to defend modern soldiers. Readers mistook the fictional tale for a real report, and as frightened, sleep-deprived troops shared rumors in muddy trenches, imagination and memory blurred together. Historians later concluded that most sightings were likely tricks of light, smoke, and exhaustion, or simply stories that grew in the telling. Yet the legend stuck.

149. Living Beneath the Battlefield

For long stretches of the war, many soldiers barely lived above ground at all. In heavily shelled sectors of the Western Front, the surface became so dangerous that entire units moved underground, digging deep into hillsides and trench walls like human moles. What began as simple holes for shelter slowly expanded into sprawling tunnel systems with timber supports, staircases, bunks, kitchens, aid posts, and even small chapels. Some dugouts sank 20 to 40 feet (6–12 meters) below the surface, deep enough to survive most artillery. From above, the battlefield looked empty, but beneath the mud thousands of men were sleeping, eating, and waiting in the dark.

Life underground was safer from shells but miserable in other ways. The air was damp and stale, heavy with smoke, sweat, and the smell of wet earth. Candles and oil lamps barely pushed back the darkness. Water seeped constantly through the walls, turning floors slick with mud. Rats and lice thrived. The ceilings were often so low that men couldn't stand upright, forcing them to crouch or crawl between rooms. When artillery landed nearby, the whole structure shook and rained dirt from the roof, making soldiers fear collapse or burial alive. Some described the sensation as living inside a coffin that might cave in at any moment.

Days blurred together without sunlight. Men slept in shifts on rough wooden bunks or directly on the ground, emerging only for sentry duty or patrols before disappearing back below. In places like Vimy Ridge and Messines, the underground networks grew so extensive that they resembled small buried towns, complete with signs, storage rooms, and hundreds of feet of corridors. To many soldiers, trench warfare no longer felt like fighting on land at all, but like existing beneath it, as if the war had forced humanity underground.

150. When Forests Turned to Matchwood

In some parts of the Western Front, entire forests simply ceased to exist. Years of constant artillery fire shredded trees so completely that what had once been green woods became fields of splintered stumps and broken poles. Shell after shell tore through trunks, snapping them like matchsticks and blasting branches into flying shards. Leaves vanished. Bark was stripped away. What remained looked less like nature and more like a giant pile of kindling scattered across the mud. Soldiers began calling these areas "matchwood forests," because every tree had been smashed into thin, jagged sticks.

From a distance, the landscape looked almost lunar. No shade, no birdsong, no grass, just gray mud and blackened timber stretching to the horizon. In places like the Somme, Verdun, and Passchendaele, woods that had stood for centuries disappeared in a matter of weeks. Landmarks vanished so completely that maps became useless. Units got lost crossing open ground where forests were supposed to be. Rain filled shell craters with stagnant water, and broken roots poked up like bones from the earth. The smell of churned soil mixed with smoke and decay.

Even after the war ended, the damage lingered. Many forests had to be replanted from scratch, and some areas were so polluted with metal fragments, chemicals, and unexploded shells that trees struggled to grow back for decades. Photographs from the time show soldiers walking through what look like graveyards of trees, thin wooden spikes stretching skyward in every direction.

151. When It Was Simply "The Great War"

When the fighting began in 1914, nobody called it "World War I." The name didn't exist yet, because no one imagined there would ever be a second one. At first, most people believed the conflict would last only a few months. Newspapers spoke confidently of "the war" or "the present war," assuming it would be short and decisive. In Britain it was often called simply "The Great War," meaning the biggest war anyone had ever seen, not the first of many. Others used phrases like "The European War," since most of the early fighting centered on France, Belgium, Germany, and Russia. Germans called it der Weltkrieg ("the world war") surprisingly early on, recognizing how many empires were involved, while Americans, before joining, often referred to it as "the European conflict."

As the months dragged into years and colonies from Africa, India, Australia, Canada, the Middle East, and Asia were pulled in, the scale became undeniable. Soldiers joked grimly that it was "the war to end all wars," a hopeful phrase repeated by politicians and newspapers who believed the suffering would be so terrible that humanity would never allow another one. That optimism aged badly. Only after a second global catastrophe erupted in 1939 did historians need a new label. The earlier conflict was retroactively renamed "World War I," or "the First World War," a title that quietly admitted the unthinkable: the "war to end all wars" had only been the beginning.

152. The War's Forgotten Horses

In an army that could replace men with new conscripts but struggled to replace animals, horses were often treated as more valuable than the soldiers riding beside them. World War I still depended heavily on horsepower. Before tanks and trucks fully took over, nearly everything moved by animal: artillery guns, ammunition wagons, food carts, ambulances, and supply trains. A single heavy gun might require six to eight horses just to drag it through mud. If the horses died, the gun stayed where it was, no matter how urgent the battle.

Because of that, horses were expensive, scarce, and strategically critical. A trained artillery horse could cost the equivalent of several months or even years of a soldier's pay. They had to be bred, raised for years, trained to ignore gunfire, and shipped across oceans. Replacing one wasn't quick.

Replacing a human soldier, harshly, often meant issuing another rifle to the next recruit.

This led to uncomfortable priorities. Veterinary units were sometimes better supplied than frontline medics. There are documented cases where wounded horses were evacuated by wagon while lightly wounded soldiers were told to walk. Armies kept detailed veterinary hospitals, dental care for horses, and special rations of oats and hay even when men lived on hard biscuits and weak tea. Commanders understood the math: save the horse, and you could still move food, shells, or the wounded. Lose the horse, and entire units might starve or be stranded.

The scale was enormous. All sides together used roughly 8–10 million horses and mules during the war, and millions died from shellfire, exhaustion, disease, or starvation. Soldiers often grew deeply attached to them, grooming and feeding the same animals every day. Many diaries mention grieving more openly for a dead horse than for another man, partly because the animal had been a constant companion, partly because it felt so unfair that something so loyal had no choice in the war at all.

153. Ancient Beasts in a Modern War

In the Middle East, British, Australian, New Zealand, and Indian forces relied heavily on camels. Thousands were organized into full camel corps, especially in Sinai and Palestine, where wheeled vehicles simply sank into soft sand. A single camel could carry 300–400 pounds (135–180 kilograms) of supplies and travel long distances without water, making it perfect for desert patrols and raids. Soldiers rode them for days across empty landscapes, rifles and machine guns strapped to their saddles, sometimes dismounting to fight on foot before climbing back on and vanishing into the dunes. The Imperial Camel Corps became so common that entire battles featured lines of camels instead of horses, an image that looked centuries old despite the presence of modern rifles and artillery.

Elsewhere, even stranger sights appeared. In parts of India and Southeast Asia, elephants were used to haul heavy artillery pieces, timber, and ammunition through jungle terrain where wheels couldn't pass. Their strength allowed them to drag guns up muddy slopes or across rivers that would have stopped tractors cold. Photographs show elephants harnessed to cannons or supply sleds, moving war material through thick forests like living cranes. Oxen and buffalo pulled carts in Africa. Donkeys and mules carried loads in mountain regions where nothing else could climb.

To soldiers arriving from the Western Front, it felt surreal. One month they might be slogging through Belgian mud behind barbed wire. The next, they were riding camels past palm trees, escorting caravans, or watching elephants drag artillery through the brush. The same war that produced tanks, machine guns, and poison gas also relied on animals that hadn't changed since ancient empires.

154. Battles for the Bridges

In a war that often looked like endless trenches and open fields, some of the most important battles were fought not for hills or towns, but for simple pieces of infrastructure: bridges. Rivers were natural barriers that could stop entire armies cold. Artillery, supply wagons, ambulances, and thousands of marching men could not simply wade across deep water. Without a bridge or a crossing point, an advance stalled instantly. So a single narrow span of wood or steel could become more valuable than a whole city.

Commanders planned offensives around these choke points. If you captured a bridge intact, your army could pour across in hours. If the enemy blew it up, repairs might take days or weeks under fire. That delay could mean running out of ammunition, food, or reinforcements. In fast-moving moments of the war, especially in 1914 and again in 1918, the difference between victory and failure sometimes came down to whether engineers could throw a temporary bridge across a river before nightfall.

Because of this, bridges were prime targets. Retreating armies often wired them with explosives and destroyed them at the last possible second. Engineers carried demolition charges specifically for this job. Meanwhile, advancing troops raced to seize crossings before they were blown, sometimes charging straight at the structure under machine-gun fire. Entire units were sacrificed just to hold one bridge long enough for the rest of the army to cross.

When bridges were gone, soldiers improvised. Combat engineers built "pontoon bridges" from floating metal or wooden sections lashed together, sometimes overnight. Others used ferries, barges, or planks laid over barrels. These makeshift crossings were shaky, crowded, and terrifying under shellfire. A single artillery hit could dump dozens of men and horses into the water. Still, they kept coming, because without that link, nothing behind the line could move forward.

Railway bridges were even more critical. One destroyed rail crossing could cut off thousands of tons of shells and food per day. Whole offensives slowed or collapsed simply because trains couldn't pass. Maps often marked bridges with heavy red circles, like arteries in a body. Block one, and everything downstream weakened.

155. Walls Made of Mud

For all the machine guns, artillery, and poison gas, one of the most important pieces of equipment on the Western Front wasn't a weapon at all. It was a simple burlap sack filled with earth. Sandbags shaped the entire battlefield. Without them, trenches would have collapsed, flooded, or offered almost no protection. With them, armies built miles of walls strong enough to stop bullets and even absorb shell fragments.

Every trench you see in photos, the neat parapets, the raised firing steps, the curved corners, was held together by thousands upon thousands of these bags. Soldiers filled them by hand using small shovels, tying them off and stacking them like bricks. A single firing bay might require hundreds. A whole trench sector might need tens of thousands. Across the Western Front, millions were used at any given time.

They worked because dirt stops bullets surprisingly well. A tightly packed sandbag could catch rifle rounds and shrapnel that would tear straight through wood or thin metal. Several layers thick could even blunt the blast of nearby shells. When artillery hit, the bags burst open and spilled dirt rather than exploding into deadly fragments like stone or concrete would. In a strange way, mud was safer than brick.

But sandbags were also endless labor. Rain rotted the fabric. Rats chewed holes through them. Shellfire shredded walls in seconds. After every bombardment, soldiers spent hours repairing damage, refilling sacks, rebuilding parapets, and stacking them again. It was common to work all night simply replacing what had been destroyed that afternoon. Trench life often meant digging and filling bags more than actually fighting.

They had other uses too. Men built dugout roofs from them, lined sleeping areas for insulation, propped them under stretchers as pillows, or used them as makeshift seats. Some were stuffed into coats as extra protection. Others became emergency barricades when raids broke through. If a section collapsed, the first order was always the same: "Get sandbags up."

Ironically, the war consumed so many that shortages became serious. Civilians at home were asked to donate old sacks. Farmers and factories shipped millions overseas. Entire supply trains carried nothing but empty bags. The front was constantly hungry for more.

156. The Trench Watch Revolution

Before World War I, most men didn't wear watches on their wrists at all. Timepieces were carried in waistcoat pockets on chains, and wristwatches were widely seen as delicate jewelry for women. But trench warfare made pocket watches almost useless. Reaching into your coat while climbing a ladder, fixing bayonets, or waiting for an artillery barrage could be slow, clumsy, or even fatal. Attacks were timed to the minute. Barrages lifted at exact seconds. "Stand-to" happened before dawn on the dot. In modern industrial war, seconds mattered, and soldiers needed both hands free.

So men improvised. They began strapping small pocket watches to their wrists with leather bands or sewing loops onto sleeves. Manufacturers quickly noticed and started producing purpose-built "trench watches" with tougher cases, thicker glass, luminous numbers, and sometimes metal cage grills over the face to stop shrapnel cracks. Dials were painted with glowing radium so time could be read in pitch darkness inside dugouts or during night attacks. For the first time, timekeeping became a piece of battlefield equipment, as essential as a rifle or compass.

The war quietly created an entire new industry. Swiss and American makers like Omega, Longines, Waltham, Elgin, and Zenith supplied thousands of rugged military watches, and many of those brands built their reputations on reliability under fire (companies like Casio wouldn't appear until decades later, but the idea of the tough, utilitarian wristwatch traces directly back to these trench models). When millions of soldiers returned home already used to wearing watches on their wrists, the fashion never went away. The modern men's wristwatch was essentially born in the trenches.

But there was a hidden cost. The glowing paint that made night reading possible contained radium, a radioactive substance. Factory workers, often young women, painted tiny numbers by hand and were told to shape their brushes with their lips for fine tips, unknowingly swallowing radium dust every day. Years later many suffered horrific jaw decay, anemia, bone fractures, and cancers in what became some of the first major industrial radiation poisoning cases. What began as a small wartime convenience (being able to check the time in the dark) helped expose the dangers of radiation and changed workplace safety laws forever.

157. From Shrapnel to Souvenirs

After heavy shelling, the battlefield floor changed completely. Explosions churned the earth like a plow, flipping mud, sandbags, and buried debris to the surface. When the smoke cleared, the ground glittered with fragments of war: jagged pieces of shrapnel, twisted shell casings, flattened bullets, and shards of steel torn from artillery rounds. Soldiers learned to spot them instantly. They called the fragments "trench teeth," because the sharp bits of metal stuck out of the dirt like broken fangs.

During quieter hours, men casually scavenged the ground, pockets filling with scraps that had screamed through the air only hours earlier. It became a strange ritual. After surviving a bombardment, some would walk the cratered earth almost like beachcombers, picking through the wreckage for interesting shapes or large fragments. A curved piece of brass might become a ring. A shell driving band could be hammered flat into a bracelet. Spent bullets were carved into crosses, pendants, or tiny sculptures. Larger shell casings were engraved with names, dates, or the word "France" and turned into vases or cups.

Entire dugouts sometimes doubled as miniature workshops. Using penknives, files, or bits of sandpaper, soldiers polished metal until it shone gold or copper. Others etched unit badges, hometowns, or sweethearts' initials into the surface. Some mailed these pieces home as gifts; others kept them in their packs as lucky charms or proof that they had survived another day.

158. Between the Trenches and Home

British soldiers had a slang word for home: "Blighty," a term borrowed from Hindi *bilāyat*, meaning Britain or the homeland. In the trenches, it took on an almost magical meaning. Blighty wasn't just a place. It meant warmth, clean sheets, real food, and safety far from artillery. So when men spoke of a "Blighty wound," they didn't mean just any injury. They meant one perfectly balanced between danger and relief: serious enough to be evacuated back to England, but not so severe that it killed or permanently crippled them.

A bullet through the arm. Shrapnel in the calf. A fractured hand.

Something painful but survivable. Something that meant a hospital bed and a ship home instead of another winter in the mud.

It created a strange, uncomfortable psychology. After months in the front line, with lice, shellfire, and friends dying daily, some soldiers quietly admitted they wouldn't mind a "nice little Blighty." Rumors circulated of men exposing a hand above the parapet a second too long, or standing a bit too high during an advance, hoping for a grazing wound. A few even shot themselves in the foot, though this was rare and harshly punished if discovered, sometimes treated as self-inflicted injury or desertion.

If a soldier was suspected of deliberately wounding himself to escape the front, the army treated it not as fear or exhaustion but as a crime. These injuries were officially labeled "self-inflicted wounds" or "self-mutilation," and officers took them very seriously. Military doctors examined the damage closely, looking for signs that the shot had come from close range, such as powder burns, torn fabric, or the angle of entry. A bullet through the hand or foot fired from only a few inches away was suspicious. Witnesses were questioned, rifles inspected, and if the story didn't add up, the man could be arrested and charged.

Punishments were harsh and meant to discourage others. Minor cases might mean loss of pay, extra drills, confinement, or being sent straight back to the trenches once healed. More serious cases went to court-martial and could lead to months in prison, demotion, or "Field Punishment No. 1," where a soldier was strapped upright to a post or wheel for hours a day in public view, exposed to the weather as a warning to everyone else. In the early years of the war, some armies even imposed the death penalty for desertion or deliberate injury. Britain alone executed more than 300 soldiers for offenses including cowardice and self-inflicted wounds. Most never acted on the thought, but the fact that the idea existed at all spoke volumes.

159. Eating the Enemy's Rations

Trenches rarely stayed neatly "British" or "French." Along much of the Western Front the Allied armies were mixed together, with neighboring sectors sometimes only a few hundred yards apart. British, Canadian, Australian, and French units regularly rotated through one another's lines, borrowed dugouts, shared roads, or took over recently captured enemy trenches. After an attack, soldiers might suddenly find themselves living in a German or French position for days or weeks, using whatever supplies had been left behind. That meant eating whatever food was available too.

Raids and advances often ended with an unexpected prize: enemy rations. German black bread, sausages, tinned meats, and pickles were eagerly collected, while French trenches were famous for their bread, cheese, and especially wine. French troops were officially issued wine as part of their daily ration, sometimes half a liter (about a pint) or more, something British soldiers almost never received. To men used to hard biscuits, bully beef, and endless tea, these captured supplies felt like luxury. Letters home frequently joked that "the Boche eat better than we do" or that French bread tasted like a feast.

160. The Frozen Trenches

Cold weather on the Western Front wasn't just uncomfortable, it was its own kind of enemy. For nearly four to five months each year, roughly November through March, temperatures hovered near freezing or below it almost constantly. In northern France and Belgium, winter days often sat around 30–40°F (0–5°C), while nights regularly dropped below 25°F (−4°C), and during cold snaps could fall near 10–15°F (−9°C to−12°C). Snow didn't cover the ground all winter, but there were often dozens of snow or sleet days each season, mixed with freezing rain that soaked uniforms by day and turned them stiff with ice by night. Worse than the snow was the endless cycle of thaw and freeze: trenches filled with water during the day, then hardened into icy sludge after sunset.

Men slept in damp greatcoats with boots still on because removing them meant frozen leather in the morning. Rifles iced up. Fingers went numb so quickly that loading ammunition or pulling a trigger became clumsy and painful. Water bottles froze solid. Tea turned lukewarm within minutes. Frostbite and trench foot multiplied as wet socks never fully dried. Sentries stamped their feet for hours just to keep blood moving, and some woke to find the duckboards glazed with ice like a skating rink.

161. From Private to President

From the moment a civilian's name was called in the draft to the moment a president or king made a decision, the war followed a rigid chain of command that stretched from muddy trenches to marble government halls. A conscript began at the very bottom as a private, the lowest rank and the backbone of every army, carrying a rifle, digging trenches, and following orders without question. Ten or twelve privates formed a section or squad led by a corporal. Several squads made a platoon commanded by a lieutenant. Four platoons formed a company under a captain. Several companies became a battalion led by a major or lieutenant colonel. Multiple battalions formed a regiment or brigade under a colonel or brigadier. Brigades grouped into divisions commanded by major generals, divisions into corps led by lieutenant generals, and several corps into entire field armies under full generals. Above them sat theater commanders planning entire fronts, then the national high command or general staff coordinating strategy for the whole war. At the very top were civilian leaders, presidents, prime ministers, or monarchs, who technically held ultimate authority and decided when to attack, negotiate, or continue fighting. In theory, orders flowed cleanly down this pyramid from the head of state to the newest private. In practice, a decision made in a quiet office hundreds of miles away could take days to reach the front, finally arriving as a shouted command from a mud-stained sergeant telling exhausted men to climb a ladder and go "over the top." For most soldiers, the vast hierarchy above them felt invisible. They rarely saw anything higher than their company officer, yet their lives were shaped by choices made by people they would never meet.

162. When Friends Went to War Together

One recruiting idea that seemed comforting at first ended up making the war's losses far more devastating at home. Early in the conflict, Britain raised what were called "Pals battalions," encouraging friends, brothers, factory workers, and even entire football teams or neighborhoods to enlist together. Posters promised that men could serve "shoulder to shoulder with your mates," and thousands signed up believing it would feel less frightening if everyone they knew went with them. Training camps often looked like hometown reunions, with clerks, miners, shopkeepers, and students sleeping in the same tents and joking that they'd bring their local rivalries to the front.

But when these battalions finally went into battle, they fought together and died together. On the first day of the Somme in 1916, some Pals units were nearly wiped out within hours. In places like Accrington, Barnsley, Leeds, and Sheffield, hundreds of men from the same streets fell in a single morning. Back home, the losses didn't trickle in one by one, they arrived all at once. Telegram boys walked door to door down entire blocks, knocking again and again. Schools lost former students by the dozens. Factories lost whole shifts of workers. Football clubs lost entire squads. In some towns, almost every family knew someone who would never return.

What had begun as a clever recruiting tactic turned into a shared tragedy. Instead of grief spread over months or years, whole communities were struck in a single blow, leaving empty classrooms, silent workshops, and gaps in family trees that never fully healed.

163. The Trains That Started the War

Mobilization in 1914 was so massive and mechanical that it was almost impossible to hide, and once it began, other nations could see it happening in real time. Railways were the backbone of every army's war plan, and moving millions of men required thousands of trains running on precise schedules. The moment mobilization orders were issued, ordinary life changed overnight. Civilian trains were canceled or delayed as tracks were handed over to the military. Railway stations filled with reservists hugging families goodbye, clerks pinning orders to notice boards, and long lines of soldiers climbing into crowded carriages with rifles and packs. Steam engines hissed and belched smoke day and night as troop trains rolled east or west without stopping. From a distance, it looked less like preparation and more like an exodus.

There was nothing secret about it. Horses, artillery pieces, wagons, and supply carts clogged roads near the borders. Telegraph wires buzzed constantly with coded military messages. Diplomats, journalists, and spies stationed in foreign cities simply had to step outside to see the evidence. Embassy staff reported that platforms were jammed with uniforms and that trains left every few minutes loaded with troops. Intelligence officers counted railcars through binoculars. In some countries, mobilization notices were even printed openly in newspapers or nailed to town halls, summoning every able-bodied man to report immediately. Church bells rang. Postmen delivered orders. Entire towns seemed to empty overnight.

The problem was that mobilization looked exactly like an invasion. There was no such thing as a slow or "defensive" buildup. War plans depended on strict timetables: trains had to run in a precise order, each one delivering a specific unit to a specific place at a specific hour. If the sequence stopped, the entire system collapsed into chaos. So once a country started loading trains, it was nearly impossible to pause or reverse. Leaders feared that waiting even a day could mean the enemy reached the border first with hundreds of thousands of men already in position.

As a result, mobilization triggered panic. If Russia began moving troops, Germany felt compelled to mobilize immediately. If Germany moved, France followed. Each government watched the others through reports and rumors, convinced that delay meant disaster. Diplomats were still arguing for peace while, at the same time, millions of soldiers were already rolling toward the front in packed railcars. In this way, the railways turned Europe into a giant machine. Once the first gears started turning, the rest were forced to move with them, and stopping the war became almost impossible before it had even officially begun.

164. The Night the Taxi Fleet Became an Army

When the German army surged toward Paris in September 1914, the French government suddenly faced a desperate problem: there weren't enough trains or trucks to move reinforcements fast enough to stop them. Rather than wait, officials turned to something completely ordinary, the city's taxi fleet. Almost overnight, hundreds of bright red Parisian taxicabs were commandeered, their meters still attached, their drivers still in caps and jackets, and ordered to the front.

On the night of September 6–7, around 600 taxis lined up beneath streetlamps and drove through the dark in long convoys, carrying thousands of soldiers toward the Battle of the Marne. Each car squeezed in five men plus gear, rifles sticking out of windows, boots muddying the seats where passengers had sat only hours earlier. Drivers followed military officers instead of street maps, headlights dimmed, engines rattling along country roads normally used by farmers. Some taxis even kept their meters running out of habit, and the government later reimbursed the fares as if it had been an ordinary ride across town.

In purely military terms, the taxis didn't move enough troops to decide the battle by themselves. But psychologically, the image mattered enormously. Civilians and soldiers alike saw an entire city mobilizing, with everyday workers and their cars becoming part of the war effort overnight. Newspapers celebrated the "Taxis of the Marne" as a symbol of national unity, proof that even shopkeepers and cab drivers were now fighting the war.

165. Buried Alive in the Trenches

For many soldiers, the most frightening danger in the trenches didn't come from bullets or shrapnel at all, but from the earth itself. Dugouts, the small underground shelters carved into trench walls, were meant to be safe havens where men slept, wrote letters, or hid during bombardments. Some were shallow holes roofed with timber and sandbags. Others were dug 10–30 feet (3–9 meters) deep with wooden stairs, bunks, and candle shelves, looking almost like cramped underground bedrooms. But all of them depended on mud walls and rough beams for support, and under heavy shellfire, that wasn't enough.

When artillery struck nearby, the ground shook like an earthquake. Walls cracked. Dust rained from the ceiling. Then, without warning, entire sections collapsed. Tons of wet clay, timber, and sandbags poured down the stairwell, sealing exits in seconds. Men inside were often trapped before they even understood what had happened. Rescue was slow and desperate. Comrades clawed at the mud with shovels, helmets, or bare hands, racing against time while more shells continued to fall. Sometimes they reached their friends quickly. Often they didn't.

Many of the dead showed no wounds at all. Instead, they had simply suffocated. Air pockets vanished, candles went out, and the weight of soil crushed the space smaller and smaller until breathing became impossible. Survivors described hearing faint tapping or muffled shouting from underground that gradually faded. In some sectors, entire dugouts disappeared, burying a dozen or more men at once. After major bombardments, burial parties sometimes found bodies days later, still seated on benches or lying on bunks as if asleep.

Ironically, the deeper the dugout, the safer it seemed from shells, but the more deadly it became if it collapsed. Soldiers learned to fear heavy bombardments not just for the explosions above, but for the thought of being entombed below. Many later said they preferred taking their chances in the open trench rather than sleeping too deep underground.

166. When the French Army Refused to Attack

By 1917, the French army had been fighting almost continuously for nearly three years, and the strain was showing in every muddy trench. Hundreds of thousands were already dead from Verdun and the Somme, entire villages back home had lost their young men, and yet generals still promised that the next big offensive would finally end the war. In the spring of 1917, General Robert Nivelle launched exactly such a promise: a massive assault that he claimed would break the German lines within forty-eight hours. Instead, it turned into a slaughter. Machine guns and artillery tore apart the attacking waves. In just a few weeks, France suffered roughly

100,000–120,000 casualties for almost no ground. Survivors returned to the trenches furious and exhausted. They felt tricked, sacrificed for nothing, and asked to die again for the same result.

Then something rare and terrifying happened: the army didn't run from the enemy, it simply refused to move. Entire units obeyed defensive orders but would not go "over the top." Some companies stayed in their trenches and stacked their rifles. Others marched away singing protest songs or boarded trains without permission. In some sectors, soldiers shouted, "We'll defend France, but we won't attack." It wasn't chaos or revolution. It was quiet defiance. Men were done with suicidal assaults. At its peak, the unrest affected parts of nearly half the French divisions on the Western Front, tens of thousands of soldiers in total. For a moment, the French high command feared its own army might collapse completely.

The government kept the crisis secret, terrified the Germans might discover how fragile the line really was. Instead of mass executions, the new commander, Philippe Pétain, chose a different approach. He improved rations, increased leave, rotated exhausted units more often, and promised no more pointless attacks. Discipline still returned, but not without punishment: around 3,000 court-martials were held, hundreds sentenced to death, and roughly fifty actually executed as examples. The message was clear, mercy mixed with firmness. The mutinies faded, but the damage lingered. For nearly a year afterward, France avoided large offensives and mostly fought defensively, waiting for American troops to arrive. For the first time in the war, it had become obvious that the greatest threat wasn't always the enemy's guns, it was an army simply too exhausted to keep fighting.

167. When Armies Began to Break from Within

France wasn't the only country whose soldiers reached their limit. By 1917–1918, the strain of industrial warfare was cracking armies across Europe and beyond, sometimes more dangerously than enemy fire ever could. In Russia, the situation spiraled fastest. Years of defeat, hunger, and poor leadership shattered discipline entirely. Soldiers stopped saluting officers, formed their own "soldiers' committees," voted on whether to obey orders, and sometimes simply walked away from the front. Desertions reached into the hundreds of thousands. Some units even turned on their own commanders. Rifles meant for the Germans were pointed inward instead. The army didn't just mutiny, it dissolved, helping trigger the Russian Revolution and forcing Russia out of the war altogether.

Italy nearly followed. After the catastrophic defeat at Caporetto in 1917, entire formations collapsed in panic. Retreating soldiers threw away rifles, clogged roads, and fled for miles. Tens of thousands were captured, and others simply disappeared into the countryside. Officers responded brutally, with harsh discipline and executions meant to restore order. The line eventually stabilized, but trust between soldiers and commanders never fully recovered.

Britain avoided mass mutiny, but the strain still showed in quieter ways. There were strikes, refusals, and small protests over endless offensives and poor leave. Some exhausted units quietly resisted orders or delayed attacks. Colonial troops, especially from India, Africa, and the Caribbean, sometimes protested unequal treatment, lower pay, and racist discipline. A few refused labor assignments or demanded better conditions, reminding commanders that loyalty had limits. These were rarely called "mutinies" officially, but they revealed deep frustration beneath the surface.

Then came Germany's breaking point. By late 1918, food shortages were severe, cities were starving, and soldiers knew the war was lost. When German naval commanders ordered the fleet to sail for one last "glorious" suicide battle against Britain, the sailors refused outright. Ships stayed in harbor. Arrests triggered riots. The unrest spread from ports to factories to entire cities. Workers joined in. Flags changed. Within days, what began as a naval mutiny became a national revolution. The Kaiser abdicated, the government collapsed, and Germany asked for an armistice. The war ended not because its army was destroyed in battle, but because the country behind it simply stopped fighting. By the final year of the war, governments feared their own soldiers almost as much as the enemy.

THIRTEEN

Conclusion

World War I officially ended at the eleventh hour of the eleventh day of the eleventh month in 1918. The guns stopped. Soldiers climbed cautiously out of trenches. Church bells rang across Europe. Crowds flooded streets in Paris, London, and New York. After more than four years of industrial slaughter, the silence must have felt unreal. But the war did not truly end that morning. It simply changed form.

Empires that had ruled for centuries vanished almost overnight. The German, Austro-Hungarian, Ottoman, and Russian empires collapsed, redrawing the map of Europe and the Middle East in ways that would echo for generations. New nations appeared. Old borders disappeared. Political revolutions erupted. Entire economies staggered under debt and reconstruction. Millions of wounded men returned home to cities that no longer felt the same.

The human cost was almost beyond comprehension. Around 16–20 million people were dead. Tens of millions more were wounded. Some carried visible scars: missing limbs, damaged lungs, blinded eyes. Others carried invisible ones: nightmares, trembling hands, silence that never fully lifted. A whole generation had grown up in mud, noise, and loss. And yet, out of that destruction, the modern world took shape.

Air power, tanks, mass production, propaganda, daylight saving time, rationing systems, plastic surgery, blood banks, intelligence networks, global finance, women in heavy industry, psychological warfare; so many parts of the twentieth century were either born or transformed during those four years. Even everyday language changed. We still talk about "front lines," "campaigns," and "being in the trenches," often without realizing the phrases were forged in barbed wire and artillery smoke.

The war also shifted power across the globe. Europe emerged exhausted and indebted. The United States emerged richer and stronger. Colonial troops returned home with new expectations. Women who had run factories demanded a larger role in society. The seeds of future conflicts were planted in peace treaties that satisfied almost no one.

Perhaps the most haunting part is this: in 1914, millions believed the war would be short, glorious, and decisive. By 1918, the illusion of quick, clean war had shattered forever. World War I taught humanity that industrial conflict could consume entire nations, not just armies. It blurred the line between soldier and civilian. It proved that factories, farms, banks, and even clocks could become weapons.

World War I was once called "the war to end all wars." History proved otherwise. Yet understanding it remains essential. Not just for trivia nights or surprising facts, but because so much of our modern world, politically, economically, socially, and even linguistically, was shaped in those trenches.

Every statistic in this book hides a human story. Every innovation was born from urgency. Every strange detail, from trench slang to war bonds to blackout curtains, was part of a much larger transformation.

The war may have ended in 1918, but its shadow stretches across the century that followed.

And now, more than a hundred years later, we are still living in the world it created.

277 SHOCKING WORLD WAR II FACTS

Scott Matthews

FOURTEEN

Introduction

In the early decades of the twentieth century, much of the world believed it was moving steadily toward stability and modernity. Cities expanded upward and outward. Radio signals crossed oceans. Passenger planes shrank continents. Electricity illuminated streets that had once gone dark at sunset. Medicine advanced, and factories multiplied. International trade tied distant economies together.

To many observers, the devastation of World War I had taught humanity a lasting lesson. The scale of that catastrophe, its slaughter, starvation, and shattered empires, seemed so extreme that surely no nation would willingly plunge into something similar again. Diplomacy, global institutions, and economic interdependence were supposed to prevent another such collapse.

They were wrong.

Beneath the outward appearance of recovery and progress, the world remained tense and uncertain. Many people were unhappy with the peace settlements that had followed World War I, and long-standing disputes over territory continued to cause friction between nations. Economic problems, including inflation, widespread unemployment, and heavy national debts, placed enormous strain on societies across the globe. At the same time, extreme political movements gained influence by offering clear promises of renewal and strength during periods of fear and instability.

Governments responded to these pressures by investing heavily in new armies, air forces, and naval fleets, believing that military power was the best way to protect their interests. Strategic planners worked carefully on invasion schedules and mobilization plans that were organized down to precise timetables. International alliances grew more rigid, binding countries together in ways that left little room for compromise, while propaganda campaigns increasingly shaped public opinion and fueled hostility toward rival states.

The international system appeared stable on the surface, but in reality, it was fragile and easily disturbed. Only a small increase in tension was needed to push it toward open conflict.

During the 1930s, that pressure mounted. Territory was seized. Treaties were ignored. Smaller nations vanished from maps. Each move was justified as necessary, temporary, or defensive. Each made the next crisis more dangerous. By the end of the decade, the world was standing at the edge of another catastrophe.

When war finally erupted, it didn't remain local for long. Within months, armies were crossing borders on multiple continents. Cities burned under aerial bombardment. Shipping lanes became killing grounds. Civilians found themselves drafted into the struggle, whether they wore uniforms or not.

What followed wasn't merely a continuation of earlier conflicts: it was warfare on a scale never before attempted.

World War II became the most destructive confrontation in human history. It fused ideology, industry, science, and nationalism into a single, relentless machine. Large formations of tanks advanced across continents, submarines hunted shipping lanes beneath the oceans, and bomber fleets carried the war deep into civilian areas. Rockets crossed national borders, while scientists in secret laboratories worked urgently to develop weapons powerful enough to destroy entire cities in moments.

The battlefield expanded everywhere: deserts, jungles, frozen plains, crowded ports, remote islands, and capital streets. Soldiers endured exhaustion, terror, and conditions that tested the limits of survival. Civilians rationed food, built shelters, evacuated children, labored in factories, and learned to live under constant threat from the air. Occupied populations navigated fear, collaboration, and resistance. Prisoners marched, starved, and died in staggering numbers.

When the fighting finally stopped, the toll defied comprehension. Tens of millions were dead. Entire regions lay in ruins. Cities had been flattened. Communities erased. Trauma followed survivors for decades. New political orders emerged from the wreckage, reshaping international relations, borders, and power structures for generations to come.

The world that followed wasn't simply rebuilt; it was transformed.

This book is not a conventional chronological textbook. It does not attempt to narrate every campaign in detail or catalogue every general and treaty. Instead, it approaches the war through moments: striking, unsettling, revealing details that illuminate what this global catastrophe truly looked like from the ground, the cockpit, the factory floor, the laboratory, and the living room.

Inside these pages, you will encounter:

The strange episodes.

The brutal realities.

The overlooked details.

The astonishing improvisations.

The human decisions that bent history in unexpected directions.

You will read about soldiers and spies, engineers and nurses, prisoners and pilots, factory workers and children. About inventions born of desperation. About accidents that altered campaigns. About acts of courage that went unnoticed and mistakes whose consequences echoed for decades.

Some of these facts will surprise you.

Some will disturb you.

Some may change how you think about modern warfare entirely.

Each stands alone, yet together they form a mosaic of a conflict that reshaped the planet and continues to influence politics, technology, and culture today. This is not only the story of how World War II unfolded. It is a collection of moments showing what happens when ideology, fear, ambition, and industrial power collide on a global scale.

This is *Shocking World War II Facts*.

FIFTEEN

A War That Engulfed the World

World War II is often remembered through its most famous battles and turning points, but the reality is that the conflict reached nearly every corner of the globe. From the cities of Europe to the deserts of North Africa, from the jungles of Southeast Asia to the vast expanses of the Pacific Ocean, the war drew in nations, colonies, and peoples on an unprecedented scale. Millions of individuals who had little influence over political decisions found themselves caught in a struggle that crossed borders and continents. This chapter explores the truly global nature of World War II, including the spread of conflict across multiple theaters, the involvement of colonial forces, and the ways in which the war reshaped regions far beyond Europe. It reveals how interconnected the world had become and how a crisis in one part of the globe could rapidly expand into a worldwide confrontation. It was a war that did not remain confined to a single front but instead transformed into a conflict that affected the entire world in ways that are still felt today.

1. Manchuria as an Early Spark

In September 1931, Japan set in motion one of the earliest crises that later blended into World War II when its forces moved into Manchuria, a resource-rich area of northeastern China. Japanese officers used an explosion along a railway near the Japanese-occupied city of Mukden, an incident whose circumstances were immediately disputed, as justification for a rapid military occupation. Within months, large areas of territory were under Japanese control, and a new puppet regime was installed to legitimize the takeover. At the time, this didn't look like the beginning of a world-spanning conflict; to many governments, it appeared to be another regional war in a turbulent post-World War I landscape. Yet in hindsight, historians often treat Manchuria as one of the first cracks in the fragile international order, a sign that armed expansion could succeed even in an age supposedly governed by diplomacy.

2. International Protests and a Quiet Departure

The reaction to Japan's move into Manchuria revealed how weak global enforcement mechanisms had become during the interwar years. China appealed to the League of Nations, an organization established after World War I to prevent future conflicts through diplomacy and collective security. The League of Nations sent investigators and eventually condemned the occupation. Japan rejected the criticism, also known as the Lytton Report, and, rather than reverse course, withdrew from the League entirely in 1933, signaling that it no longer felt bound by that system of collective security. This episode mattered far beyond East Asia. Other governments watched closely and drew their own conclusions about how much resistance territorial expansion might provoke. The Manchurian crisis didn't yet ignite a global war, but it demonstrated that treaties and international pressure alone were proving insufficient to stop determined states: an unsettling precedent as the 1930s continued to unfold.

3. Ethiopia and the Limits of Collective Security

In October 1935, Italy launched a full-scale invasion of Ethiopia, then commonly called Abyssinia, turning another regional crisis into a test of the international system meant to preserve peace. Under the leadership of Benito Mussolini, Italian forces advanced from neighboring colonies using modern weapons against a largely under-equipped defender. The government in Addis Ababa appealed again to the League of Nations, which imposed economic sanctions on Italy but avoided measures that might provoke war, such as cutting off vital oil supplies. Those limited penalties failed to halt the invasion, and by 1936, Ethiopia had been conquered and absorbed into a new Italian empire in East Africa. To many observers, the episode was unsettling proof that aggressive expansion could succeed even when openly condemned, further weakening confidence in diplomatic institutions and encouraging other powers to test how far they might go.

4. Spanish Civil War

When civil war erupted in Spain in 1936, it quickly became more than an internal struggle; it became a "clash of ideologies" that divided the world. The conflict was fought between two main groups: the Republicans, who supported the country's democratically elected government, and the Nationalists, a rebel group of conservative military officers led by General Francisco Franco. The struggle drew in outside powers eager to shape Europe's political direction and to use Spain as a military laboratory. Germany and Italy supported Franco's Nationalists, seeing an opportunity to install a fellow fascist-style dictator in Western Europe. Meanwhile, the Soviet Union sent aid to the Republicans. Because major democracies like Britain and the U.S. remained officially neutral, thousands of private citizens from around the world, known as the International Brigades, traveled to Spain to fight against the spread of fascism. Fascism is a far-right political system characterized by dictatorial power, extreme nationalism, and the forceful suppression of any opposition. The war reached a horrific peak with the 1937 bombing of Guernica, a chilling preview of how civilian populations would be targeted from the air in the coming years.

5. China Drawn into Full-Scale War

In July 1937, fighting flared between Japanese and Chinese troops near the Marco Polo Bridge outside Beijing, turning years of tension into open conflict between Japan and China. What began as a confused nighttime confrontation over troop movements quickly escalated into a massive invasion. This escalation forced the Chinese government, led by Generalissimo Chiang Kai-shek, the head of the Nationalist Party (Kuomintang) and the country's military leader, to abandon his previous policy of cautious compromise and mobilize for a "war of resistance." As Japanese forces captured major coastal cities, Chiang Kai-shek relocated his government deep inland to the mountain city of Chongqing, vowing to wear down the invaders through a prolonged struggle of attrition. The conflict was marked by devastating air raids and atrocities that shocked the international community, yet Chiang Kai-shek's forces remained the primary barrier to total Japanese control of the mainland. Although often viewed abroad as a separate Asian conflict, this war tied down millions of Japanese troops and reshaped global diplomacy. When Europe eventually descended into war in 1939, the fighting in China didn't pause; under Chiang's continued leadership, it merged into the broader Allied effort: the collective military struggle of the "Allied Powers," an alliance of nations including Great Britain, the Soviet Union, and eventually the United States, who united to defeat the aggression of the Axis powers (Germany, Italy, and Japan).

6. Appeasement and Territorial Gambles

While Asia burned, Europe moved closer to crisis through a series of calculated risks and hesitant responses driven by the ambitions of Adolf Hitler, the leader of the Nazi Party, who had risen to power in Germany with a promise to undo the "humiliations" of World War I. In 1936, Hitler ordered German troops to march back into the Rhineland, a strategically vital strip of German land bordering France that had been strictly demilitarized by international treaty to act as a safety buffer. Though this was a blatant violation of post-war agreements, it met no military resistance. Two years later, Germany absorbed Austria and then pressed claims on parts of Czechoslovakia. Britain and France, desperate to avoid another continent-wide slaughter, pursued a policy known as appeasement: negotiation rather than confrontation. This culminated in the Munich Agreement of 1938, which handed over disputed Czech territory to Germany in exchange for Hitler's promises of peace. While many celebrated the deal as a triumph for diplomacy, the victory was short-lived. Within months, German forces occupied the rest of Czechoslovakia, making it increasingly clear that Hitler's goals weren't limited to reclaiming lost territory but were aimed at total European dominance.

7. A Border War in the Mongolian Region

In the summer of 1939, fighting erupted far from Europe along the remote frontier between Mongolia and Japanese-controlled territory in Manchuria, near the Khalkhin Gol River. Forces from Japan clashed repeatedly with Mongolian troops backed by the Soviet Union (USSR), a vast communist state led by Joseph Stalin that spanned Eurasia and sought to protect its eastern borders from Japanese expansion. In August and September, Soviet armored units and artillery, coordinated with air power under the command of future war hero Georgy Zhukov, eventually encircled and crushed major Japanese formations. The defeat was costly for Tokyo and carried consequences well beyond the battlefield. Japanese leaders quietly abandoned plans for further northern expansion into Siberia and instead shifted attention southward toward Southeast Asia and the Pacific, a strategic decision that would later shape the course of the wider war.

Though largely overshadowed by events in Europe, Khalkhin Gol was a turning point in Asia before the global conflict formally ignited.

8. A Pact That Shocked Europe

As tensions mounted across Europe in 1939, diplomacy produced one of the most shocking agreements in history: a non-aggression pact between Nazi Germany and the Soviet Union. On the surface, the two countries, led by Adolf Hitler and Joseph Stalin, publicly promised not to attack one another. This stunned the world because the two leaders were bitter ideological enemies; Hitler's fascism and Stalin's communism were completely opposed. However, the treaty contained secret clauses that weren't revealed to the public. In these hidden terms, the two dictators agreed to carve up Eastern Europe between them. They planned to invade and divide Poland and decided that the Baltic states (Estonia, Latvia, and Lithuania) would fall under Soviet control. This deal was a strategic "win" for both dictators and served as the final green light for global conflict. For Germany, it meant that Hitler could invade Poland without the fear of the Soviet Union attacking him from the east, allowing him to focus his military strength in one direction. For the Soviet Union, the agreement bought Stalin vital time to build up his military and established a "buffer zone" of occupied territory in Eastern Europe to keep any future German threats far from the Soviet heartland. The signing of this pact was the final green light for war. With his eastern border secured by this temporary friendship, Hitler was ready to launch his invasion.

9. The Attack That Opened the European War

In the early hours of September 1, 1939, German forces crossed into Poland, launching a coordinated assault that many historians treat as the formal beginning of World War II in Europe. Armored columns advanced along multiple fronts while aircraft struck railways, bridges, and cities, aiming to paralyze Polish defenses before they could fully mobilize. German propaganda claimed the invasion was defensive, but the operation followed months of planning and was made politically possible by the recent non-aggression pact with the Soviet Union. Polish troops resisted fiercely, but they were outmatched in equipment and air support. Within days, refugees clogged roads and rail lines, governments across Europe rushed to emergency meetings, and it became clear that the diplomatic crises of the 1930s had finally tipped into open continental war.

10. Declarations That Globalized a Conflict

Germany's invasion of Poland forced other powers to decide whether years of warnings and guarantees would finally be backed by action. On September 3, 1939, the United Kingdom and France formally declared war on Germany after ultimatums demanding withdrawal from Poland went unanswered. The announcements were brief and legalistic, but their implications were enormous: what had begun as a regional invasion was now a war between Europe's major powers. Crowds gathered around radios in cities and villages, soldiers were mobilized, and navies began positioning themselves across the Atlantic and Mediterranean. Although little immediate fighting followed on the Western Front, the diplomatic threshold had been crossed. The long sequence of crises stretching back to Manchuria and Ethiopia had culminated in a confrontation that now threatened to spread far beyond Poland's borders.

11. A Second Army from the East

As Polish forces struggled to slow the German advance in September 1939, another blow arrived from an unexpected direction. On September 17, troops from the Soviet Union crossed Poland's eastern frontier, acting under the secret provisions of the recent German–Soviet agreement. Soviet officials claimed that the Polish state had collapsed and that they were moving in to protect local populations, but the action effectively sealed Poland's defeat. Already stretched thin, Polish units found themselves facing two invading powers at once, while political leaders fled abroad to continue resistance in exile. Within weeks, the country was divided between its occupiers, and millions of civilians came under new, often brutal administrations. The double invasion shocked observers abroad and confirmed that the European war was no longer limited to a single aggressor but was already reshaping the balance of power across the continent.

12. Finland's Winter Struggle

Only months later, another front opened in the north when the Soviet Union attacked Finland in November 1939 after negotiations over territory and security guarantees broke down. Expecting a swift victory, Soviet planners instead encountered fierce resistance from Finnish troops who used skis, camouflage, and intimate knowledge of forests and frozen lakes to offset overwhelming numbers. Fighting took place in temperatures that plunged far below zero, with weapons freezing and soldiers suffering severe frostbite alongside combat wounds. Although Finland was eventually forced to cede territory in March 1940, it preserved its independence and inflicted unexpectedly heavy losses on the invaders. The campaign drew international attention, exposed weaknesses in Soviet military preparedness, and demonstrated how the war was already spreading into new and unforgiving environments only months after it began.

13. Denmark's Sudden Fall

In April 1940, Germany abruptly expanded the war northward by attacking Denmark, seeking to secure supply routes for Swedish iron ore, a high-quality mineral essential for the production of German steel, tanks, and ships. Because Germany lacked sufficient domestic resources, these shipments from neutral Sweden were the lifeblood of its war machine. The German assault also aimed to block any future presence of the Allied Powers: the international coalition led by Britain and France that had formed in September 1939 to oppose German aggression. The assault came with almost no warning. German troops crossed the border at dawn while aircraft flew low over Copenhagen, dropping leaflets urging surrender rather than resistance. Denmark's small and lightly equipped military faced an overwhelming force, and government leaders feared that continued fighting would lead to the destruction of cities and civilian casualties. After only a few hours of combat, Danish authorities agreed to surrender, making it one of the fastest national defeats of the entire war. Strategically, the occupation gave Germany control of airfields, ports, and sea lanes into the Baltic Sea, a large body of water in Northern Europe that is nearly enclosed by land, serving as the primary maritime highway connecting Germany, Scandinavia, and the Soviet Union. By controlling Denmark, Germany effectively locked the "gate" to this sea, signaling to Europe that the conflict was spreading into new regions vital for resources and transportation.

14. Norway's Fjords and Frozen Battles

On the same day as the Danish operation, German forces struck Norway, whose long coastline and deep fjords, which are long, narrow inlets with steep cliffs or slopes created by glaciers that reach far inland, made it crucial for Atlantic naval access. These natural harbors provided ideal hiding spots for warships and were vital for protecting the iron ore shipments coming from Sweden. Unlike Denmark, Norway resisted, and British and French units soon landed to support its defense. Fighting erupted around ports, mountain passes, and snowbound roads, while warships clashed offshore and paratroopers seized key airfields inland. For weeks, the campaign remained uncertain, but Germany steadily poured in reinforcements by sea and air. By early June 1940, Allied troops withdrew, and Norwegian authorities fled into exile, leaving the country under occupation. The campaign gave Germany valuable submarine bases along the Atlantic coast and demonstrated how air power, speed, and control of infrastructure could overcome difficult terrain in modern warfare.

15. Overrunning of France in Weeks

In May 1940, the conflict in Western Europe reached a stunning climax when German armies surged through Belgium, the Netherlands, and Luxembourg before driving into France itself. Allied commanders expected the main thrust to follow heavily fortified borders, but German armored divisions instead cut through the Ardennes, a densely forested region long believed to be unsuitable for tanks. This surprise maneuver split the defending forces and triggered a massive civilian flight, as roads filled with millions of refugees. Within just a few weeks, German troops reached the English Channel coast, Paris fell, and French leaders were forced to request an armistice. By June 1940, the French surrender was official. The speed of the collapse shocked the world and completely overturned long-held assumptions about defensive warfare, leaving Britain isolated in Western Europe and marking one of the most dramatic turning points of the early war.

16. Trapping of Allied Forces

In mid-May 1940, German armored spearheads, fast-moving groups of tanks and motorized vehicles designed to punch a hole through enemy lines and race deep into the rear, tore through northern France and Belgium. This "lightning" maneuver cut off large Allied armies from the south, forcing British and French units to retreat toward the port city of Dunkirk. Located on the coast of the English Channel near the Belgian border, Dunkirk sat roughly forty-seven miles (seventy-five kilometers) from the British coast. The town's beaches and harbor became the final escape route for soldiers surrounded by advancing German troops on land and attacked by the Luftwaffe (the German air force) from the sky.

17. Encirclement on the Channel Coast

By May 24, 1940, nearly 400,000 Allied soldiers from the United Kingdom and France were crowded into sand dunes, narrow streets, and improvised defensive lines around the port city of Dunkirk. German forces closed in from land while aircraft bombed harbor facilities, destroying docks and blocking many large ships from approaching. Thousands of men were forced to wait for days in the open, exposed to strafing attacks and artillery fire, wading into cold water in hopes of reaching rescue vessels offshore. Many feared that the capture of the entire British Expeditionary Force was unavoidable. What looked like the destruction of Britain's army in Western Europe was instead becoming a desperate race against time, as commanders scrambled to assemble any vessel capable of crossing the Channel.

18. Operation Dynamo and the Little Ships

The crisis at Dunkirk triggered a dramatic rescue effort beginning on May 26, 1940, when British naval planners launched an emergency evacuation code-named Operation Dynamo. Coordinated from headquarters in southern England, the plan relied not only on warships but also on hundreds of civilian craft pressed into service, fishing trawlers, ferries, tugboats, pleasure boats, and river launches, many of them crewed by volunteers. These small vessels ferried troops from shallow beaches to destroyers and transports waiting farther offshore while German aircraft attacked relentlessly from above. Smoke from burning fuel tanks drifted across the coast, and wrecked ships littered the harbor approaches. By the time the operation ended on June 4, roughly 338,000 Allied soldiers had been carried to safety, though nearly all heavy equipment had been left behind. The evacuation transformed a looming catastrophe into a defining moment of wartime survival and ensured Britain could continue fighting.

19. Attacks Across the Channel

After the fall of France in June 1940, Germany turned its focus toward forcing the United Kingdom out of the war. Beginning in July, the German air force launched sustained strikes against merchant shipping in the English Channel and radar installations along Britain's southern coastline. These tall towers, using radio waves to detect approaching aircraft, formed an early-warning shield that allowed defenders precious minutes to prepare. The attacks were intended to weaken Britain's ability to respond in the air and to clear the way for a planned cross-Channel invasion known as Operation Sea Lion. At first, the campaign focused on infrastructure rather than cities, signaling that Germany hoped to defeat Britain militarily before risking a costly amphibious landing.

20. Britain's Integrated Air Defense System

To counter the growing air threat, Britain relied on a carefully coordinated defensive network unlike anything previously attempted on such a scale. Radar stations, coastal observers, and command centers were linked by telephone lines and plotting rooms that tracked enemy formations in real time. Instead of keeping fighters circling endlessly in the sky, controllers directed squadrons to take off only when needed, conserving fuel and allowing pilots to meet raids at optimal altitudes. German bombers and escort fighters repeatedly struck airfields in counties closest to France, such as Kent and Sussex, hoping to cripple this system and destroy defending aircraft on the ground. The struggle soon became one of endurance and organization as much as raw firepower, with each side testing whether technology, logistics, and coordination could decide control of the skies before an invasion was attempted.

21. Pilots from Many Nations

The aerial defense of Britain depended heavily on young fighter pilots who flew exhausting schedules, sometimes scrambling into combat several times a day. While many were British, hundreds came from countries already under Axis occupation: nations conquered by the "Axis Powers," the military alliance led by Nazi Germany, Fascist Italy, and later Imperial Japan. These pilots included skilled airmen from Poland and Czechoslovakia who had escaped their homelands to continue the fight. They were joined by volunteers from Commonwealth nations, a global association of countries that were formerly part of the British Empire, such as Canada, Australia, and New Zealand, which shared a common allegiance to the British Crown. These volunteers brought valuable combat experience and formed some of the most effective units of the campaign. Air battles erupted daily above farmland, seaside towns, and crowded suburbs, turning ordinary landscapes into contested airspace. Losses mounted on both sides, and replacement pilots were rushed through training to keep squadrons operational. By August 1940, the fighting had hardened into a grinding contest of attrition: a tactical struggle where each side attempted to wear down the other's resources and personnel. The survival of the country became increasingly dependent on whether its air defenses could remain intact longer than those of its opponent.

22. Night Raids over London

In September 1940, German strategy shifted away from airfields toward sustained bombing of major population centers, especially London. These nighttime assaults, later known collectively as the Blitz, dropped high-explosive bombs and incendiaries that ignited widespread fires, flattened neighborhoods, and forced civilians into underground stations and public shelters. Other industrial cities were also struck repeatedly as ports, factories, and rail yards burned. The campaign continued through the winter and into the spring of 1941, yet aircraft production and air defenses remained active despite the destruction. Public morale, though shaken, didn't collapse. By October, German leaders postponed plans for an invasion indefinitely, marking the first major strategic failure of their westward expansion and ensuring that the war in Europe would continue rather than end swiftly in the air.

23. Submarines in the Supply Lines

As Britain resisted invasion in 1940, Germany intensified a campaign at sea designed to starve the United Kingdom into submission. German submarines, called U-boats, short for the German word *Unterseeboot*, meaning "undersea boat," slipped into the Atlantic shipping lanes to attack merchant vessels carrying food, fuel, and weapons from North America. These ships usually traveled in convoys, tightly grouped formations meant to make defense easier, but early in the war, many lacked sufficient escort warships or air cover. U-boats often attacked at night on the surface, firing torpedoes and vanishing into darkness before counterattacks could begin. Sinkings mounted rapidly, alarming British planners who understood that losing cargo ships faster than they could be replaced threatened the nation's ability to survive the war at all.

24. Escorts, Sonar, and Closing the Ocean Gaps

Britain and its allies gradually learned how to fight back against the submarine menace. Warships were equipped with sonar, an underwater detection system that used sound waves to locate submerged vessels, and depth charges, explosive barrels dropped into the sea to damage or destroy submarines below. Aircraft began patrolling shipping routes as well, forcing U-boats to dive and slowing their attacks. Long stretches of ocean that aircraft couldn't yet reach, known as the "air gap," proved especially dangerous until longer-range planes and escort carriers were introduced. Convoy systems were tightened, and intelligence efforts tracked German naval communications. The campaign became a battle of production as much as tactics: Germany rushed to build more submarines, while Britain and the United States expanded shipyards to replace lost vessels faster than they could be sunk. Control of the Atlantic would become one of the war's decisive struggles.

25. A New Front in the Mediterranean

In June 1940, Italy entered the conflict on Germany's side, opening new fronts around the Mediterranean Sea and in North Africa. Italian forces advanced from Libya into British-controlled Egypt, aiming to threaten the Suez Canal, a vital man-made waterway that served as a shortcut for ships traveling between Europe and the "colonies" (territories ruled by distant nations) in Asia and East Africa. For Britain, losing the canal would mean losing its quickest access to the resources of its global empire and the critical oil supplies of the Middle East. Early fighting revealed major problems with Italian equipment, coordination, and long supply lines stretching across the harsh, trackless desert terrain. British counteroffensives, aided by troops from across the British Empire, including India and Australia, soon pushed Italian units back, capturing large numbers of prisoners and alarming the leadership in Rome. Naval clashes and air raids spread across the Mediterranean as both sides tried to protect convoys, organized groups of merchant ships protected by warships, carrying fuel, food, and ammunition to distant armies. What had begun as a European war was now clearly spilling into the deserts and sea routes that connected three continents, turning the Mediterranean into a high-stakes battleground for global survival.

26. Rommel and the Desert See-Saw

To stabilize the collapsing Italian position, Germany sent an expeditionary force to North Africa in early 1941 under General Erwin Rommel. His units, known as the Afrika Korps, quickly launched bold counterattacks that drove British troops back across hundreds of miles of desert. The fighting became a mobile tug-of-war, with armored columns racing between isolated forts and supply depots while aircraft bombed roads and ports. Desert warfare placed enormous strain on logistics: vehicles consumed fuel at staggering rates, water was scarce, and spare parts had to be hauled over vast distances. Victories often depended less on battlefield brilliance than on whether one side could keep trucks, tanks, and troops supplied. The North African front soon turned into one of the war's most fluid and unpredictable theaters.

27. A Coup That Alarmed Berlin

In early 1941, Germany turned anxious attention toward Yugoslavia, a multi-ethnic state created after World War I that included Serbs, Croats, Slovenes, and several other South Slavic groups. The country's political balance suddenly collapsed when a coup overthrew a government that had recently aligned itself with the Axis. The change infuriated Adolf Hitler, who feared that instability in the Balkans could expose Germany's southern flank and disrupt crucial supply routes, especially those linked to Romanian oil fields. The episode convinced German leaders that Yugoslavia couldn't be left neutral or uncertain while larger military plans were underway. Within days, invasion orders were issued. What had looked like a regional political crisis quickly became the trigger for a new military campaign, one that would pull southeastern Europe directly into the widening war.

28. Blitzkrieg in Southeastern Europe

In April 1941, German and Italian forces launched simultaneous invasions of Yugoslavia and Greece, opening another major front only weeks before the planned assault on the Soviet Union. Heavy bombing struck cities, including the Yugoslav capital, Belgrade. Along with the bombing, armored columns and airborne troops crossed borders from multiple directions. Because attacks came at once from several sides, organized resistance collapsed rapidly. Within weeks, both countries were occupied or partitioned, carved into zones governed by different Axis powers and collaborators. The victories secured Germany's southern approaches, safeguarded supply routes near Romania, and extended Axis influence toward the eastern Mediterranean. Yet the campaigns also consumed precious weeks, delaying the much larger invasion of the Soviet Union that German planners were already preparing farther east.

29. Crete and the Age of Airborne Assaults

In May 1941, Germany attempted one of the most daring operations of the early war: the capture of the Mediterranean island of Crete almost entirely by parachute troops. The island, which had become an Allied stronghold after the fall of mainland Greece, controlled important sea routes and airfields. German paratroopers descended from transport planes under intense fire, suffering heavy casualties as defenders shot them while they were still landing and scrambling for their weapons. Fighting raged around villages and airstrips, and only after days of brutal combat did German forces secure enough runways to fly in reinforcements. Crete eventually fell, but at a staggering cost. The losses alarmed German commanders, who concluded that such large airborne invasions were too risky to repeat. The battle shaped later planning and revealed how experimental and costly modern warfare had become by 1941.

30. A Massive Army

Even as fighting continued around the Mediterranean, Germany quietly assembled enormous forces along the western border of the Soviet Union. At dawn on June 22, 1941, Adolf Hitler launched Operation Barbarossa, a vast invasion stretching hundreds of miles from the Baltic to the Black Sea. This attack was a profound act of betrayal, as it formally broke the Molotov-Ribbentrop Pact: the "non-aggression" agreement signed just two years earlier in which both nations had promised not to fight one another. The sudden strike caught the Soviet leadership by surprise, shattering the diplomatic peace that had allowed both dictators to carve up Eastern Europe in 1939. Three immense formations drove toward key objectives: Leningrad in the north, Moscow in the center, and Ukraine in the south. Aircraft smashed airfields and rail junctions, destroying hundreds of Soviet planes on the ground in the opening hours. German planners believed rapid armored thrusts and encirclement tactics would bring victory before winter. Instead, the invasion instantly transformed the war into a continental struggle of unprecedented scale across forests, rivers, and open land.

31. Encirclements and Catastrophic Losses

During the summer of 1941, German forces advanced deep into Soviet territory using mobile formations of tanks, trucks, and infantry to surround entire enemy armies in vast "pockets." Cities such as Minsk and Smolensk fell after fierce fighting, while hundreds of thousands of captured soldiers were marched westward under brutal conditions. The German policy toward prisoners proved especially lethal, with millions subjected to starvation, forced marches, and executions rather than being treated according to international norms. Civilians fled burning towns as front lines swept east, and destruction spread across enormous swaths of countryside. Although the German advance appeared unstoppable in its early months, the sheer distances involved, growing casualties, and stubborn Soviet resistance hinted that the campaign was becoming something far larger and far more dangerous than its planners had anticipated.

32. Encirclement of a Northern Metropolis

By September 1941, German and allied forces had reached the outskirts of Leningrad, today known as St. Petersburg, cutting most overland routes into the city and beginning what would become one of the longest sieges in modern warfare. Instead of launching an immediate frontal assault, German commanders chose to surround the metropolis and bombard key infrastructure, hoping that hunger, cold, and isolation would force surrender without the cost of street fighting. Rail links were severed, warehouses destroyed, and utilities disrupted as shells and bombs fell across residential districts. Millions of civilians, along with soldiers and factory workers producing weapons inside the city, suddenly found themselves trapped behind tightening lines. The encirclement turned daily survival into a strategic issue and marked the opening phase of a blockade that would last far longer and prove much deadlier than most observers initially expected.

33. Starvation and the Frozen Escape Route

As winter set in during late 1941, conditions inside besieged Leningrad deteriorated rapidly. Food rations dropped to only a few hundred calories a day, and tens of thousands of people died each month from hunger and exposure. The city's main lifeline ran across Lake Ladoga, where trucks and sled convoys crossed the frozen surface during winter in a hazardous supply route later called the "Road of Life." These journeys took place under constant artillery fire and air attack, and vehicles sometimes plunged through thin ice. Though never sufficient to fully relieve suffering, the route prevented complete collapse and allowed limited evacuations, turning a frozen lake into one of the war's most fragile and vital arteries.

34. The Final Push Toward Moscow

Farther south in autumn 1941, German forces renewed their drive toward Moscow, hoping that capturing the Soviet capital would cripple political leadership, transportation networks, and morale. Early advances brought forward units within sight of the city's outer suburbs, prompting emergency defensive measures and the evacuation of government offices eastward. Yet logistical problems mounted quickly. Seasonal rains transformed unpaved roads into deep mud, immobilizing tanks and trucks and slowing supply convoys. Rail lines struggled to keep pace with the rapidly shifting front, while exhausted troops fought in worsening weather. Soviet commanders rushed reinforcements into defensive belts surrounding the capital, digging trenches and fortifying villages in preparation for a last stand as temperatures plunged and the battle for central Russia entered a decisive phase.

35. Winter Counterblows in the East

By early December 1941, freezing temperatures and stretched supply lines had left German units around Moscow dangerously exposed. Many soldiers lacked adequate winter clothing, vehicles froze overnight, and fuel shortages slowed movement. Soviet forces, strengthened by newly deployed divisions and reorganized defenses, launched coordinated counterattacks along broad sections of the front. Ski troops played a critical role in this offensive: specialized mobile infantry units equipped with skis that allowed them to glide over deep snow that would trap a normal soldier, enabling them to launch surprise attacks from the forest. These ski troops and other mobile units exploited the frozen ground to strike German flanks and rear areas, pushing the invaders back dozens of miles from the capital. In some critical sectors, the Germans were forced to retreat as far as 150 miles (about 250 kilometers) away. The reversal shocked German commanders, who had expected the campaign to end months earlier. Although the fighting remained brutal, the counteroffensive marked the first major collapse of Germany's momentum in the east and demonstrated that the Soviet Union retained both the manpower and the will to continue a war that had already grown far beyond its planners' original expectations.

36. Rising Tensions in the Pacific

By late 1941, relations between Japan and the United States had deteriorated sharply. Japan had been fighting a prolonged war in China since 1937 and sought access to oil, rubber, and other raw materials in Southeast Asia to sustain its military expansion. In response, the United States and its allies imposed economic sanctions, including an embargo that cut off oil exports to Japan, resources essential for its navy and industry. Diplomatic negotiations continued throughout the year, but both sides prepared for the possibility of war. Japanese leaders faced a difficult choice: abandon expansionist goals or seize the resources they needed by force. As tensions rose, military planners began to consider a bold strategy that would attempt to disable American power in the Pacific before it could respond.

37. A Surprise Strike Across the Pacific

In late 1941, Japanese military planners prepared a high-risk operation designed to weaken the United States before it could interfere with expansion in Asia. The plan called for a long-range naval strike against the American Pacific Fleet stationed at Pearl Harbor, located on the island of Oahu in Hawaii, thousands of kilometers from Japan. Aircraft carriers, warships that carry and launch planes, would sail secretly across the northern Pacific, maintaining radio silence to avoid detection. The goal was to destroy battleships, aircraft, and fuel supplies in a single coordinated attack, buying Japan time to secure resource-rich territories in Southeast Asia. The strategy relied on complete surprise. If successful, it could delay the American response for months. If it failed, Japan risked provoking a powerful industrial nation into a prolonged war that it might not be able to win.

38. The Morning Attack

On the morning of December 7, 1941, Japanese aircraft launched their attack on Pearl Harbor in two waves, catching the base largely unprepared. Bombers and torpedo planes targeted battleships anchored in the harbor, while fighters strafed airfields to destroy American aircraft before they could take off. Within minutes, explosions tore through ships, including the battleship USS *Arizona*, which sank after a massive internal blast. Sailors scrambled to return fire as smoke and flames spread across the water. In total, more than 2,400 Americans were killed, and many ships were sunk or heavily damaged. However, key targets, including aircraft carriers, repair facilities, and fuel depots, remained intact, largely because they were absent or missed. Instead of securing a decisive advantage, the attack united American public opinion, leading to a formal declaration of war the following day.

39. Declarations of Global War

The attack on Pearl Harbor immediately transformed the conflict into a truly global war. On December 8, 1941, the United States formally declared war on Japan, marking a decisive shift in American policy after years of avoiding direct involvement. The following days widened the conflict even further. Japan's allies, Germany and Italy, declared war on the United States, bringing the world's largest industrial power into both the Pacific and European theaters simultaneously. What had previously been partially connected wars in Europe, Africa, and Asia now merged into a single, coordinated global struggle. Governments began to align their strategies, industries shifted to wartime production on an enormous scale, and millions of new soldiers were mobilized. The entry of the United States ensured that the war would expand not only geographically but also in resources, technology, and intensity.

40. Simultaneous Offensives Across the Pacific

In December 1941, immediately following the attack on Pearl Harbor, Japan launched a series of nearly simultaneous offensives across Southeast Asia and the Pacific. These attacks were carefully coordinated to strike multiple Allied positions at once, overwhelming defenders before they could organize an effective response. Japanese forces targeted British, American, and Dutch territories, focusing on key ports, airfields, and communication centers. The goal was to secure a defensive perimeter and gain access to vital natural resources such as oil, rubber, and minerals needed to sustain a long war. Because many Allied forces were unprepared or spread too thin, Japanese troops often achieved rapid successes. Within weeks, vast areas of territory had been captured, creating the impression that Japan's military expansion might be unstoppable.

41. The Fall of the Philippines

One of Japan's main objectives was the Philippines, a group of islands under American control that stood directly between Japan and Southeast Asia. Japanese aircraft struck airfields shortly after Pearl Harbor, destroying many planes on the ground and leaving defenses weakened. Ground forces soon landed and advanced toward the capital, Manila, forcing American and Filipino troops to retreat to the Bataan Peninsula. There, they held out for months under severe shortages of food, medicine, and supplies. When resistance finally collapsed in April 1942, tens of thousands of exhausted prisoners were forced to march long distances under brutal conditions in what became known as the Bataan Death March. The fall of the Philippines removed a major obstacle to Japanese expansion and demonstrated the harsh realities of captivity during the Pacific War.

42. Singapore and the Collapse of a Fortress

At the same time, Japanese forces advanced down the Malaya peninsula toward Singapore, a heavily fortified British naval base often described as the "Gibraltar of the East." British planners had expected any attack to come from the sea, but Japanese troops moved rapidly overland, using bicycles and light equipment to travel quickly through jungle terrain that defenders had considered difficult to cross. Air superiority allowed Japanese aircraft to strike supply lines and defensive positions, weakening resistance. By February 1942, Singapore was surrounded, and after a short but intense battle, British forces surrendered. More than 80,000 troops were taken prisoner, making it one of the largest defeats in British military history. The fall of Singapore shocked Allied governments and severely damaged confidence in colonial defenses across Asia.

43. Securing Oil in the Dutch East Indies

A key objective of Japanese expansion was control of the Dutch East Indies, a region rich in oil and other natural resources essential for modern warfare. Without reliable fuel supplies, Japan's navy, air force, and industry couldn't continue operating effectively. Japanese forces moved quickly to capture major oil fields and refineries, often encountering limited resistance as Allied defenses struggled to coordinate across vast distances. Naval battles were fought in surrounding seas, but Japanese fleets gained control, allowing transport ships to move troops and supplies with increasing security. By early 1942, most of the region had fallen under Japanese control, providing the resources needed to sustain further military operations. These victories gave Japan a temporary strategic advantage, but they also stretched its forces across a vast territory that would later become difficult to defend.

44. A Carrier Battle

In May 1942, opposing fleets met in the Coral Sea northeast of Australia in a battle that marked a new kind of naval warfare. For the first time, ships on both sides never directly saw each other; instead, aircraft launched from carriers searched for and attacked enemy vessels over long distances. Japan aimed to capture Port Moresby in New Guinea. Securing this port would have allowed Japan to dominate the region and threaten Australia's supply lines: the vital maritime routes used to transport food, fuel, military equipment, and fresh troops from the United States. If these lines had been cut, Australia would have been isolated, making it much harder for the Allies to launch a comeback in the Pacific. American and Australian forces moved to intercept the Japanese fleet. Over several days, both sides exchanged heavy air strikes, damaging or sinking major ships and losing dozens of aircraft. Although both sides suffered heavy losses, the Japanese advance toward Port Moresby was halted, marking their first major strategic setback of the Pacific war. The battle proved that aircraft carriers had replaced heavily armored battleships as the dominant force at sea. It demonstrated that in modern naval warfare, the side that controlled the air above the ocean would ultimately control the waves below.

45. The Turning Point at Midway

In June 1942, Japanese forces attacked Midway Atoll, expecting to draw out and destroy the remaining American carriers. Instead, they encountered a prepared defense. As Japanese aircraft rearmed on their carriers, American dive bombers arrived overhead, striking at a vulnerable moment. Within minutes, multiple Japanese carriers were set ablaze, their decks crowded with fuel and ammunition. The loss of these ships and their highly trained pilots was devastating. Japan could replace ships over time, but experienced aircrews were far harder to rebuild. The battle marked a major shift in the Pacific War, as Japan lost the ability to carry out large-scale offensive operations in the same way it had before.

46. From Expansion to Defense

After the Battle of Midway, Japan's rapid expansion slowed dramatically. Instead of advancing across the Pacific, Japanese troops were forced to defend a vast area of newly conquered territory stretching from Southeast Asia to remote island chains. Supply lines became longer and more difficult to protect, while Allied forces began planning counteroffensives. Control of key islands, airfields, and shipping routes became increasingly important as both sides prepared for prolonged conflict. The early phase of nearly uninterrupted Japanese victories had come to an end, replaced by a more balanced struggle in which industrial production, logistics, and long-term strategy would determine the outcome. The war had entered a new stage, where the initiative was beginning to shift.

47. Guadalcanal and the First Allied Offensive

In August 1942, Allied forces launched their first major offensive in the Pacific by landing on the island of Guadalcanal in the Solomon Islands chain. The island was strategically important because Japanese forces were building an airfield there that could threaten supply routes between the United States and Australia. American Marines landed and quickly captured the unfinished airstrip, later naming it Henderson Field. What followed were months of intense fighting on land, at sea, and in the air. Japanese forces launched repeated attempts to retake the island, often landing troops at night to avoid detection. Conditions were harsh, with heat, disease, and supply shortages affecting both sides. Guadalcanal marked a turning point because it shifted the initiative to the Allies, who were now beginning to move from defense to offense.

48. A War of Attrition in the Jungle

The campaign on Guadalcanal became a prolonged struggle of attrition, meaning a fight where each side attempts to wear the other down over time through continuous losses. Battles were fought in dense jungle, along narrow ridges, and around key positions such as Henderson Field. Night naval battles took place in nearby waters, where ships often engaged at close range in darkness. Both sides suffered heavy casualties not only from combat but also from malaria, malnutrition, and exhaustion. Supplies were difficult to deliver, and reinforcements often arrived under dangerous conditions. Japanese forces gradually weakened as their supply lines stretched too far, while American industrial capacity allowed a steady flow of replacements. By early 1943, Japan withdrew its remaining troops, marking its first major land defeat of the war and signaling a shift in momentum across the Pacific.

49. Expanding Across Multiple Fronts

By late 1942, World War II had become a truly global conflict, with major battles taking place simultaneously across Europe, North Africa, and the Pacific. In North Africa, Axis and Allied forces fought across deserts for control of strategic routes and resources. In the Soviet Union, massive armies clashed along an enormous front stretching thousands of miles. Meanwhile, in the Pacific, naval and island campaigns determined control of vast ocean regions. This multi-front war placed enormous demands on manpower, equipment, and logistics. Nations had to coordinate strategies across continents while maintaining supply lines that stretched across oceans and deserts. The scale of the conflict forced governments to mobilize entire societies, turning factories, farms, and civilian populations into essential parts of the war effort.

50. The Battle for Stalingrad Begins

In the summer of 1942, German forces launched a major offensive toward Stalingrad, a massive industrial city stretching along the banks of the Volga River in southern Russia. The city was a vital objective for two reasons: strategically, it was a major transport hub for moving fuel and grain from the south to the rest of the Soviet Union; and symbolically, capturing a city named after the Soviet leader, Joseph Stalin, would have been a devastating propaganda blow to Soviet morale. The German army, also known as the

Sixth Army, led by General Friedrich Paulus, advanced rapidly across the open steppe, aiming to seize the city. At the same time, other units drove further south toward the Caucasus, a region rich in oil fields that Hitler desperately needed to fuel his global war machine. By the time the Germans reached the outskirts of Stalingrad in August, the Luftwaffe (German air force) had reduced much of the city to rubble through intense firebombing. The conflict quickly devolved into a nightmare of urban warfare, or "Rattenkrieg" (Rat's War), as the Germans called it. Both sides committed millions of troops to the struggle, turning the city into a meat grinder. The battle was no longer just about territory; it became a test of wills that would eventually decide the future course of the war on the Eastern Front.

51. Street Fighting in Stalingrad

By late 1942, the battle for Stalingrad had turned into a brutal struggle fought at extremely close range. German and Soviet soldiers battled for control of factories, apartment blocks, and even individual rooms. The destruction was so extensive that rubble often became defensive positions, making it difficult for tanks and large units to maneuver. Fighting was constant, with snipers, machine guns, and grenades used in tight spaces. Soviet forces adopted a tactic of staying as close to German positions as possible, reducing the effectiveness of German artillery and air power. Civilians who remained in the city endured extreme conditions, sheltering in ruins while the fighting raged around them. The battle became a test of endurance, with both sides suffering heavy losses but neither willing to retreat.

52. Encirclement of the Sixth Army

In November 1942, Soviet forces launched a massive counteroffensive around Stalingrad, targeting the weaker Axis units guarding the flanks of the German army. These forces, which included Romanian and Hungarian troops, were less well equipped than the main German formations. The Soviet attack broke through their lines and advanced rapidly, linking up behind the city and surrounding the German Army. This maneuver, known as an encirclement, trapped more than 250,000 German and Allied soldiers inside Stalingrad. Cut off from supplies, they relied on limited air deliveries that proved insufficient to sustain them. As winter tightened its grip, the trapped forces faced severe shortages of food, fuel, and ammunition. What had begun as an offensive operation turned into a desperate struggle for survival.

53. Surrender in the Winter Cold

By early 1943, conditions inside the encircled German forces at Stalingrad had become unbearable. Starvation, freezing temperatures, and constant Soviet pressure weakened the trapped army. Attempts to break through the encirclement failed, and relief efforts from outside were unable to reach the city. Despite orders to hold their position, German resistance gradually collapsed. In February 1943, the remaining troops surrendered, marking one of the largest defeats in German military history. Hundreds of thousands had been killed, captured, or wounded. The loss of the Sixth Army was a major turning point on the Eastern Front, ending German advances into the Soviet Union and shifting momentum toward the Red Army, the official name for the Soviet Union's military forces.

54. The Desert Advance

By mid-1942, Axis forces under Erwin Rommel had pushed across North Africa from Libya into Egypt, bringing the war dangerously close to the Suez Canal. This canal was one of the most important routes in the world, linking the Mediterranean Sea to the Indian Ocean and allowing Britain to move troops and supplies quickly between Europe, Asia, and its overseas territories. If it fell, Allied communication lines would be severely disrupted. The advance finally stalled near El Alamein, a narrow stretch of desert between the Mediterranean coast and impassable terrain to the south. This geography meant that neither side could easily outflank the other, forcing a direct confrontation. Both armies dug in, building defensive lines and preparing for a decisive battle that would determine control of North Africa.

55. Breaking the Axis Line at El Alamein

In October 1942, British forces launched a carefully planned offensive at El Alamein, combining artillery barrages, infantry advances, and coordinated tank assaults to break through Axis defenses. The battle lasted nearly two weeks, with heavy fighting as minefields were cleared and fortified positions attacked. Gradually, Allied forces created gaps in the defensive lines, allowing armored units to push through. Once the line was broken, Axis forces were forced into a retreat westward across Libya, abandoning equipment as they withdrew. The victory marked the first major land defeat of German-led forces in the war and boosted Allied morale at a critical moment. It also secured Egypt and the Suez Canal, ensuring that this vital supply route remained open and allowing the Allies to begin pushing Axis forces out of North Africa entirely.

56. Landings in North Africa

In November 1942, Allied forces launched Operation Torch, a large amphibious invasion of North Africa: attacks launched from the sea onto defended coastlines. Troops from the United States and the United Kingdom landed along the coasts of Morocco and Algeria, territories controlled by the Vichy French government, which had been aligned with Germany. The goal was to open a second front in North Africa and trap Axis forces between advancing Allied armies from both east and west. After initial resistance and negotiation, many French forces ceased fighting and joined the Allies. The landings marked the first large-scale American ground operation in the European–African theater and signaled a growing Allied ability to coordinate complex operations across long distances.

57. Axis Forces in Tunisia

Following the landings of Operation Torch, Axis forces in North Africa found themselves caught between two advancing armies. From the east, British forces pushed westward after their victory at El Alamein, while American and British units moved east from newly secured positions in Algeria. The remaining Axis troops, including German and Italian units, retreated into Tunisia, where they attempted to hold defensive positions. Fighting in this region was intense, with both sides struggling over supply lines, mountainous terrain, and key ports. However, the Axis position became increasingly untenable as Allied forces tightened their grip, cutting off escape routes and reducing access to supplies. What had once been a campaign of movement across open desert turned into a confined struggle with limited options for retreat.

58. The Collapse of Axis North Africa

By May 1943, Axis resistance in North Africa had collapsed. Surrounded and cut off from reinforcement, more than 250,000 German and Italian troops surrendered in Tunisia. This marked the complete loss of Axis presence on the African continent and removed the threat to the Suez Canal. The victory gave the Allies control of the Mediterranean's southern shores and provided a launching point for further operations into southern Europe. It also demonstrated the growing strength of Allied cooperation, combining resources, troops, and planning across multiple nations. With

North Africa secured, attention shifted toward the next phase of the war: an invasion of Axis-controlled Europe.

59. Invasion of Sicily and the Opening of Italy

In July 1943, Allied forces launched Operation Husky, a massive invasion of the island of Sicily, located just off the "toe" of the Italian mainland. This was one of the largest amphibious operations of the war, involving a coordinated assault by land, sea, and air. British and American forces, led by Generals Bernard Montgomery and George S. Patton, landed on the island's southern and eastern shores to open a direct path into Southern Europe, often referred to by Winston Churchill as the "soft underbelly" of the Axis powers. Despite facing strong resistance from German and Italian divisions, the Allied forces used their superior air power and naval support to push the Axis troops across the rugged, mountainous terrain of the island. The fighting was intense, especially around the slopes of Mount Etna, but the momentum remained with the Allies. As the invasion progressed, it exposed deep-seated weaknesses within the Italian military and triggered political instability in Rome. The Italian people and many government officials were becoming weary of a war that had now reached their own soil. By August 1943, the Allies had successfully captured the island, giving them control of critical airfields and shipping routes that secured the central Mediterranean for their convoys. The capture of Sicily marked the end of the African and Mediterranean island campaigns and the beginning of the grueling struggle for the Italian mainland.

60. The Fall of Mussolini

In July 1943, the invasion of Sicily exposed deep weaknesses within Italy and shook confidence in its leadership. Benito Mussolini, who had ruled as a dictator since the 1920s, faced growing criticism from military leaders and government officials who believed the war was being lost. On July 25, 1943, he was removed from power by members of his own government and arrested on the orders of the king. A new Italian administration began secret negotiations with the Allies, seeking a way out of the conflict. Mussolini's fall marked a major political shift within the Axis alliance, showing that one of Germany's key partners was beginning to collapse under the pressure of military defeats.

61. Changing Sides in the War

In September 1943, the new Italian government signed an armistice with the Allies, effectively withdrawing from the war against them. However, the announcement created immediate confusion across the country, leaving Italian forces without clear orders as German troops moved quickly to take control. Instead of leaving Italy, Germany treated the armistice as a betrayal and launched operations to occupy the country. Italian soldiers were disarmed, captured, or forced to choose between joining German forces or resisting them. Some units fought alongside the Allies, while others were taken prisoner. The sudden shift turned Italy into a new battleground, where former allies were now fighting each other.

62. Germany's Occupation

After Italy's surrender, German forces rapidly moved to secure key cities, transportation routes, and defensive positions across the Italian peninsula. Key cities, railways, and communication routes were occupied, while Italian units were disarmed or captured. German commanders understood that Italy's geography, long, narrow, and dominated by mountains, could be used to slow any invasion. They began constructing defensive lines across the peninsula, positioning troops behind rivers, hills, and fortified positions. These defenses were designed not to win a quick victory but to delay Allied progress for as long as possible, turning Italy into a prolonged battleground that would absorb large numbers of troops and resources.

63. Mussolini Restored

At the same time, German forces carried out a dramatic rescue of Benito Mussolini, who had been imprisoned after his removal from power. In a carefully planned airborne and commando operation, he was freed and brought under German protection. Mussolini was then placed at the head of a new pro-German government in northern Italy, creating what was effectively a separate state aligned with Germany. This division split the country into two: the south, controlled by Allied forces and the new Italian government, and the north, under German occupation and Mussolini's authority. The situation led to internal conflict, as resistance groups formed to fight against German control and the new regime. Italy became not only a front line in the war but also a country divided by civil war, with fighting taking place between opposing Italian forces and foreign armies.

64. A Slow and Costly Advance

Allied forces began moving north through Italy, but the campaign proved far more difficult than expected. The terrain, mountains, rivers, and narrow valleys favored the defenders, allowing German forces to build fortified lines and delay progress. Battles were fought for control of key positions, including towns, roads, and bridges, often at high cost. Progress was slow, measured in miles rather than large advances, and each defensive line required intense fighting to break through. The campaign tied down large numbers of troops on both sides, turning Italy into a prolonged and difficult front. While it didn't bring a quick victory, it forced Germany to divert resources that might otherwise have been used elsewhere.

65. Fire from the Sky over Germany

By 1943, the Allies had begun a sustained strategic bombing campaign against Germany, aimed at weakening its capacity to wage war by targeting industry, transportation, and production centers. Strategic bombing focused on factories, railways, and fuel facilities rather than front-line troops. During the day, American bombers attempted more precise strikes, while at night, British aircraft carried out large-scale raids designed to overwhelm defenses. Cities such as Hamburg were hit with massive bombing campaigns, including incendiary bombs that started widespread fires. In some cases, these fires merged into firestorms, intense blazes that created powerful winds and consumed entire neighborhoods. The bombing caused heavy destruction and civilian casualties, but it also forced Germany to divert aircraft, anti-aircraft weapons, and manpower away from the front lines to defend its cities.

66. The Battle of Kursk Begins

In July 1943, German forces launched a major offensive against Soviet positions near Kursk (a city in western Russia), aiming to regain momentum after earlier defeats. The front line in this area formed a large bulge, making it a target for an encirclement attack from both north and south. However, Soviet commanders had anticipated the assault and built extensive defensive systems. These included multiple layers of trenches, barbed wire, anti-tank obstacles, and dense minefields designed to slow advancing units. When the German attack began, their tanks and infantry encountered fierce resistance and prepared defenses, reducing the effectiveness of their initial assault and turning what was meant to be a fast breakthrough into a prolonged battle.

67. The Largest Tank Battle

As the fighting around Kursk intensified, it developed into one of the largest armored battles ever fought. Thousands of tanks from both sides clashed across open fields and defensive positions, with close-range engagements and heavy losses. One of the most famous encounters took place near Prokhorovka on July 12, where hundreds of German and Soviet tanks collided in a chaotic, smoke-filled whirlwind of fire. The noise and dust were so thick that tank commanders often couldn't tell friend from foe until they were right on top of each other. Despite the massive scale of the attack and the introduction of powerful new German tanks, such as the *Panther* and *Tiger*, German forces failed to achieve a decisive breakthrough. The Soviet defenses, which were deeper and more sophisticated than anything the Germans had faced before, held firm. Reserves, extra troops, and equipment held back for emergencies were committed by Soviet commanders at key moments to plug gaps in the line. The failure of the Kursk offensive marked the final turning point on the Eastern Front.

68. The Red Army Pushing West

After halting the German advance at Kursk, Soviet forces launched a series of counteroffensives that pushed German troops westward. Large areas of previously occupied territory were recaptured, including important cities and industrial regions. The Red Army, strengthened by increasing production and experience, began to maintain the initiative. German forces, which had once advanced rapidly, were now forced into defensive positions, attempting to slow the Soviet advance. The scale of operations remained immense, with millions of soldiers involved and continuous fighting across a vast front. From this point onward, the momentum on the Eastern Front increasingly shifted toward the Soviet Union.

69. The Planning of D-Day

By early 1944, Allied leaders finalized plans for a massive invasion of German-occupied France, intended to open a western front against Germany and relieve pressure on the Soviet Union. The operation required unprecedented coordination between land, sea, and air forces. Thousands of ships, landing craft, and aircraft were assembled, while troops trained extensively for amphibious assaults. To increase the chances of success, the Allies also carried out an elaborate deception campaign, creating dummy armies, dummy equipment, and false radio signals to mislead German commanders into believing that the invasion would take place elsewhere, particularly near the Pas de Calais. The goal was to delay German reinforcements when the real landings began. After years of preparation, the Allies were ready to attempt one of the largest military operations in history.

70. The Landings in Normandy

On June 6, 1944, Allied forces launched the invasion of Normandy, commonly known as D-Day. Thousands of ships crossed the English Channel, carrying troops toward heavily defended beaches along the northern coast of France. The landings were divided across several sectors, each assigned to different Allied forces. Soldiers faced strong resistance as they approached the shore, with machine guns, artillery, and obstacles designed to destroy landing craft. Despite heavy casualties, especially on beaches such as Omaha, troops managed to establish footholds. Airborne units dropped behind enemy lines to disrupt defenses and secure key routes. By the end of the day, the Allies had successfully landed large numbers of troops and equipment, marking the beginning of a sustained campaign to push inland.

71. Breaking Out of Normandy

After securing the beaches in Normandy, Allied forces faced weeks of difficult fighting as they attempted to advance inland. The region's landscape, known as bocage, consisted of small fields separated by thick hedgerows, which limited visibility and favored defenders. German troops used these natural barriers to slow the advance, forcing Allied units to fight for each field and road. Progress was slow and costly, but continuous pressure, combined with air superiority and increasing reinforcements, gradually weakened German defenses. In late July 1944, Allied forces launched a breakout operation, using concentrated air bombardment to break through German lines. Once the defenses collapsed, armored units advanced rapidly, beginning the liberation of France.

72. The Liberation of Paris

As Allied forces advanced deeper into France, resistance movements in Paris began to intensify against the German occupation. In August 1944, fighting broke out in the city as resistance fighters took control of key buildings and streets. Allied troops advanced toward Paris, and German forces, facing pressure on multiple fronts, withdrew. On August 25, 1944, the city was liberated. Crowds filled the streets as Allied soldiers entered, marking a symbolic and strategic victory. The liberation of Paris not only restored a major European capital but also signaled that German control in Western Europe was beginning to collapse. The focus of the war in the west now shifted toward pushing into Germany itself.

73. A Risky Airborne Gamble

In September 1944, the Allies launched an ambitious operation called Operation Market Garden, aiming to end the war quickly by advancing into Germany through the Netherlands. The plan combined airborne troops, soldiers dropped by parachute, with ground forces moving north to link up with them. Airborne divisions were tasked with capturing a series of key bridges over rivers and canals, allowing armored units to cross quickly and bypass German defenses. If successful, the operation could have opened a direct route into Germany's industrial heartland. However, the plan depended on precise timing and underestimated German strength in the area. Some bridges were captured, but others proved heavily defended, and delays slowed the advance. The operation ultimately failed to achieve its objectives, showing that even bold strategies could falter when conditions on the ground didn't match expectations.

74. A Narrow Corridor Under Pressure

As part of Operation Market Garden, Allied ground forces advanced along a single narrow road through the Netherlands, attempting to reach airborne units holding bridges farther ahead. This route became highly vulnerable, as German forces attacked from both sides, cutting supply lines and isolating forward units. In places such as Arnhem, airborne troops held their positions for days despite being surrounded, but reinforcements failed to arrive in time. The difficulty of maintaining such a narrow corridor revealed the risks of prioritizing speed over security. When the operation ended, the Allies had gained some territory but failed to secure the final objectives, leaving the war in Western Europe far from over.

75. Germany's Last Major Offensive

In December 1944, Hitler launched a massive, surprise counteroffensive through the Ardennes Forest, the same rugged terrain he had used to invade France in 1940. His goal was to split the British and American armies, capture the vital Belgian port of Antwerp, and force the Western Allies to sign a separate peace treaty. This became known as the Battle of the Bulge because the German attack pushed a sixty-mile (or ninety-seven-kilometer) "bulge" into the Allied front lines. Taking advantage of poor weather that limited Allied air power, German troops broke through lightly defended lines and created a large bulge in the front. The sudden attack caught Allied commanders off guard, and intense fighting followed as both sides struggled for control. Towns and road junctions became key objectives, and supply shortages affected troops on both sides during the harsh winter conditions.

76. Holding the Line and Pushing Back

Despite early German success in the Battle of the Bulge, Allied forces regrouped and reinforced key positions. Small groups of American soldiers held critical crossroads, such as the town of Bastogne, where they were completely surrounded but famously refused to surrender. These pockets of resistance slowed the German advance, forcing their tanks to burn through limited fuel while waiting for roads to clear. As the weather finally cleared in late December, the Allied air forces returned to the skies with a vengeance. They targeted German supply lines, the convoys of trucks carrying the fuel and ammunition needed to keep the tanks moving. Without gasoline, many German *Tiger* and *Panther* tanks were simply abandoned in the snow. By January 1945, a massive Allied counterattack led by General Patton's Third Army pushed the front back to its original position. The failed offensive was a catastrophe for Germany; it exhausted its final reserves for the defense of the homeland. With the "bulge" flattened and the German army depleted, the path into the heart of Germany was now wide open, and the end of the war in Europe was finally in sight. As weather conditions improved, Allied air forces returned, targeting German supply lines and movements. Gradually, the German offensive lost momentum, and counterattacks pushed the front back to its previous positions by January 1945. The failed offensive exhausted Germany's remaining reserves of troops, fuel, and equipment. It was the last major attempt by Germany to regain the initiative in the west, and after its failure, the path into Germany itself became increasingly open to Allied forces.

77. The Soviet Advance

By early 1945, the Soviet Union had built up massive forces along the eastern front and launched a large-scale offensive into German-held territory. Beginning in January, Soviet armies pushed westward from Poland toward Germany, advancing rapidly across frozen ground that allowed tanks and vehicles to move more easily. German defenses, weakened by earlier losses, struggled to hold the line. Entire regions were overrun as Soviet troops captured cities, railways, and supply centers. The speed of the advance surprised many observers, as Soviet forces covered vast distances in a short time. Civilians fled westward ahead of the front, while German units attempted to regroup and delay the advance. The offensive brought Soviet forces to the borders of Germany itself, marking the beginning of the final assault on the country.

78. Crossing into Germany

At the same time, Allied forces in the west prepared to cross into Germany. One of the key obstacles was the Rhine River, a major natural barrier that German forces used as a defensive line. In March 1945, Allied troops managed to capture a bridge over the river intact, allowing them to move forces across more quickly than expected. Additional crossings followed, supported by large numbers of engineers building temporary bridges under difficult conditions. Once across the Rhine, Allied armies advanced deeper into Germany, capturing industrial regions and surrounding enemy forces. The coordinated pressure from both east and west placed Germany in an increasingly difficult position, as it faced advancing armies on multiple fronts with limited resources remaining.

79. The Encirclement of Berlin

By April 1945, the Red Army had positioned over 2.5 million troops and 6,000 tanks on the outskirts of the German capital. On April 16, they launched their final massive assault, beginning with a thunderous barrage from thousands of heavy artillery, large-caliber guns, and rocket launchers, such as the famous *Katyusha*, designed to destroy fortifications from a distance. Multiple Soviet armies, led by Marshals Zhukov and Konev, raced to be the first to reach the city center. By April 25, Berlin was completely surrounded, cutting off all escape. The defending German forces were a desperate mix of exhausted regular soldiers and the Volkssturm, a national militia consisting of "volunteers" as young as sixteen and as old as sixty, most of whom had little combat experience and were armed with basic anti-tank weapons like the *Panzerfaust*. Fighting took place street by street as Soviet forces pushed into the city. Artillery bombardments and air attacks caused widespread destruction, reducing large areas to rubble. The encirclement meant that German forces inside the city were isolated, with little chance of reinforcement or supply. The battle for Berlin became the final major confrontation in Europe, signaling that the war was nearing its end.

80. The Final Battle

By April 1945, Soviet forces had surrounded Berlin, launching a full-scale assault on the German capital. The climax of the battle took place at the Reichstag, the German parliament building, which became a symbol of the

Nazi regime. Soviet soldiers fought through the smoke-filled halls in a brutal struggle for every floor. Supply lines had collapsed, and communication between units became increasingly difficult. Civilians remained trapped in the city as the battle intensified, sheltering underground while bombardments continued. The fighting was among the most intense of the war, marking the final major confrontation in Europe.

81. Hitler's Death and the Collapse of Leadership

As Soviet troops closed in on Berlin, the leadership of Nazi Germany faced complete collapse. On April 30, 1945, as Soviet troops were just blocks away from his underground bunker, Adolf Hitler committed suicide. The government's command passed to the remaining officials, but the situation was beyond recovery. German forces in Berlin, cut off from reinforcements and supplies, could no longer sustain organized resistance. Within days, the city fell to Soviet troops, and the central government effectively ceased to function. With its capital captured and leadership gone, Germany's ability to continue the war was destroyed. The fall of Berlin made surrender inevitable, as Allied forces advanced across the remaining territory and German command structures disintegrated.

82. Germany's Unconditional Surrender

After the fall of Berlin and the collapse of central leadership, Germany's remaining officials sought to end the fighting. On May 7–8, 1945, representatives of the German military signed documents of unconditional surrender, agreeing to cease all hostilities. The surrender meant that German forces across Europe were ordered to lay down their arms. The date became known as Victory in Europe Day, or V-E Day, marking the end of the war on the European continent. However, the exact end of the conflict remained a subject of debate in some contexts, as formal arrangements and occupation agreements continued afterward. Despite these complexities, May 1945 is widely recognized as the moment when Nazi Germany was defeated, and the European war came to a close.

83. The Pacific War Continues

Although fighting had ended in Europe, the war in the Pacific continued. Japan still controlled territory across parts of Asia and the Pacific, and Allied forces prepared for a final push toward the Japanese home islands. The fighting in this region was intense, with battles taking place on islands where defenders often fought to the end rather than surrender. Allied strategy focused on capturing key islands that could serve as bases for air attacks and supply routes. At the same time, naval forces enforced blockades that limited Japan's access to resources. The conflict in the Pacific had already been long and costly, and planners expected that an invasion of Japan itself would result in even greater casualties on both sides.

84. Firebombing and the Destruction of Cities

By 1945, Allied forces intensified bombing campaigns against Japanese cities in an effort to weaken industrial production and reduce morale. Using large numbers of aircraft, they dropped incendiary bombs designed to start fires in densely built urban areas. One of the most devastating raids took place in Tokyo in March 1945, where fires spread rapidly through wooden buildings, destroying large sections of the city. These attacks caused massive destruction and high civilian casualties. At the same time, Japan's ability to respond was weakened by fuel shortages and the loss of experienced pilots. The bombing campaigns demonstrated the increasing scale of destruction in modern warfare, where entire cities could be targeted as part of military strategy.

85. The Bombing of Hiroshima

On August 6, 1945, the United States dropped an atomic bomb on the Japanese city of Hiroshima. The weapon released energy from a nuclear reaction, producing an explosion far more powerful than conventional bombs. A blinding flash was followed by an intense blast wave and extreme heat that destroyed buildings across a wide area. Many people were killed instantly, while others suffered severe burns and injuries. The explosion also released radiation, energy that can damage human tissue, which caused long-term illness and death among survivors. It is estimated that approximately 70,000–80,000 people were killed immediately, with the total death toll rising to around 140,000 by the end of 1945 due to injuries and radiation exposure. Because Hiroshima was a military and industrial center, it had been selected as a target, but the scale of destruction shocked observers. The bombing demonstrated a new level of destructive capability, where a single weapon could devastate an entire city in moments.

86. Nagasaki and the Impact of Nuclear Warfare

Three days later, on August 9, 1945, a second atomic bomb was dropped on the city of Nagasaki. Although the terrain of the city limited some of the blast's spread, the explosion still caused widespread destruction and heavy casualties. It is estimated that approximately 40,000 people were killed instantly, with the total number of deaths rising to around 70,000 by the end of 1945 as a result of injuries and radiation exposure. The use of two atomic bombs within days highlighted the destructive potential of nuclear weapons and signaled that further attacks could follow. At the same time, the Soviet Union declared war on Japan and launched a large-scale invasion of Japanese-held territory in Manchuria, adding additional pressure. Faced with the combined impact of atomic bombings and military advances, Japanese leaders began to consider surrender. The events marked the beginning of a new era in warfare, where the threat of nuclear weapons would shape global politics for decades to come.

87. The Decision to Surrender

After the atomic bombings of Hiroshima and Nagasaki and the entry of the Soviet Union into the war against Japan in August 1945, Japanese leaders faced a situation with few remaining options. Continued resistance risked further destruction, while surrender raised concerns about political and national consequences. Within the Japanese government, intense debate took place over whether to accept Allied terms. Ultimately, Emperor Hirohito intervened, supporting the decision to surrender in order to prevent further loss of life. This moment was unusual, as the emperor rarely took direct part in political decisions. The decision marked a turning point, as it set in motion the formal end of World War II, though the process would unfold over several days.

88. The Emperor's Broadcast

On August 15, 1945, Emperor Hirohito addressed the Japanese people in a radio broadcast, announcing the decision to accept Allied terms. This was the first time many citizens had ever heard the emperor's voice. The speech used formal and indirect language, referring to the need to "endure the unendurable" to achieve peace. For many listeners, the meaning wasn't immediately clear, but it soon became understood that Japan had agreed to surrender. The date became known as Victory over Japan Day, or V-J Day, and is often considered the practical end of the war, as fighting largely ceased following the announcement. However, the formal conclusion of the conflict had not yet taken place.

89. The Formal Surrender Ceremony

Although Japan announced its surrender in August, the official signing took place on September 2, 1945, aboard the American battleship USS *Missouri* in Tokyo Bay. Representatives of Japan signed documents accepting unconditional surrender in the presence of Allied officials. This ceremony formally ended the war in Asia and is often considered the definitive end of World War II. However, the exact end date of the conflict is sometimes debated, as different events marked different stages of its conclusion. While August 15 marked the announcement of surrender, September 2 marked its formal completion.

90. When Did World War II Really End?

Although World War II is commonly said to have ended in 1945, historians sometimes cite different dates depending on the context. The armistice on August 15, 1945, marked the end of active fighting, while the formal surrender on September 2 finalized the conflict. A peace treaty between Japan and the Allies was signed in 1951, officially restoring diplomatic relations. In Europe, Germany's defeat in May 1945 ended fighting there, but formal arrangements and political changes continued for years afterward. Some scholars even note that no formal peace treaty was ever signed between Japan and the Soviet Union, with relations normalized later through agreements rather than a full treaty. These variations show that the "end" of the war wasn't a single moment but a process that unfolded over time.

SIXTEEN

Dictators, Democracies, and Decisions

World War II was not only a clash of armies but also a struggle shaped by political systems, leadership, and critical decisions made under pressure. The rise of authoritarian regimes in Germany, Italy, and Japan challenged the existing international order, while democratic nations were forced to respond to growing aggression and instability. Choices made by leaders, whether to resist, negotiate, or expand, played a decisive role in determining the course of the war. This chapter examines the political forces behind the conflict, including the ambitions of dictators, the responses of democratic governments, and the key decisions that escalated tensions into full-scale war. It looks at how ideology, diplomacy, and miscalculation combined to shape events, often with far-reaching consequences.

91. A Fragile Peace and Unstable Democracies

After World War I ended in 1918, many hoped that the world had entered a more peaceful era. Instead, the postwar settlement created new tensions that weakened many governments. The Treaty of Versailles imposed heavy penalties on Germany, including financial reparations, territorial losses, and military restrictions. While intended to prevent future conflict, these measures instead fueled resentment and economic instability. At the same time, new nations emerged in Eastern Europe, but many were politically fragile and divided along ethnic lines. Democratic governments struggled to maintain authority in this environment. Many countries faced high inflation, unemployment, and political violence. In Germany, for example, the Weimar Republic, a democratic government, was attacked by both communist and nationalist groups. Communism is a political and economic system in which the government or community owns all property and resources, aiming to create a society without social classes. Across Europe, faith in democracy began to weaken as people lost trust in leaders who seemed unable to solve economic crises. This instability created conditions in which more extreme political movements could gain support by promising order, strength, and national revival.

92. Lenin's New Economic Policy and Strategic Retreat

In the early 1920s, the newly formed Soviet Union faced serious economic and social problems after years of revolution and civil war. Agricultural production had collapsed, cities were struggling with food shortages, and widespread unrest threatened the survival of the Bolshevik government. In response, Vladimir Lenin introduced the New Economic Policy (NEP) in 1921, a temporary shift away from strict communist control. The NEP allowed limited private business activity, especially in agriculture and small industries, while the state retained control over major sectors, such as heavy industry and banking. This mixed system helped stabilize the economy, increase food production, and reduce public unrest. However, it also showed that even revolutionary leaders sometimes had to compromise their ideological goals to maintain power. The policy strengthened the Soviet state in the short term, but it also raised questions about the future direction of the country, setting the stage for later struggles over how the Soviet Union should develop under new leadership.

93. The March on Rome and the Seizure of Power

In October 1922, Italy became one of the first countries in Europe to turn toward authoritarian rule when Benito Mussolini and his fascist movement took control. Italy had emerged from World War I on the winning side, but many citizens felt "cheated" by the peace settlement, believing their country had not gained enough territory or respect. Economic problems, high unemployment, and political unrest created an atmosphere of instability. During this time, Italy was a battleground between two opposing ideologies: socialism, a theory arguing that the community should own or control the means of production to ensure that wealth is distributed equally, and fascism, a far-right system that places the nation above the individual and uses a dictator to suppress opposition through force. Mussolini, a former socialist who had turned into a radical nationalist, organized his supporters into paramilitary groups known as the "Blackshirts." These groups used violence and intimidation against political opponents, especially socialists and trade unions, which are organized groups of workers formed to protect their rights and interests. In October 1922, thousands of fascist supporters began the March on Rome. While the march was largely a show of force rather than a military invasion, it created so much pressure that King Victor Emmanuel III feared a civil war. Instead of using the army to stop them, he invited Mussolini to form a government. This decision marked the beginning of a fascist dictatorship that would last for more than two decades, providing a blueprint for other future dictators, including Adolf Hitler.

94. Fascism as a Model of Authoritarian Rule

After gaining power, Mussolini gradually transformed Italy from a constitutional monarchy into a one-party dictatorship. Elections were manipulated, opposition parties were banned, and the press was placed under strict control. The state promoted a powerful nationalist message, emphasizing unity, strength, and loyalty to the leader, who was known as *Il Duce*. Political dissent was suppressed through secret police and imprisonment, creating an atmosphere of fear that limited resistance. Fascism presented itself as an alternative to both liberal democracy and communism. It rejected the idea of individual political freedoms in favor of a strong, centralized state that would guide the nation toward greatness. Mussolini's regime also promoted militarism and expansion, arguing that Italy needed to become a major power. His success in consolidating control attracted attention in other countries, particularly in Germany, where similar ideas were gaining support. Fascist Italy became an early example of how democratic systems could collapse under pressure, providing a model that would influence other authoritarian movements in the years leading up to World War II.

95. The Beer Hall Putsch and a Failed Coup

In November 1923, Adolf Hitler attempted to seize power in Germany through a coup known as the Beer Hall Putsch. At the time, Germany was facing a severe economic crisis, including hyperinflation that made money nearly worthless and widespread political instability. Hitler, who led the National Socialist German Workers' Party (Nazi Party), believed the government was weak and could be overthrown by force. On November 8, Hitler and around 2,000 supporters stormed a large political meeting in Munich, hoping to gain support from local leaders and then march on

Berlin to take control of the country. The following day, the group marched through the streets, but they were met by police forces. A brief exchange of gunfire ended the attempted coup, leaving several people dead, and the march quickly collapsed. Hitler was arrested soon afterward and charged with treason. Although the putsch failed, it revealed Hitler's ambitions and brought him national attention. Instead of ending his political career, the event would ultimately help transform him into a prominent figure in German politics.

96. Prison, Propaganda, and Political Strategy

After the failed coup, Adolf Hitler was put on trial in early 1924. Rather than weakening him, the trial became a platform for his ideas. He used the courtroom to criticize the German government and promote his nationalist and anti-Semitic beliefs (the prejudice, discrimination, or hatred directed specifically toward Jewish people), gaining sympathy from some sections of the public who saw him as a patriot rather than a criminal. He was found guilty of treason but received a relatively lenient sentence of five years in prison, of which he served only about nine months. During his imprisonment, Hitler wrote *Mein Kampf* ("My Struggle"), a book outlining his ideology and long-term goals. It included his belief in racial hierarchy, his desire to expand German territory in Eastern Europe, and his deep hostility toward Jews and communism. Importantly, the failure of the Beer Hall Putsch led him to change tactics. Instead of trying to seize power by force, he decided that the Nazi Party would pursue control through legal political means, using elections, propaganda, and influence within existing institutions. This strategic shift would later prove far more effective.

97. Stalin's Reign

In Russia, when Vladimir Lenin suffered a series of strokes beginning in 1922 and died in January 1924, a fierce power struggle began among the leading Bolsheviks: the radical wing of the Russian Social Democratic Labor Party that had successfully seized power during the 1917 Russian Revolution. These "Bolsheviks" (meaning "those of the majority") were committed to establishing a communist state and overthrowing the old imperial system of the Tsars. Joseph Stalin, who held the seemingly administrative position of General Secretary of the Communist Party, used his control over party appointments to build a massive network of loyal supporters. While other leaders focused on public speeches and theory, Stalin focused on the "paperwork" of the party, placing his allies in key positions across the vast country and gradually removing rivals such as

Leon Trotsky, the brilliant but less politically maneuverable commander of the Red Army. By the late 1920s, Stalin had effectively secured control over the Soviet government. He turned what had originally been a collective leadership of top Bolshevik officials into a centralized system centered entirely around his own absolute authority. This shift marked the beginning of a period of total state control over every aspect of Soviet life, from the economy to personal expression, as Stalin prepared to modernize the Soviet Union at any cost.

98. The Five-Year Plans and Forced Industrialization

In 1928, Joseph Stalin launched the first of several Five-Year Plans, aiming to rapidly transform the Soviet Union from a largely agricultural society into an industrial power. The plans focused on heavy industry, including the production of steel, coal, and machinery, as the government believed that industrial strength was essential to both economic independence and military security. Massive factories were built, and millions of people moved from rural areas into cities to work in new industries. At the same time, agriculture was reorganized through a process called collectivization, in which small farms were merged into large, state-controlled units. Many peasants resisted the loss of their land and livestock, resulting in widespread repression. The state responded with force, seizing grain and punishing those who opposed the system. This contributed to severe food shortages and famines, particularly in the early 1930s. While industrial output increased significantly, the human cost was immense, and the policies strengthened the government's control over both the economy and the population.

99. Purges, Fear, and Absolute Control

By the mid-1930s, Joseph Stalin had consolidated power in the Soviet Union to such an extent that he began eliminating real and perceived rivals in a series of campaigns known as the Great Purges. Between 1936 and 1938, party officials, military leaders, intellectuals, and ordinary citizens were arrested, imprisoned, or executed. Many were accused of vague crimes such as "counter-revolutionary activity" or disloyalty to the state, often based on forced confessions obtained under torture. Public trials were staged to demonstrate the consequences of opposing the regime, while the secret police, known as the NKVD, carried out mass arrests across the country. Millions of people were sent to labor camps, where harsh conditions led to high mortality rates. Even senior officers in the Red Army were removed, weakening the military's leadership on the eve of war. The purges created a climate of fear in which few dared to speak openly, allowing Stalin to maintain near-total control over the Soviet state while ensuring that any opposition was quickly and decisively crushed.

100. Political Violence and Militarism in Japan

During the early 1930s, Japan experienced growing political instability as military leaders gained increasing influence over the government. Many officers believed that Japan needed to expand its territory to secure natural resources and protect itself from foreign powers. Civilian politicians who supported diplomacy and international agreements were often seen as weak, and some became targets of violent opposition. In May 1932, a group of naval officers assassinated Prime Minister Inukai Tsuyoshi, an event known as the May 15 Incident. The attackers hoped to replace civilian leadership with a more aggressive, nationalist government. Although the coup itself didn't fully succeed, the response was relatively lenient, and public sympathy for the perpetrators weakened respect for democratic institutions. Over time, the military gained greater control over national policy, shaping decisions on foreign expansion and war. By the mid-1930s, Japan was increasingly governed by leaders who favored military solutions, setting the stage for further conflict in Asia and the Pacific.

101. Economic Crisis and the Collapse of Democracy

The global economic crisis that began in 1929, known as the Great Depression, had a devastating impact on many countries, but it was especially severe in Germany. The economy depended heavily on foreign loans, particularly from the United States, and when those loans were withdrawn, businesses collapsed, banks failed, and unemployment rose dramatically. By the early 1930s, millions of Germans were unemployed, and many families struggled to afford basic necessities. This economic hardship weakened faith in democratic government. The Weimar Republic, Germany's post–World War I government, appeared unable to solve the crisis, and political parties became increasingly divided. Extremist movements on both the left and right gained support by promising strong leadership and quick solutions. Street violence between rival groups became common, and elections produced unstable coalitions that couldn't govern effectively. As confidence in democratic institutions declined, more people began to support parties that offered radical change, creating the conditions that allowed authoritarian leaders to rise to power through legal means.

102. Hitler's Legal Path to Dictatorship

In January 1933, Adolf Hitler was appointed Chancellor of Germany after his Nazi Party became the largest political force in the country. Although he had not won an outright majority, conservative leaders believed they could control him and use his popularity to stabilize the government. This decision would prove to be a critical miscalculation. Soon after taking office, Hitler moved quickly to expand his power. In February 1933, the Reichstag building, home of the German parliament, was set on fire. The government blamed communist groups and used the crisis to suspend civil liberties, allowing the arrest of political opponents. In March, the Enabling Act was passed, giving Hitler the authority to make laws without parliamentary approval. This effectively ended democratic rule in Germany. Political parties were banned, trade unions were dissolved, and opposition leaders were imprisoned. Within months, Germany had been transformed from a democracy into a one-party dictatorship, with power concentrated entirely in Hitler's hands.

103. Rearmament and the Breaking of Versailles

After consolidating power, Adolf Hitler began to openly challenge the Treaty of Versailles, the agreement that had ended World War I and imposed strict limits on Germany's military. The treaty restricted the size of the German army, banned tanks and aircraft, and prohibited the remilitarization of certain regions. Hitler rejected these restrictions, arguing that Germany needed to restore its strength and dignity. In 1935, Germany reintroduced conscription, requiring men to serve in the military, and began expanding its armed forces far beyond the treaty's limits. The government also invested heavily in new weapons, including modern aircraft and armored vehicles.

104. Propaganda, Control, and the Nazi State

At the same time as Germany was rearming, the Nazi regime worked to control public opinion and shape society. Propaganda played a central role in maintaining support for the government. Under the direction of Joseph Goebbels, the Ministry of Propaganda controlled newspapers, radio broadcasts, films, and cultural events. Messages were carefully designed to promote loyalty to the state, glorify Hitler as a strong leader, and present Germany as a nation rising from humiliation to power. The regime also targeted groups it considered enemies, especially Jewish people, who were blamed for Germany's problems. Laws passed in the mid-1930s, such as the

Nuremberg Laws, stripped Jewish citizens of their rights and excluded them from many areas of public life. Education, youth organizations, and public ceremonies were used to spread Nazi ideology, particularly among younger generations. By controlling both information and daily life, the government created an environment in which dissent was dangerous, and conformity was encouraged, strengthening its hold over the population as it prepared for expansion.

105. Appeasement and the Rhineland Gamble

In March 1936, Adolf Hitler took a major risk by sending German troops into the Rhineland, a region along Germany's western border that had been designated as a demilitarized zone under the Treaty of Versailles. This area was intended to serve as a buffer between Germany and France, reducing the chances of another conflict. The German military at the time was still relatively weak, and many officers were concerned that France might respond with force. However, no military action was taken. France, facing political uncertainty at home, hesitated to act without British support, and the British government viewed Germany's move as taking place within its own territory. This response reflected a broader policy known as appeasement, in which leaders hoped that allowing limited demands might prevent a larger war. The success of this gamble strengthened Hitler's position at home and convinced him that his opponents were unlikely to intervene, encouraging more aggressive actions in the years that followed.

106. The Anschluss and Expansion Without War

In March 1938, Germany annexed Austria in an event known as the Anschluss, meaning "union." Many Austrians supported unification with Germany, but the move also involved significant pressure and the threat of military force. German troops entered Austria without resistance, and a controlled referendum was later held to legitimize the annexation, producing an overwhelming but heavily influenced result in favor of joining Germany. The annexation was another clear violation of international agreements, yet once again, there was no military response from Britain or France. The incorporation of Austria increased Germany's population, territory, and access to resources, strengthening its position in Central Europe. It also placed Germany in a stronger strategic position, surrounding Czechoslovakia and opening the way for further expansion. Like the remilitarization of the Rhineland, the Anschluss demonstrated that Germany could alter the map of Europe without facing immediate consequences, further emboldening its leadership.

107. The Munich Agreement and the Sudetenland

In 1938, Adolf Hitler turned his attention to Czechoslovakia, specifically the Sudetenland, a border region with a large ethnic German population. He claimed that these communities were being mistreated and demanded that the territory be handed over to Germany. Czechoslovakia had a strong army and defensive fortifications, but it was diplomatically isolated and depended on support from Britain and France. In September 1938, leaders from Britain, France, Germany, and Italy met in Munich to resolve the crisis. Czechoslovakia itself wasn't invited to the negotiations. The resulting agreement allowed Germany to annex the Sudetenland in exchange for Hitler's promise that he would make no further territorial demands. British Prime Minister Neville Chamberlain returned home, declaring that the agreement had secured "peace for our time." However, the decision weakened Czechoslovakia by stripping away its defenses and industrial regions, while convincing Hitler that the Western powers would continue to avoid confrontation.

108. The End of Appeasement and the Road to War

The Munich Agreement didn't bring lasting peace. In March 1939, Germany violated its promises by occupying the rest of Czechoslovakia, demonstrating that Hitler's ambitions extended far beyond uniting German-speaking populations. This action shocked many in Britain and France, as it made clear that appeasement had failed to prevent further aggression. In response, both countries began to change their policies. They guaranteed the independence of Poland, warning that any attack on the country would lead to war. At the same time, Germany increased its military preparations and began making demands regarding the Polish city of Danzig and the surrounding territory. Diplomatic tensions rose rapidly across Europe as alliances hardened and negotiations broke down. By mid-1939, the situation had become increasingly unstable, with many leaders recognizing that another major conflict was becoming unavoidable. The system that had seemed fragile for years was now close to collapse.

109. Hitler's Pact with the Soviet Union

Adolf Hitler's decision to sign an agreement with the Soviet Union in August 1939 wasn't based on trust, but on strategy. Germany's leaders remembered the outcome of World War 1, when fighting on two fronts, against France and Britain in the west and Russia in the east, had stretched resources and contributed to defeat. Hitler was determined to avoid repeating that mistake. At the same time, negotiations between the Soviet Union, Britain, and France had stalled. Joseph Stalin was concerned that the Western powers might be trying to push Germany and the Soviet Union into conflict while staying out of the fighting themselves. By reaching an agreement with Germany instead, Stalin gained time to rebuild his military after the purges of the late 1930s, which had removed many experienced officers. For Hitler, the pact ensured that when Germany invaded Poland, it would not immediately face Soviet resistance. For Stalin, it created a buffer zone between the Soviet Union and Germany. Both leaders viewed the agreement as temporary, expecting that conflict between them would eventually arise.

110. Calculations, Misjudgments, and the Road to War

The final days before the invasion of Poland were shaped by a series of calculated decisions and dangerous assumptions. Hitler believed that Britain and France, despite their warnings, would avoid another large-scale war, as they had done during earlier crises such as the Rhineland and Czechoslovakia. Previous success without consequences had reinforced his confidence that opponents would continue to back down. At the same time, British and French leaders believed that firm guarantees to Poland might deter Germany, or at least limit the scale of conflict. However, they lacked the immediate capacity to provide direct military support to Poland if war broke out. This created a situation in which commitments were made, but practical responses were uncertain. When Germany invaded Poland on September 1, 1939, these miscalculations became clear. Britain and France declared war two days later, but Poland faced the initial assault largely alone. What followed wasn't the limited conflict some leaders had hoped for, but the beginning of a global war shaped by earlier decisions, hesitations, and misunderstandings.

111. Different Leadership Styles

When the war began in 1939, the major powers were led by figures with very different styles of leadership, which shaped how each country fought. In Germany, Adolf Hitler increasingly took direct control of military decisions, often relying on his own judgment rather than professional advice. His leadership was centralized, personal, and driven by ideology, with little tolerance for disagreement. In contrast, Britain and France were led by civilian governments that had to balance military needs with political opinion. Decisions were slower and often cautious, especially in the early stages of the war. In the Soviet Union, Joseph Stalin ruled through a highly centralized system, but his earlier purges had removed many experienced military officers, weakening the Red Army's leadership. In Japan, decision-making was divided between civilian leaders and powerful military factions, often leading to competing strategies. These differences meant that the war wasn't only a clash of armies but also a clash of leadership styles, each with its own strengths and weaknesses.

112. The "Phoney War" and Strategic Hesitation

After Britain and France declared war on Germany in September 1939, many expected immediate large-scale fighting in Western Europe. Instead, a period of relative quiet followed, often called the "Phoney War." For several months, there was little direct combat between German forces and the Western Allies along the French-German border. French strategy relied heavily on defense, particularly the Maginot Line, a system of fortifications designed to prevent a German invasion. Military planners believed that a strong defensive position would wear down any attack. At the same time, British forces were still mobilizing and building up strength. Leaders in both countries hoped that economic pressure, such as a naval blockade, might weaken Germany over time without the need for immediate large-scale offensives. This hesitation allowed Germany to consolidate its gains in Poland and prepare for future campaigns. The lack of early action also revealed a gap between expectations and reality, as leaders struggled to adapt to a new, fast-moving, industrialized form of warfare.

113. Hitler's Risky Strategy in the West

After the defeat of Poland in 1939, German leadership turned its attention to Western Europe, where France and Britain remained at war with Germany. Many military planners initially expected a repeat of World War I, with a major attack through Belgium followed by slow, grinding battles along fortified lines. Early German plans reflected this idea, proposing a direct advance that could have led to another stalemate. However, a different approach began to take shape. German General Erich von Manstein proposed a bold alternative: instead of attacking where the Allies expected, German forces would move through the Ardennes, a heavily forested region between Belgium and France. This area was considered difficult terrain for tanks and large armies and, therefore, lightly defended. Hitler approved the plan, despite its risks, because it offered the possibility of a rapid and decisive victory. The strategy depended on speed, coordination, and surprise. If it failed, German forces could become trapped. But if it succeeded, it could break through Allied defenses and avoid the kind of prolonged war that Germany wanted to prevent.

114. The Ardennes Gamble and Allied Misjudgment

When Germany launched its offensive in May 1940, Allied leaders believed the main attack would come through northern Belgium, as it had in World War I. As a result, British and French forces moved north to meet the expected advance, leaving the Ardennes region relatively weakly defended. Many commanders considered the area unsuitable for large-scale armored movement, assuming that dense forests and narrow roads would slow any attack. This assumption proved to be a critical mistake. German armored divisions moved quickly through the Ardennes, crossing difficult terrain faster than expected and concentrating their forces at key points. Once they reached the Meuse River, German units broke through French defenses and advanced rapidly toward the English Channel. This maneuver split the Allied forces, trapping large numbers of British and French troops in northern France and Belgium. The speed of the advance shocked Allied commanders, who struggled to respond to a form of warfare that emphasized mobility and coordination rather than static defense. The success of the Ardennes plan demonstrated how assumptions based on past wars could lead to dangerous miscalculations in a new kind of conflict.

115. Command Breakdown and the Collapse of France

As German forces broke through the Ardennes in May 1940 and advanced rapidly toward the English Channel, Allied command structures struggled to respond. French and British leaders had expected a slower, more predictable campaign, and their communication systems weren't prepared for the speed of German advances. Orders were often delayed, misunderstood, or based on outdated information, making it difficult to coordinate an effective defense. French command relied on centralized decision-making, meaning that field commanders often had to wait for instructions rather than act independently. This slowed reactions at critical moments. Meanwhile, German forces operated with more flexible command structures, allowing local commanders to exploit opportunities quickly. The rapid advance cut off Allied armies in the north, while German units continued pushing deeper into France. The collapse wasn't only military but also organizational, as confusion and a lack of coordination made it increasingly difficult to mount a unified response against a fast-moving, adaptive opponent.

116. Leadership Decisions and the Fall of France

As the situation worsened, French political leaders faced a difficult choice: continue fighting or seek an armistice. By June 1940, German forces had captured Paris, and much of northern France was under occupation. The government was divided. Some leaders, including Prime Minister Paul Reynaud, wanted to continue the fight from overseas colonies, while others believed further resistance would only lead to greater destruction. Reynaud eventually resigned, and Marshal Philippe Pétain, a respected World War I general, took power. Pétain argued that continuing the war would cause unnecessary suffering and chose to request an armistice with Germany. The agreement, signed in June 1940, divided France into occupied and unoccupied zones, with a new government established in the town of Vichy. While officially neutral, this regime cooperated with Germany in many areas. The decision to surrender reshaped the balance of the war. Britain was left to face Germany largely alone in Western Europe, while France's defeat gave Germany control over significant resources and strategic positions.

117. Churchill's Leadership and the Decision to Resist

In May 1940, as German forces advanced rapidly through Western Europe, Britain faced the possibility of defeat. Neville Chamberlain resigned as prime minister, and Winston Churchill took his place at a moment of crisis. Unlike some members of the British government who considered negotiating with Germany, Churchill was determined to continue the fight, even if Britain stood alone. Churchill believed that any agreement with Hitler would only delay further conflict and weaken Britain's position. In a series of speeches, he made it clear that the country would resist invasion and continue the war regardless of the cost. His message wasn't one of easy victory but of endurance, emphasizing that survival itself was the goal. At the same time, the government began preparing for a possible invasion, strengthening defenses and organizing resources for a prolonged conflict. This decision to resist shaped the course of the war. By refusing to negotiate, Britain remained in the fight and continued to serve as a base for future Allied operations, ensuring that Germany would not achieve complete dominance in Western Europe.

118. Hitler's Strategic Choice and the Limits of Power

After the fall of France in June 1940, Adolf Hitler faced a major strategic decision. With much of Western Europe under German control, he could attempt to force Britain out of the war or turn his attention elsewhere. A full invasion of Britain, known as Operation Sea Lion, was considered, but it required control of the air and sea, which Germany didn't yet have. Instead, Germany began an air campaign aimed at weakening Britain's defenses and forcing a political settlement. Hitler still believed that Britain might eventually agree to negotiate, especially if it faced continued pressure. This assumption influenced his decision not to commit immediately to a risky cross-channel invasion. The delay allowed Britain time to strengthen its defenses and adapt to the new phase of the war. It also revealed a limitation in German strategy: success on land didn't automatically translate into control over air and sea power. Hitler's choice to postpone the invasion and rely on pressure rather than decisive action would have long-term consequences, as Britain remained in the war and continued to resist German expansion.

119. Decision-Making in the Battle of Britain

During the summer of 1940, German leadership aimed to defeat Britain by destroying its air defenses. The Luftwaffe (German air force) began a sustained campaign targeting radar stations, airfields, and aircraft production facilities in southern England. These attacks were designed to weaken the Royal Air Force (RAF) and clear the way for a possible invasion. German commanders believed that sustained pressure would eventually overwhelm British defenses. British leadership, however, relied on a coordinated system that allowed them to respond efficiently. Radar stations detected incoming aircraft, while central command centers directed fighter squadrons to intercept them at the right moment. This system helped conserve resources and avoid unnecessary losses. Fighter Command, led by Air Chief Marshal Hugh Dowding, carefully managed limited aircraft and pilots, prioritizing defense over risky offensives. The outcome of the battle depended not only on equipment but also on decision-making. British leaders focused on maintaining their defensive network, while German strategy depended on breaking it quickly. As the campaign continued, it became clear that control of the air would not be easy to achieve.

120. Strategic Shifts and the Blitz

In September 1940, German strategy changed. Instead of continuing to focus primarily on airfields and radar installations, the Luftwaffe shifted to bombing major cities, especially London. This campaign, known as the Blitz, aimed to damage infrastructure and reduce civilian morale, with the expectation that sustained bombing would pressure Britain into seeking peace. The shift, however, had unintended consequences. By reducing attacks on airfields and radar stations, German forces allowed the RAF time to recover and rebuild. British defenses remained operational, and aircraft production continued despite the damage caused by bombing. Civilians adapted by using shelters, underground stations, and emergency services to cope with the attacks. The bombing caused widespread destruction and loss of life, but it didn't achieve its primary goal of forcing Britain out of the war. By October 1940, plans for a German invasion were postponed indefinitely. The decision to change targets marked a turning point, as it reduced pressure on British air defenses and allowed them to remain a significant obstacle to German expansion.

121. Mussolini's Independent War and Strategic Overreach

After Germany's rapid victories in 1939–1940, Benito Mussolini feared that Italy might be left out of the rewards of war. Although Italy had not been fully prepared for a large-scale conflict, Mussolini decided to enter the war in June 1940, believing that Germany's success would lead to a quick victory. His decision was driven more by ambition and prestige than by military readiness. Soon after, Mussolini launched a series of independent campaigns without fully coordinating with German leadership. In October 1940, Italian forces invaded Greece from Albania, expecting an easy victory. Instead, Greek forces resisted strongly and pushed the Italians back into Albanian territory. At the same time, Italian forces in North Africa advanced into Egypt but soon faced strong British counterattacks. These campaigns revealed weaknesses in planning, logistics, and equipment. Italian forces often lacked sufficient supplies and coordination, while their opponents adapted quickly. Mussolini's decision to act independently expanded the war into new regions, but it also exposed the limits of Italy's military strength and created problems that Germany would soon have to address.

122. German Intervention and the Cost of Alliance

Italy's setbacks forced Adolf Hitler to intervene in regions he had not originally planned to prioritize. In early 1941, German forces were sent to North Africa to support Italian troops, forming the Afrika Korps under General Erwin Rommel. These forces helped stabilize the situation and pushed British units back across the desert, temporarily restoring Axis momentum in the region. At the same time, Germany prepared to intervene in the Balkans after Italy's failed invasion of Greece. German leaders were concerned that instability in southeastern Europe could threaten vital supply routes, particularly access to oil from Romania. In April 1941, German forces invaded both Yugoslavia and Greece, quickly defeating resistance and securing the region. While these interventions were successful in the short term, they came at a strategic cost. Resources and attention were diverted away from other plans, including preparations for the invasion of the Soviet Union. The need to support weaker allies showed that alliances could create new obligations, forcing leaders to adjust their strategies in ways that complicated their overall war plans.

123. Hitler's Decision to Invade the Soviet Union

In June 1941, Adolf Hitler made the decision to invade the Soviet Union, opening what would become the largest front of the war. The operation, known as Operation Barbarossa, involved millions of soldiers advancing across a vast frontier. The decision wasn't only strategic but also ideological. Hitler viewed the Soviet Union as both a political enemy and a source of land and resources that Germany needed to secure its future. German planning focused on a rapid campaign. Leaders believed that Soviet forces would collapse within a few months, allowing Germany to achieve victory before winter. The strategy relied on speed, coordination, and large-scale encirclements to destroy Soviet armies quickly. Early successes appeared to confirm these expectations, as German forces advanced deep into Soviet territory during the summer of 1941. However, the decision to launch such a massive invasion also meant committing resources to a long and uncertain campaign. By opening an eastern front while still at war with Britain, Germany entered a conflict that would strain its military and economic capacity far beyond those of earlier campaigns.

124. Underestimation and Strategic Miscalculation

German leadership underestimated both the size and resilience of the Soviet Union. Intelligence reports had suggested that the Red Army had been weakened by internal purges, and early victories reinforced the belief that resistance would collapse quickly. However, the scale of the Soviet Union's resources, territory, and population made it far more difficult to defeat than expected. As German forces advanced, supply lines became longer and more difficult to maintain. Roads were poor, distances were vast, and the infrastructure needed to support a fast-moving army was limited. At the same time, Soviet forces continued to mobilize new units, replacing losses and preparing for counterattacks. The Soviet government also relocated key industries eastward, beyond the reach of German advances, allowing production to continue. The assumption of a quick victory proved to be one of the most significant miscalculations of the war. As the conflict continued into the winter, German forces faced conditions for which they were unprepared, while Soviet resistance grew stronger. What had been planned as a short campaign became a prolonged and costly struggle that would reshape the course of the war.

125. Stalin's Shock and Sudden Recovery

When Germany invaded the Soviet Union on June 22, 1941, Joseph Stalin was reportedly caught off guard despite multiple intelligence warnings. For months, Soviet sources, including spies in Europe, had warned of a possible German attack. However, Stalin believed that Hitler would not risk a two-front war while Britain remained unconquered. He also feared that responding too aggressively to border tensions might provoke Germany prematurely. In the first days of the invasion, Stalin withdrew from public view, and confusion spread within the Soviet leadership. However, within a short period, he reasserted control. On July 3, 1941, Stalin addressed the Soviet population by radio, framing the conflict not merely as a war between governments but as a patriotic struggle for survival. This shift in messaging mobilized broader national support beyond communist ideology. The early shock revealed weaknesses in Soviet preparedness, but Stalin's decision to remain in Moscow and organize national resistance played a key role in stabilizing morale during the invasion's most dangerous phase.

126. Centralized Command and the Price of Absolute Authority

Stalin governed through strict centralization, meaning that major military decisions were often controlled from the top. While this allowed for rapid coordination of national resources, it also created serious problems during the early stages of the invasion. Soviet commanders were frequently afraid to act independently, fearing punishment if they made incorrect decisions. This hesitation sometimes slowed responses at critical moments. Earlier political purges had removed many experienced officers from the Red Army, weakening its leadership structure. As a result, the army struggled with coordination and communication during the first months of the war. Over time, however, Stalin adjusted his approach. He gradually allowed greater operational flexibility to capable commanders such as Georgy Zhukov, who would later play a major role in defending Moscow and leading counteroffensives. The Soviet system combined harsh discipline with massive mobilization. Factories were relocated east of the Ural Mountains, entire industries were reorganized, and millions of civilians were drafted into war production. While centralized authority created early setbacks, it also enabled the Soviet Union to reorganize on a vast scale, transforming initial disaster into long-term resistance.

127. Japan's Strategic Debate: North or South Expansion

During the late 1930s and early 1940s, Japanese leaders were divided over how the country should expand its influence. One group within the military supported a strategy known as "strike north," which focused on expanding into Siberia and confronting the Soviet Union. This approach aimed to secure land and resources while aligning Japan more closely with Germany's war in Europe. However, a series of border conflicts between Japanese and Soviet forces, particularly in 1939, ended in decisive Soviet victories. These defeats demonstrated the risks of confronting the Soviet Union directly and weakened support for northern expansion. At the same time, Japan faced increasing pressure from Western powers, especially the United States, which opposed its actions in China and Southeast Asia. As a result, attention shifted toward a "strike south" strategy, focusing on resource-rich regions such as Southeast Asia and the Pacific. These areas contained vital supplies like oil, rubber, and metals, which Japan needed to sustain its economy and military operations. This shift in strategy would soon bring Japan into direct conflict with Western powers.

128. The Oil Embargo

By 1941, tensions between Japan and the United States had reached a critical point. The United States had imposed economic sanctions, including restrictions on oil exports, in response to Japanese expansion in China and Southeast Asia. Since Japan depended heavily on imported resources, especially oil, these measures created a strategic dilemma. Leaders had to choose between reducing expansion and securing resources by force. Japanese leadership concluded that negotiation was unlikely to resolve the situation on favorable terms. Instead, they planned a preemptive strike to weaken American power in the Pacific. The goal was to destroy the U.S. Pacific Fleet, buying time for Japan to secure key territories before the United States could respond effectively. On December 7, 1941, Japanese aircraft attacked the U.S. naval base at Pearl Harbor in Hawaii. The attack caused significant damage to ships and aircraft and resulted in heavy casualties. While it achieved tactical surprise, it also led the United States to declare war. This decision transformed the conflict into a global war involving major powers across multiple continents and oceans.

129. Roosevelt's "Germany First" Strategy

After the attack on Pearl Harbor in December 1941, the United States entered the war facing two major enemies: Japan in the Pacific and Germany in Europe. This created a strategic dilemma. While public attention was focused on Japan, American and British leaders agreed that Germany posed the greater long-term threat due to its industrial strength, technological development, and control over much of Europe. As a result, President Franklin D. Roosevelt and Prime Minister Winston Churchill adopted what became known as the "Germany First" strategy. This approach prioritized defeating Germany before concentrating fully on Japan, even though the United States continued to fight in the Pacific. The reasoning was that if Germany were allowed to consolidate its power, it would later become far more difficult to defeat. This decision shaped the entire course of the war. Resources, production, and long-term planning were directed toward Europe, while the Pacific war was fought with more limited means in the early years. It demonstrated how strategic priorities were set not only by immediate threats but also by assessments of long-term danger.

130. Building and Coordinating a Global Alliance

Fighting a global war required cooperation between countries with different political systems, priorities, and military structures. The United States, Britain, and the Soviet Union formed the core of the Allied coalition, despite significant differences in ideology and leadership. Coordinating their efforts required constant communication and negotiation. A series of conferences helped establish shared goals and strategies. Leaders met to discuss military plans, resource allocation, and the overall direction of the war. One key principle that emerged was the demand for "unconditional surrender," meaning that the Axis powers would not be allowed to negotiate terms but would have to accept complete defeat. Cooperation extended beyond strategy. Industrial production, supply systems, and military operations had to be coordinated across continents. For example, the United States supplied large quantities of equipment and materials to its allies, while joint operations were planned to apply pressure on multiple fronts. Despite disagreements and tensions, the ability of Allied leaders to coordinate their efforts became a major factor in their eventual success. The war was no longer being fought by individual nations alone but by a coalition that combined resources on a global scale.

131. Increasing Control over Military Decisions

As the war progressed, Adolf Hitler increasingly took direct control over military decisions, reducing the influence of experienced generals. Early German successes had relied on flexibility and rapid adaptation, but over time, leadership became more centralized and less responsive to changing conditions on the battlefield. Hitler often issued detailed orders from headquarters, even when he lacked accurate, up-to-date information about the situation at the front. One of the most significant features of this approach was his insistence on holding ground at all costs. Retreats, even when they were strategically necessary, were often forbidden. German units were ordered to defend positions until the last possible moment, which frequently led to encirclement and the destruction of entire formations. Opportunities to withdraw and reorganize were lost, weakening the army's ability to sustain prolonged operations. At the same time, disagreements between Hitler and his generals over priorities became more common. Resources were sometimes spread across multiple objectives rather than concentrated where they were most effective. This combination of rigid command and divided focus gradually reduced Germany's ability to respond to setbacks, turning early advantages into long-term strategic problems.

132. Allied Flexibility and Coordinated Strategy

In contrast to the increasingly centralized and rigid command structure in Germany, Allied leadership developed a more flexible and cooperative approach as the war progressed. Although early coordination between Britain, the United States, and the Soviet Union was often difficult, these countries gradually established systems that allowed them to plan and operate together on a global scale. One key feature of this approach was the delegation of authority to experienced commanders in the field. Leaders such as Dwight D. Eisenhower and Georgy Zhukov were given the responsibility to make operational decisions based on local conditions, allowing armies to adapt more quickly to changing situations. At the same time, major strategic decisions were coordinated through conferences and joint planning bodies, ensuring that efforts across regions aligned with a common goal. The Allies also demonstrated a willingness to learn from setbacks. Early defeats led to changes in tactics, improvements in communication, and better integration of land, sea, and air forces. Over time, this adaptability allowed them to coordinate large-scale operations across multiple fronts, applying pressure simultaneously and gradually reducing the ability of Axis forces to respond effectively.

133. Opening a Second Front

One of the most important strategic debates among Allied leaders concerned when and where to open a second major front against Germany in Western Europe. The Soviet Union, which had been fighting large-scale battles on the Eastern Front since 1941, pushed strongly for an invasion of France to relieve pressure on its forces. Joseph Stalin argued that without a second front, the Soviet Union would continue to bear the main burden of the war. British and American leaders, however, were cautious. Early in the war, they believed they weren't yet prepared for a large-scale invasion of heavily defended territory. Instead, they chose to launch operations in North Africa and later in Italy, gradually building experience and weakening Axis forces. These decisions reflected both strategic caution and practical limitations in manpower, equipment, and coordination. By 1944, Allied leaders agreed that the time had come to open a second front in Western Europe. The decision required careful planning and coordination, as it would involve one of the largest amphibious operations in history. The timing and location of the invasion were chosen to maximize the chances of success while forcing Germany to fight on multiple fronts simultaneously.

134. Planning a Coordinated Invasion

The plan for the invasion of Western Europe, later known as Operation Overlord, required unprecedented coordination between Allied nations. Leaders had to consider not only military strength but also logistics, weather conditions, and the element of surprise. Large numbers of troops, vehicles, and supplies needed to be transported across the English Channel, while air and naval forces had to secure the area to support the landings. Deception played a crucial role in the planning process. This involved the use of false information, dummy equipment, and controlled communications designed to mislead German intelligence. At the same time, commanders prepared for the complexity of the operation itself. Multiple landing sites were selected, each with specific objectives, and forces from different countries were assigned to work together. The success of the invasion would depend on precise timing and coordination across land, sea, and air. The planning phase demonstrated how Allied leadership combined strategy, deception, and cooperation to prepare for one of the most critical operations of the war.

135. Leadership and the Decision to Launch D-Day

By early June 1944, Allied leaders had completed preparations for the invasion of Western Europe, but the final decision to launch the operation depended heavily on weather conditions. The invasion required calm seas, low tides, and enough light for airborne and naval forces to operate effectively. However, forecasts for early June were uncertain, and poor weather could delay the operation by weeks. General Dwight D. Eisenhower, the Supreme Allied Commander, was responsible for making the final decision. Postponing the invasion risked losing momentum and possibly revealing the plan to German forces, while proceeding under poor conditions increased the danger for troops landing on heavily defended beaches. After reviewing updated weather reports, Eisenhower chose to proceed with the invasion on June 6, 1944. The decision carried enormous consequences. Thousands of ships, aircraft, and soldiers were already in position, and reversing the operation would have been extremely difficult. By committing to the invasion, Allied leadership accepted the risks involved, relying on careful planning and coordination to achieve success.

136. Commanding Under Pressure

Once the invasion began, Allied commanders had to respond to rapidly changing conditions on the ground. Communication was often difficult, and units faced unexpected resistance in some areas. On several beaches along the Normandy coast in France, especially Omaha Beach, troops encountered strong defenses, including fortified positions, machine-gun fire, and obstacles designed to slow the landing forces. Commanders had to make quick decisions with limited information. In some cases, landing forces were scattered, requiring officers and soldiers to reorganize under fire. Naval and air support played a crucial role in suppressing defenses, while engineers worked to clear obstacles and open routes inland. Despite heavy casualties, Allied forces gradually secured their positions and established a foothold in France. The ability of commanders to adapt to unfolding events was essential to the success of the operation. The invasion demonstrated how leadership under pressure required not only planning but also flexibility and the capacity to make critical decisions in real time.

137. Stalin, Roosevelt, and Churchill: Coordinating Victory

As the war progressed into its later stages, cooperation among Allied leaders became increasingly important. The leaders of the United States, Britain, and the Soviet Union, Franklin D. Roosevelt, Winston Churchill, and Joseph Stalin, met at a series of conferences to coordinate strategy and plan for the final defeat of Germany. Despite their shared goal, the three leaders had different priorities shaped by their countries' positions and experiences in the war. The Soviet Union, having suffered enormous losses, pushed for continued pressure on Germany and the opening of additional fronts to reduce the burden on its forces. Britain and the United States focused on coordinating large-scale operations in Western Europe while maintaining supply lines and global commitments. These meetings also addressed the future of Europe, including the occupation of Germany and the political structure of liberated territories. Although disagreements were common, the ability of these leaders to maintain cooperation was crucial. Their decisions ensured that Germany faced sustained pressure from multiple directions, accelerating the collapse of its military position.

138. Political Decisions and the Shape of the War's End

As Allied forces advanced into German territory in 1944 and 1945, leaders began making decisions about how the war would end and what would follow. Leaders discussed how Germany would be governed after defeat. Plans were made to divide the country into occupation zones, each controlled by one of the major Allied powers. Similar discussions took place regarding Eastern Europe, where the Soviet Union had already established a strong military presence. These decisions weren't purely military; they were also political, shaping the postwar world. As the war drew to a close, cooperation between the Allies began to show signs of strain, as differences in ideology and interests became more pronounced. Even before the fighting had fully ended, the foundations of future tensions were already being laid.

139. Final Decisions in Berlin and the Collapse of Leadership

By April 1945, as Soviet forces closed in on Berlin, Adolf Hitler faced a situation he had long claimed would never happen: total defeat. For years, he had framed the war as a struggle in which victory or destruction were the only possible outcomes. He rejected the idea of surrender entirely, believing that if Germany couldn't win, it didn't deserve to survive. This belief shaped his final decisions. Hitler also feared capture by Soviet forces, whose advance into Germany had been accompanied by intense fighting and widespread destruction. He was determined not to be taken prisoner or publicly displayed as a defeated leader. In his final days, he dictated political statements blaming others for Germany's failures and insisting that the war had been lost due to betrayal rather than strategic mistakes. On

April 30, 1945, as Soviet troops fought nearby, Hitler ended his life in his underground bunker. His death was both a personal decision and a reflection of his refusal to accept defeat or negotiate. Even in the final moments, leadership remained tied to ideology rather than reality, leaving no organized transition or clear direction as Germany collapsed around him.

140. Leadership Decisions and the End of the War in Asia

By the summer of 1945, the United States faced a difficult decision about how to end the war with Japan. Although Japan had lost much of its navy and air power, its leadership showed no clear willingness to surrender. Previous battles, such as those on Pacific islands, had demonstrated that Japanese forces often fought to the end, raising concerns that an invasion of the Japanese mainland could result in extremely high casualties on both sides. The final decision rested with U.S. President Harry S. Truman, who had taken office in April 1945 after the death of Franklin D. Roosevelt. Truman was informed about a secret program known as the Manhattan Project, which had developed atomic weapons capable of causing unprecedented destruction. Military planners presented the bomb as a way to force a rapid surrender without the need for a full-scale invasion. On August 6 and August 9, 1945, atomic bombs were dropped on Hiroshima and Nagasaki. At the same time, the Soviet Union entered the war against Japan, launching a major offensive in Manchuria. Together, these events placed enormous pressure on Japanese leadership. Within days, Emperor Hirohito intervened to support surrender, marking a rare direct political role. The decision to use atomic weapons remains one of the most debated choices in modern history, as leaders weighed the goal of ending the war quickly against the devastating human consequences.

SEVENTEEN

Intelligence & Hidden War

Behind the visible battles of World War II existed another conflict: one fought in secret. Intelligence gathering, codebreaking, and covert operations played a crucial role in shaping the outcome of campaigns, often determining success or failure long before troops engaged on the battlefield. Information became one of the most valuable weapons of the war. This chapter explores the hidden side of the conflict, from the breaking of encrypted messages to the development of advanced surveillance and deception strategies. It highlights the importance of intelligence networks and the individuals who worked behind the scenes, often without recognition, to gain an advantage over the enemy. It was a war where knowledge could be as powerful as firepower and where secrets could decide the fate of nations.

141. Early Codebreaking and the Polish Enigma Breakthrough

Before the war officially began, one of the most important intelligence battles was already underway: the effort to read German encrypted communications. Germany used a machine called Enigma, which looked like a heavy typewriter but functioned as a complex scrambling device. It was used to turn ordinary military orders into ciphertext: a jumble of letters that looked like nonsense to anyone who didn't have the correct "key" to unlock it. To a layperson, the Enigma was a mechanical puzzle of incredible complexity. Each time an operator pressed a key, three or more internal rotors (spinning wheels) would turn, constantly changing the electrical pathway and producing a different letter. Because the machine's settings were changed every single day, there were over 150 quintillion (150 followed by eighteen zeros) possible combinations. The Germans were so confident in this complexity that they believed the code was absolutely unbreakable. In the early 1930s, however, Polish mathematicians made a crucial breakthrough. Instead of using traditional linguistics (looking for patterns in language), they used mathematical analysis to figure out the internal wiring of the machine. By 1932, a mathematician named Marian Rejewski successfully reconstructed the Enigma's logic. The Poles even developed devices called "bombes," early mechanical computers designed to automate the process of guessing the daily settings. As the threat of war grew, Poland realized it could no longer keep up with the increasing complexity of German updates alone. In July 1939, just weeks before the invasion of their country, Polish intelligence shared their secret "Enigma clones" and their mathematical findings with their British and French allies.

142. Bletchley Park and the Birth of Ultra Intelligence

After receiving the Polish discoveries, Britain established a secret codebreaking center at Bletchley Park, located northwest of London. There, mathematicians, linguists, engineers, and analysts worked together to break German encrypted communications. Among them were individuals from a wide range of backgrounds, including academics, crossword puzzle experts, and chess players, all selected for their ability to recognize patterns and solve complex problems. One of the key challenges was the constant change in Enigma settings. To keep up, British codebreakers used machines known as "bombes," which could rapidly test different configurations. Over time, they began to read large volumes of German messages, an intelligence source later known as Ultra. Ultra intelligence provided detailed information about German movements, supply lines, and strategic plans. However, it had to be used carefully. If Germany realized its codes had been broken, it would change its systems. As a result, intelligence from Enigma was often disguised or used indirectly to avoid revealing the secret. This balance between using information and protecting its source became a constant challenge throughout the war.

143. Early Intelligence Failures and Missed Signals

Despite advances in codebreaking, intelligence during the early stages of the war was far from perfect. Information was often incomplete, delayed, or difficult to interpret, and even accurate intelligence could be ignored if it didn't fit existing expectations. This was especially true before major German offensives, when warning signs were sometimes overlooked. Before the German invasion of the Soviet Union in June 1941, multiple intelligence reports suggested that an attack was imminent. These warnings came from various sources, including intercepted communications and foreign agents. However, Soviet leader Joseph Stalin remained skeptical, believing that Germany would not risk a two-front war while still fighting Britain. As a result, many preparations were delayed, and Soviet forces were caught off guard when the invasion began. Intelligence also depended on interpretation. Commanders had to decide which reports were reliable and how to act on them. In several cases, assumptions about enemy behavior led leaders to dismiss important information. These early failures demonstrated that intelligence was only as effective as the decisions made from it.

144. Espionage Networks and Secret Agents Across Europe

Alongside codebreaking, espionage played a key role in gathering intelligence. Governments recruited agents to operate behind enemy lines, collecting information about troop movements, industrial production, and political developments. These networks often relied on local resistance groups, who provided knowledge of terrain and conditions. In occupied Europe, resistance movements became an important source of intelligence for the Allies. Members risked arrest or execution to pass on information through coded messages, hidden transmitters, or couriers. Some agents used false identities and lived for months or years within enemy-controlled areas, maintaining contact with intelligence services abroad. However, espionage was extremely dangerous. Many networks were infiltrated or discovered by counterintelligence forces, leading to arrests and executions. Both sides used deception, false information, and double agents to manipulate their opponents. The intelligence war was often invisible, yet it had a direct impact on military operations, as information gathered in secret could influence decisions on the battlefield.

145. The Double-Cross System and Controlled Spies

During the war, British intelligence developed a system that turned enemy spies into controlled sources of information. Known as the Double-Cross System, it involved capturing German agents sent to Britain and persuading them, through cooperation, coercion, or negotiation, to work for the Allies instead. Rather than simply arresting these agents, British intelligence used them to send carefully crafted messages back to Germany.

These messages appeared to provide valuable intelligence, but in reality, they were designed to mislead German command. The system was managed by a specialized group that coordinated what information was sent and ensured that all reports remained consistent. This required careful planning, as even small contradictions could raise suspicion. Over time, the British gained significant control over the flow of intelligence reaching Germany from within the United Kingdom. By managing these agents, they were able to shape enemy expectations and influence strategic decisions without the Germans realizing that their own network had been compromised.

146. Operation Mincemeat and the Use of a False Identity

In 1943, Allied planners needed to mislead German forces about where the next major invasion would take place. The target was Sicily, but if Germany anticipated the attack, it could reinforce the island, making the invasion far more difficult. To distract attention, British intelligence devised a plan to convince the enemy that the invasion would occur elsewhere. The operation involved placing false documents on the body of a man dressed as a British officer. The documents suggested that Allied forces were planning attacks in Greece and Sardinia rather than in Sicily. The body was then released off the coast of Spain, a country that was officially neutral but had contacts with German intelligence. The expectation was that the documents would be recovered and passed on to German authorities. The plan depended on credibility. The identity, personal items, and documents were carefully prepared to appear genuine. When the information reached German command, it contributed to a misinterpretation of Allied intentions, drawing attention away from the actual target.

147. Deception at a Strategic Scale

The success of operations like Mincemeat demonstrated how intelligence could influence entire military campaigns. By shaping what the enemy believed, Allied planners could influence where forces were deployed and how resources were used. In the case of Sicily, German leadership diverted attention and defensive preparations to areas they believed were under threat, reducing their readiness where the actual invasion occurred. This approach was part of a broader strategy that combined multiple forms of deception, including false radio transmissions, misleading reports from double agents, and visible preparations designed to suggest attacks in different locations. Intelligence wasn't only used to gather information but also to create a controlled picture of reality for the enemy. Such operations required careful coordination between intelligence services and military planners. A successful deception could save lives by reducing resistance, while a failure could reveal the strategy and strengthen enemy defenses. By this stage of the war, intelligence had become a central element of planning, shaping decisions long before battles began.

148. Ultra Intelligence and the Battle of the Atlantic

Throughout the war, the Battle of the Atlantic became one of the longest and most critical campaigns, as German submarines, known as U-boats, attempted to cut off supply routes between North America and Britain. These convoys carried food, fuel, and equipment essential to the Allied war effort. If the supply lines failed, Britain's ability to continue the war would be severely weakened. Ultra intelligence, derived from breaking German Enigma codes, played a key role in countering this threat. By intercepting and decrypting German communications, Allied commanders could track the positions of U-boat groups, often referred to as "wolfpacks." This allowed convoys to be rerouted away from danger or escorted more effectively by naval and air forces. However, the use of this intelligence required caution. If the Germans realized their communications were being read, they could change their encryption systems. As a result, commanders sometimes had to allow attacks to proceed rather than reveal the true source of their information. Despite these limitations, Ultra intelligence significantly improved Allied ability to protect shipping and maintain vital supply routes.

149. Codebreaking and the Struggle for Control at Sea

The battle between German submarines and Allied convoys wasn't only fought with ships and aircraft but also with information. As German encryption methods became more complex, codebreakers at Bletchley Park faced periods where they could no longer read enemy messages. During these times, losses at sea increased, showing how closely intelligence was linked to operational success. To regain the advantage, Allied forces worked to capture German equipment, including Enigma machines and codebooks, from damaged or surrendered submarines. These materials provided crucial insight into how the system worked and helped codebreakers restore their ability to read communications. Advances in technology and analysis also improved the speed and accuracy of decryption. Over time, the combination of intelligence, improved convoy systems, and increased air coverage shifted the balance in favor of the

Allies. The ability to understand and anticipate enemy movements reduced losses and strengthened supply lines. The struggle at sea demonstrated that intelligence could be as decisive as firepower, influencing the outcome of an entire campaign.

150. Codebreaking in the Pacific War

In the Pacific, the intelligence war took a different form but was just as critical to survival. The United States focused on breaking Japanese naval codes, particularly a system known as JN-25, which was the primary "operational" code used to coordinate fleet movements. Unlike the mechanical Enigma machine, JN-25 was a book-based cipher. This means that a Japanese officer would first look up a word or phrase in a massive codebook to find a five-digit number and then add a second "random" number to it from a separate table to scramble the message further. American codebreakers, led by Commander Joseph Rochefort in a basement office in Hawaii known as Station HYPO, worked to reconstruct the code using a technique called "traffic analysis." They collected and compared thousands of intercepted radio messages to identify recurring patterns. For example, they realized that certain five-digit groups always appeared at the beginning of messages, which helped them identify the sender's rank or location. Even though the Americans could often decode only 10% to 15% of a message, those fragments were incredibly valuable. By identifying specific code words for geographic locations, which the Americans called "designators," they could estimate where the Japanese fleet was heading. By understanding where Japanese forces would strike next, American commanders could position their carriers for an ambush rather than wandering the empty ocean, turning mathematical analysis into a decisive strategic weapon.

151. Intelligence Warnings Before Pearl Harbor

Before the attack on Pearl Harbor in December 1941, the United States had already intercepted and partially decrypted a number of Japanese communications. These messages indicated rising tensions and suggested that Japan was preparing for major military action. American intelligence was aware that negotiations between the two countries were failing and that conflict was becoming increasingly likely. However, the available information didn't clearly identify where the attack would take place. Many analysts believed that Japan's next move would be directed toward Southeast Asia, where valuable resources such as oil were located. Locations like the Philippines, Malaya, or the Dutch East Indies were considered more likely targets than Hawaii, which was seen as distant and relatively secure. As a result, warnings were general rather than specific. Commanders in the Pacific were advised to remain alert, but the possibility of a direct attack on Pearl Harbor wasn't widely expected. The intelligence existed, but it didn't lead to a clear, immediate defensive response.

152. Misinterpretation, Timing, and Surprise

The failure to prevent the attack on Pearl Harbor wasn't due to a complete lack of information, but rather to how that information was interpreted and acted upon. Intelligence was fragmented across different agencies, and communication between them was limited. Key pieces of information weren't always shared quickly or effectively, leading to gaps in understanding. Timing also played a crucial role. Some intercepted messages suggesting a break in diplomatic relations were decoded only hours before the attack, leaving little time to respond. Even when warnings were sent, they often arrived too late or lacked enough detail to prompt immediate action. In addition, existing assumptions influenced decision-making. Many believed that a surprise attack on a distant naval base would be too risky for Japan. This underestimation contributed to a lack of preparedness. When the attack began on December 7, 1941, it achieved tactical surprise, demonstrating how intelligence can fail not only through absence but also through misinterpretation, delay, and misplaced confidence.

153. The Manhattan Project and Secret Science

The groundwork for a nuclear program in the United States began as early as late 1939, following a letter from Albert Einstein to President Roosevelt warning that Nazi Germany might be developing "extremely powerful bombs of a new type." However, it wasn't until August 1942 that the effort was officially organized as the Manhattan Project, a massive undertaking led by the U.S. Army Corps of Engineers under General Leslie Groves and scientific director J. Robert Oppenheimer. The goal was to harness nuclear fission, the process of splitting an atom's nucleus to release a massive amount of energy, to create a weapon of unprecedented destructive power. The project brought together scientists, engineers, and military personnel from the United States, Britain, and Canada, driven by the intense fear that Germany might achieve a nuclear breakthrough first. The scale of the project was staggering, employing over 130,000 people and costing nearly $2 billion (equivalent to roughly $35 billion today). To maintain the highest level of security, entire "secret cities" were built from scratch in remote locations. In Oak Ridge, Tennessee, massive plants used electromagnetism and gas to separate Uranium-235, the fuel needed for the bomb. Meanwhile, in Hanford, Washington, the first full-scale nuclear reactors were built to produce plutonium, an even more powerful man-made element. The actual design and assembly of the weapons took place at a central laboratory in Los Alamos, New Mexico. To protect the secret, the military used compartmentalization: a security method in which workers are given only the specific information needed for their individual tasks. Most employees at Oak Ridge had no idea they were working on a weapon; they simply monitored gauges in massive factories, unaware of the final product. Even Harry S. Truman was kept in the dark about the project until he became president in April 1945. The effort reached its climax on July 16, 1945, in the New Mexico desert with the Trinity Test, the first successful detonation of a nuclear device. The explosion was equal to roughly 21,000 tons of TNT, turning the desert sand into green glass. While the project was born from the threat of Nazi Germany, the successful test occurred months after Germany's surrender, leaving the United States with a weapon that would instead be used to end the war in the Pacific.

154. Espionage and Secrets Within the Atomic Program

Despite the strict security surrounding the Manhattan Project, information about it wasn't completely contained. Soviet intelligence managed to place agents within the program, allowing them to gather details about the development of atomic weapons. These agents passed information to the Soviet Union, providing insights that would later assist in its own nuclear program. The structure of the project, with its many sites and large workforce, posed security challenges. While most participants had limited knowledge of the overall effort, some individuals had access to critical information. Intelligence services on both sides recognized the importance of scientific developments, and efforts were made to gather or protect knowledge wherever possible. The presence of espionage within the project showed that even the most secret programs were vulnerable. Information gathered during the war contributed to the rapid development of nuclear weapons by multiple countries in the years that followed. The intelligence dimension of the Manhattan Project extended its impact beyond the war itself, shaping the balance of power in the postwar world.

155. Operation Fortitude and the Illusion of Invasion

In the months leading up to the Allied invasion of Western Europe in 1944, planners recognized that surprise would be critical. If German forces could be convinced that the main landing would occur somewhere other than the actual target, they might delay sending reinforcements, giving Allied troops time to establish a foothold. To achieve this, the Allies launched a large-scale deception plan known as Operation Fortitude. This operation was designed to mislead German intelligence about both the location and timing of the invasion. The real landing would take place in Normandy, on the northern coast of France, but Fortitude aimed to convince German commanders that the main attack would occur at the Pas-de-Calais, the narrowest point between Britain and France. This location appeared more logical because it was closer to England and offered shorter supply lines. To reinforce the deception, Allied forces generated false radio traffic, planted misleading intelligence, and used double agents to pass carefully constructed information to the Germans. These agents, some of whom were under Allied control, reported the buildup of forces in southeastern England, creating the impression that a major invasion force was waiting there. Over time, these efforts shaped German expectations, causing them to prepare for an attack in the wrong place.

156. The Creation of a Phantom Army

A key part of Operation Fortitude was the creation of an entirely fictional military formation known as the First United States Army Group (FUSAG). This "army" existed only on paper, but it was presented to German intelligence as a powerful force preparing for invasion. To make the illusion convincing, the Allies used a combination of physical props, signals, and controlled information. Inflatable tanks and aircraft were placed in fields to simulate large concentrations of equipment. Wooden structures and dummy landing craft were constructed along the coast. Meanwhile, radio operators transmitted messages that mimicked the communications of a real army, complete with the patterns and terminology expected by enemy listeners. Even the movement of units was staged to suggest training exercises and preparations for an imminent attack. The deception was further strengthened by placing General George Patton, one of the Allies' most well-known commanders, in charge of the fictitious army. German leaders considered him one of the most capable Allied generals, so his supposed involvement added credibility to the threat. As a result, even after the real invasion began in Normandy in June 1944,

German forces continued to expect a larger attack at Pas-de-Calais and held back key divisions. This delay played a crucial role in the success of the Allied landings.

157. Intelligence and the Normandy Breakout

After the Allied landings in Normandy on June 6, 1944, intelligence continued to play a decisive role in the next phase of the campaign. While German commanders initially believed the Normandy landings were a diversion, intercepted communications and reconnaissance began to reveal the true scale of the Allied buildup. However, by the time this realization spread, the delay caused by earlier deception operations had already weakened German responses. Allied intelligence units worked closely with resistance groups across France, who provided real-time information about German troop movements, supply lines, and defensive positions. These reports were transmitted through coded radio messages and helped Allied commanders plan attacks with greater precision. At the same time, Ultra intelligence from decrypted German communications revealed how German units were being redeployed, allowing Allied forces to anticipate counterattacks. One of the key moments came in late July 1944 during Operation Cobra, the Allied "breakout" from the coastal areas of Normandy. After weeks of being stuck in the dense French countryside, the Allies used a combination of three intelligence tools to shatter the deadlock: aerial reconnaissance (photos taken by planes flying overhead), intercepted communications (radio messages decoded by experts), and resistance reports (secret information sent by French citizens fighting against the occupation). By layering this information together, Allied planners identified exactly where the German defensive line was at its weakest. Using these insights, the Allies launched a massive, concentrated attack on those specific thin spots. This allowed their armored divisions to punch through the German front and finally begin racing across the open plains of France toward Paris.

158. The July Plot and Intelligence Inside Germany

In July 1944, one of the most dramatic intelligence-related events of the war came from within Germany itself. A group of German military officers and officials, convinced that the war was lost and that Hitler's leadership was leading the country to destruction, organized a plan to assassinate him and take control of the government. This plan became known as the July Plot. The central figure in the operation was Colonel Claus von Stauffenberg, who placed a bomb in a briefcase during a meeting at Hitler's headquarters in East Prussia on July 20, 1944. The explosion killed several people, but Hitler survived with relatively minor injuries. The failure of the assassination attempt led to a rapid crackdown by the Nazi regime. Although not an intelligence operation in the traditional sense, the plot revealed the extent of internal dissent within Germany and the limits of control even in a highly authoritarian system. German intelligence services, including the Gestapo, launched extensive investigations to uncover those involved. Thousands were arrested, and many were executed. The event demonstrated that even as Germany maintained strict control over information, resistance existed within its own leadership. It also highlighted that intelligence wasn't used only against external enemies but also to monitor and suppress internal opposition.

159. The Ardennes Offensive and Intelligence Misjudgment

In December 1944, Germany launched a surprise counteroffensive in the Ardennes forest region of Belgium and Luxembourg, an operation that became known as the Battle of the Bulge. The goal was to split Allied forces and capture the vital port of Antwerp. Despite the extensive intelligence capabilities of the Allies, the attack achieved a significant degree of surprise. German forces maintained strict radio silence and used landlines instead of wireless communication, limiting the amount of information available for interception. Troop movements were carried out under the cover of bad weather and dense forest, reducing the effectiveness of aerial reconnaissance. As a result, many Allied analysts believed that Germany no longer had the strength to launch a major offensive. There were warning signs. Some intelligence reports suggested unusual German activity, but these were often dismissed or interpreted as defensive preparations rather than an offensive threat. When the attack began on December 16, 1944, it initially caught Allied forces off guard, leading to heavy fighting and temporary gains for German troops. However, once the scale of the attack became clear, Allied intelligence and logistics helped coordinate a response. Improved weather allowed air support, and intercepted communications revealed German supply shortages. Within weeks, the offensive was contained and eventually pushed back. The battle showed that even advanced intelligence systems could fail when assumptions influenced interpretation.

160. Soviet Intelligence and the Final Offensive

As the war moved into its final phase in early 1945, Soviet intelligence played a key role in preparing large-scale offensives against German forces.

The Red Army gathered information through reconnaissance units, partisan networks, and intercepted communications, building a detailed picture of German defenses along the Eastern Front. One of the most important operations was the Vistula–Oder Offensive, launched in January 1945. Soviet planners used intelligence to identify weak points in German lines and to concentrate overwhelming force at specific locations. Deception was also used to conceal the true scale and timing of the attack, preventing German forces from reinforcing critical sectors. When the offensive began, Soviet forces advanced rapidly across Poland, pushing German units back toward the Oder River, only about forty-three miles (seventy kilometers) from Berlin. The speed of the advance shocked German commanders, many of whom had underestimated Soviet capabilities. Intelligence allowed Soviet forces to coordinate massive troop movements and maintain momentum, ensuring that German defenses couldn't recover.

161. Intelligence and the Race for Berlin

In early 1945, as Allied forces closed in on Germany from both the west and the east, intelligence played a key role in shaping the final advance toward Berlin. Both the Western Allies and the Soviet Union gathered information on German troop positions, defensive lines, and supply conditions, but their strategic goals differed. While the Soviets aimed to capture Berlin, Western Allied leaders prioritized avoiding unnecessary casualties and securing other key regions. Soviet intelligence, supported by reconnaissance units and partisan networks, provided detailed information about German defenses around the capital. This allowed Soviet commanders to plan a massive offensive involving multiple army groups, designed to overwhelm German positions through sheer force and coordination. At the same time, intercepted communications revealed the weakening state of German units, many of which were understrength and poorly supplied. In the west, Allied intelligence suggested that German resistance was collapsing unevenly, with some units surrendering while others continued to fight. This influenced decisions about where to advance and where to halt. Ultimately, the Western Allies stopped short of Berlin, allowing Soviet forces to take the city. Intelligence, in this case, didn't just guide military movements; it also shaped political decisions about how the war would end.

162. The Collapse of German Communications

By the final months of the war, Germany's ability to coordinate its forces had been severely weakened. Continuous bombing campaigns had destroyed railways, communication lines, and industrial centers, making it increasingly difficult for orders to reach front-line units. At the same time, Allied interception of German communications meant that many messages were no longer secure. German commanders often relied on outdated information or incomplete reports, leading to confusion and ineffective decisions. In some cases, units received orders to attack or hold positions that had already been lost. The breakdown of communication networks also made coordination among different parts of the German military increasingly difficult. Allied intelligence, on the other hand, became more effective as the war progressed. Intercepted messages, aerial reconnaissance, and reports from advancing troops provided a clearer picture of the battlefield. This allowed Allied commanders to identify weak points and exploit them quickly. The contrast between the two sides was stark. While the Allies were improving their ability to gather and use information, Germany was losing control over its own communication systems. This imbalance contributed to the rapid collapse of German defenses in 1945, as the ability to command and coordinate forces is essential in any military operation. Without it, even large armies can become disorganized and ineffective.

163. Intelligence and the Atomic Decision

As the war in Europe ended, intelligence also influenced decisions in the Pacific. American leaders were trying to determine how to bring the war with Japan to a close, and one key question was whether Japan would surrender without a full-scale invasion. Through intercepted Japanese communications, particularly diplomatic messages, American intelligence gained insight into Japan's internal debates. These messages suggested that some Japanese leaders were seeking a negotiated settlement, but others were committed to continuing the war. The information indicated that Japan was divided but not yet ready to accept unconditional surrender. At the same time, intelligence estimates predicted that an invasion of the Japanese mainland could result in extremely high casualties for both sides. These projections were based on previous battles, in which Japanese forces had fought to the last, and on reports about preparations to defend the home islands. This combination of intelligence, showing both Japan's willingness to resist and the potential cost of invasion, contributed to the decision to use atomic weapons. While not the only factor, intelligence played a role in shaping how American leaders understood their options, influencing one of the most significant decisions of the war.

164. Intelligence and the Soviet Entry into the Pacific War

Another crucial factor in the final phase of the war was the planned entry of the Soviet Union into the conflict against Japan. This decision had been agreed upon earlier by Allied leaders, but its timing and execution were closely tied to intelligence assessments. Soviet intelligence had been monitoring Japanese forces in Manchuria, where a large army was stationed. These forces were considered significant, but intelligence also suggested that they were overstretched and not fully prepared for a major offensive. Meanwhile, American intelligence recognized that a Soviet attack could further pressure Japan and accelerate the end of the war. In August 1945, shortly after the atomic bombings, the Soviet Union launched a massive offensive into Manchuria. Using detailed intelligence and overwhelming force, Soviet troops advanced rapidly, defeating Japanese forces in a matter of weeks. The speed of the offensive surprised many observers and demonstrated the effectiveness of coordinated planning. The combination of atomic attacks and the Soviet invasion created a situation in which Japanese leaders faced multiple threats at once. Intelligence on both sides helped shape these final operations, contributing to the decisions that ultimately ended the war.

165. The Lasting Impact of Wartime Intelligence

The intelligence operations of World War II had a lasting impact far beyond the conflict itself. During the war, countries developed new methods for gathering, analyzing, and protecting information, including codebreaking, signal interception, and large-scale deception. These methods proved so effective that they became permanent parts of national security systems after the war ended. Organizations created for wartime intelligence, such as codebreaking centers and cryptographic units, laid the foundation for modern intelligence agencies. Techniques developed during the war influenced how governments approached surveillance, espionage, and information security in the decades that followed. The importance of secrecy and information control became central to global politics. The war also demonstrated that intelligence could be as decisive as military strength. The ability to understand enemy plans, protect one's own communications, and influence what the enemy believed could shape entire campaigns. This realization contributed to the emergence of new forms of conflict after the war, where intelligence and information would play a central role. In this sense, World War II wasn't only a conflict of armies and weapons but also a turning point in how information itself became a powerful tool of war.

EIGHTEEN

Spies, Agents, and Double Lives

World War II created a world in which secrecy and deception became essential tools of survival and strategy. Spies operated across borders, gathering information, sabotaging operations, and influencing events from the shadows. Many lived double lives, navigating constant danger where a single mistake could mean capture or death. This chapter looks at the individuals who operated in this hidden world, including agents sent behind enemy lines, resistance fighters working in occupied territories, and the networks that supported them. It reveals the risks they faced and the crucial role they played in shaping the course of the war. It was a conflict where some of the most important battles were fought without uniforms, in silence, and far from the front lines.

166. The Cambridge Five and the Quiet Infiltration

In the 1930s, a group of students at Cambridge University in Britain began making decisions that would have long-term consequences for the intelligence war that followed. Influenced by the political climate of the time, including economic instability and the rise of fascism across Europe, several of them became sympathetic to communist ideas. Soviet intelligence identified their potential early and recruited them while they were still students, before they entered government service. Over the following years, these individuals, later known as the "Cambridge Five," moved into influential positions within British institutions, including intelligence agencies and the diplomatic corps. Because they came from trusted backgrounds and appeared loyal, they weren't initially suspected. This allowed them to pass sensitive information to the Soviet Union over an extended period. Their actions provided insight into Allied planning and intelligence operations, showing that espionage wasn't only carried out across borders but also from within. The group remained active for years, demonstrating how long-term infiltration could shape the intelligence landscape of the war.

167. Richard Sorge and the Warning from Tokyo

In the years leading up to and during the early stages of World War II, one of the most effective intelligence sources for the Soviet Union was operating in Japan. Richard Sorge, a German journalist and committed communist, worked secretly as a Soviet agent while maintaining close connections with German diplomats and Japanese officials. His position gave him access to information that was difficult for others to obtain. In 1941, Sorge reported that Germany was preparing to invade the Soviet Union, providing an early warning of Operation Barbarossa. Later that year, he delivered another critical message: Japan didn't intend to attack the Soviet Union in the near future. This information allowed the Soviet leadership to move experienced divisions from Siberia to the western front, where they were needed to defend Moscow. These reinforcements played an important role in slowing the German advance during the winter of 1941. Sorge's work demonstrated how intelligence gathered far from the battlefield could influence key decisions. However, Japanese authorities became suspicious after intercepting coded radio transmissions linked to his network, and the arrest of one of his associates led investigators to him. He was eventually arrested by Japanese authorities and later executed, with his contributions becoming widely recognized only after the war.

168. Duško Popov and the Warning That Went Unheeded

In the early years of the war, espionage often depended on individuals who lived double lives, constantly balancing trust and suspicion. One such figure was Duško Popov, a Yugoslav double agent who worked for British intelligence while pretending to serve Germany. His role required him to travel across Europe and the United States, maintaining contact with German handlers while secretly reporting back to the Allies. In 1941, Popov was sent to the United States by German intelligence with a detailed questionnaire about American military installations. Among the locations mentioned was Pearl Harbor, the major U.S. naval base in Hawaii. Recognizing the significance of these questions, Popov passed the information to American authorities, hoping it would raise concern. However, his warning didn't lead to a decisive response. Part of the problem was that intelligence agencies were cautious about trusting information from double agents, whose reliability was always uncertain. Popov himself operated under constant pressure, knowing that a single mistake could expose his role and lead to execution. His experience illustrated one of the key challenges of espionage: even accurate intelligence could be overlooked if it didn't fit existing expectations or if its source wasn't fully trusted.

169. The Abwehr and the Limits of German Espionage

Germany entered the war with its own intelligence organization, the Abwehr, responsible for espionage and counterintelligence operations. However, despite early efforts, the Abwehr struggled to build effective networks, particularly in Britain. Many of the agents it sent were quickly identified, captured, or turned by British intelligence, often within days of arrival. For individual spies, this meant entering an environment where survival was unlikely. Agents were dropped into unfamiliar territory, often with limited support and little local knowledge. Some were betrayed, while others made small mistakes that exposed them. Once captured, they faced interrogation, imprisonment, or execution. The weaknesses of the Abwehr weren't only operational but also internal. Rivalries between different intelligence organizations, as well as distrust within the Nazi system, made coordination difficult. Some officers within the Abwehr even secretly opposed Hitler, creating further instability. For the individuals involved, espionage was rarely glamorous. It was a dangerous and uncertain existence, where loyalty, deception, and survival were constantly in tension. The failure of German intelligence networks in places like Britain showed how difficult it was to operate successfully in hostile territory, especially when the enemy was already watching closely.

170. Virginia Hall and the Limping Lady

One of the most effective Allied agents operating in occupied Europe was Virginia Hall, an American who worked with British intelligence and later the United States. Her presence in the field was unusual for another reason: she had a prosthetic leg, which she nicknamed "Cuthbert," after losing her lower leg in an accident years earlier. Despite this, she volunteered for one of the most dangerous roles in the war. Operating in France after its occupation by Germany, Hall built networks of resistance fighters, organized supply drops, and helped coordinate sabotage operations. She also assisted downed Allied airmen, guiding them through escape routes out of occupied territory. Her work required constant movement and secrecy, often traveling long distances on foot or by bicycle, even with her disability. The Gestapo, Germany's secret police, became aware of her activities and referred to her as "the most dangerous of all Allied spies." Her physical condition, which might have been seen as a limitation, actually became part of her disguise, allowing her to blend in as an ordinary civilian. When her network was compromised, she was forced to flee across the Pyrenees Mountains into Spain in the winter, a difficult journey even for a fully able-bodied person. Hall later returned to France, continuing her work under even greater risk.

171. Noor Inayat Khan and the Silent Radio

In occupied France, one of the most dangerous roles in the resistance was that of a wireless operator. These agents were responsible for transmitting coded messages back to Britain, often from within enemy territory. Because radio signals could be detected, German forces used tracking equipment to locate transmissions, meaning that operators had to move frequently and limit how long they stayed on the air. Many were captured within weeks. Noor Inayat Khan, a British agent of Indian origin, was sent into France in 1943 as a radio operator. After a series of arrests destroyed much of her network, she became one of the last remaining operators in the region. Despite the risk, she continued transmitting messages, knowing that her signals were essential for coordinating resistance activities and supply drops. Living under constant threat, she moved from place to place, carrying her radio equipment and avoiding detection. Eventually, she was betrayed and captured by German forces. Even under interrogation, she refused to provide useful information and attempted escape more than once. Because she was considered highly dangerous, she was classified as a "night and fog" prisoner, a category for those who were to disappear without a trace. Noor Inayat Khan was later executed in 1944. Her story highlighted the extreme risks faced by agents in the field, where communication itself could reveal their location and where even silence under interrogation required extraordinary resilience.

172. Juan Pujol and the Imaginary Network

One of the most unusual spies of the war was Juan Pujol, a Spanish civilian who had no formal training in intelligence but was determined to fight against Nazi Germany. At first, he tried to offer his services to the British, but when they rejected him, he decided to act on his own. Posing as a pro-

German sympathizer, he convinced German intelligence to recruit him as a spy. Without ever setting foot in Britain, Pujol began sending reports to Germany based entirely on information gathered from newspapers, maps, and public sources. To make his reports appear more credible, he invented an entire network of fictional agents across Britain, each with their own personalities, backgrounds, and roles. Over time, he built a detailed imaginary organization that German intelligence believed was real. Eventually, British intelligence discovered his activities and decided to recruit him as a double agent, giving him the codename "Garbo." From that point on, his false network became a powerful tool of deception. He continued to send reports to Germany, mixing harmless truths with carefully crafted misinformation. By the time of the D-Day invasion in 1944, Pujol's network had become one of Germany's most trusted sources. His messages helped convince German commanders that the main Allied invasion would take place away from Normandy, causing them to delay sending reinforcements. Pujol later received awards from both sides, honored by Germany for his "service" and by Britain for his role in the Allied victory, making him one of the few spies to be decorated by opposing forces.

173. Nancy Wake and the Most Wanted Woman in France

Nancy Wake was one of the most active and widely pursued Allied agents operating in occupied France. Originally from New Zealand and later working for British intelligence, she became deeply involved in resistance activities, coordinating sabotage operations and helping Allied forces disrupt German control. Known by the Gestapo as "The White Mouse" because of her ability to evade capture, Wake constantly moved between safe houses, carrying messages, organizing fighters, and helping supply networks operate under occupation. She worked closely with resistance groups, helping them receive weapons, explosives, and instructions dropped by air from Britain. Her work required both physical endurance and constant awareness. At one point, after a communications breakdown, she reportedly cycled over 185 miles (about 300 kilometers) through enemy territory to reestablish contact with her network. Throughout her missions, she lived under the constant threat of arrest, knowing that capture would likely lead to interrogation and execution. Despite being one of the most wanted individuals in France, she managed to survive the war. Her story reflects the scale of civilian involvement in intelligence work, where ordinary individuals took on extraordinary risks, operating in secrecy while contributing directly to military operations.

174. Cicero and the Spy Inside the Embassy

One of the most unusual intelligence breaches of the war took place not on a battlefield but inside the British Embassy in Ankara, Turkey, a country that remained officially neutral for much of the conflict. The man at the center of it was Elyesa Bazna, a valet who worked for the British ambassador. Using his position inside the embassy, he gained access to highly sensitive documents, including reports and diplomatic communications. At night, when the building was quiet, Bazna would secretly open safes, photograph documents, and then return everything to its place before morning. He sold these photographs to German intelligence, which gave him the codename "Cicero." The information he provided included details about Allied planning and discussions, making him one of the most valuable sources the Germans had at the time. However, his story also showed the limits of intelligence. Some German officials distrusted the material, suspecting it might be a British deception, while others failed to act on it effectively. As a result, even though the information was genuine, it didn't always produce the strategic advantage it might have offered. For Bazna, the work was driven partly by money and partly by opportunity, but it carried enormous risk. Had he been discovered, he would likely have been executed. His actions revealed how espionage could occur in unexpected places, where access and timing mattered as much as ideology or loyalty.

175. Odette Sansom and Resistance Under Interrogation

For many agents, the greatest danger came not during their missions, but after capture. Odette Sansom, a British agent working in occupied France, experienced this reality firsthand. She had been sent to help coordinate resistance networks, passing information and supporting operations behind enemy lines. In 1943, she was arrested by German forces after her network was compromised. Following her capture, Odette was subjected to interrogation by the Gestapo. Like many captured agents, she was pressured to reveal information about resistance networks, contacts, and operations. Instead, she attempted to mislead her captors, claiming she was married to a high-ranking British officer, hoping this would make the Germans treat her as a more valuable prisoner rather than execute her immediately. She endured severe treatment, including physical abuse, but refused to provide useful intelligence. Her resistance under interrogation helped protect other members of her network from exposure. Eventually, she was sent to a concentration camp, where conditions were harsh, and survival was uncertain. Odette survived the war, but her experience reflected the reality faced by many agents. Espionage didn't end with capture. For those who were caught, the struggle often continued in interrogation rooms and prison camps, where silence itself became an act of resistance.

176. The Lucy Spy Ring and Intelligence from Within

One of the most mysterious and valuable intelligence networks of the war operated out of neutral Switzerland and became known as the "Lucy Spy Ring." The central figure, Rudolf Roessler, was a German exile who maintained contacts with individuals inside the German military and political system. Through these connections, he received detailed information about German plans, troop movements, and upcoming operations. What made this network unusual was the level of detail and the speed at which information arrived. Reports often reached the Soviet Union with remarkable accuracy, sometimes even before orders had fully been implemented on the battlefield. This intelligence was passed through intermediaries using coded radio transmissions, eventually reaching Soviet commanders. The exact source of Roessler's information remained unclear even after the war. Some believed it came from high-ranking officers who opposed Hitler, while others suspected that parts of the information may have been indirectly influenced by other intelligence operations. Regardless of its origin, the intelligence proved valuable in several campaigns, helping Soviet forces prepare for German actions. For those involved, the risks were extreme. Operating across borders, relying on secret contacts, and transmitting sensitive information meant that discovery could lead to execution. The Lucy Spy Ring demonstrated that some of the most important intelligence didn't come from agents behind enemy lines but from individuals within the enemy's own system.

177. Violette Szabo and the Final Stand

Violette Szabo was one of many agents sent into occupied France to support resistance operations, but her missions placed her in some of the most dangerous situations of the war. Working with British intelligence, she was responsible for coordinating local resistance groups, organizing sabotage, and maintaining communication with Allied command. During her second mission in 1944, shortly after the D-Day landings, Szabo was dropped into central France to help disrupt German movements. At one point, while traveling with resistance fighters, her group was stopped by German forces. Realizing that escape was necessary, she took up a defensive position with a submachine gun, providing covering fire so that others could attempt to flee. She fought until she ran out of ammunition and was eventually captured. Following her arrest, she was interrogated but refused to provide information about her network. She was later deported to a concentration camp, where she was executed in 1945. Szabo's story reflected the reality faced by many agents operating in occupied territories. Missions were often brief, intense, and carried out under constant threat. Capture could come suddenly, and survival was never guaranteed. In many cases, agents continued to resist even after their missions had ended, demonstrating that espionage required not only skill but also extraordinary personal courage.

NINETEEN

The Soldier

At the center of World War II were the soldiers who fought on its many fronts. They endured extreme conditions, from the frozen winters of the Eastern Front to the heat of desert campaigns and the dense terrain of jungle warfare. For many, survival depended on discipline, resilience, and the ability to adapt to constantly changing circumstances. This chapter examines the experiences of those who served, including the realities of combat, the challenges of daily life in the military, and the psychological toll of prolonged warfare. It explores the human dimension of the conflict, focusing on the individuals who carried out orders and faced the direct consequences of the war. It was a war fought not only by nations but also by individuals whose endurance shaped its outcome.

178. Mobilization and the Call to Arms in Europe

In the late summer of 1939, European nations mobilized with a speed that shocked civilian populations. In France, over six million men were called up in just a few weeks. In Germany, the system was even more efficient; by the time they invaded Poland, the *Wehrmacht* (German Defense Force) had 3.7 million men under arms. Unlike the United States' later peacetime draft, most major powers in Europe already had systems of conscription in place. Countries such as Germany, France, and the Soviet Union required young men to register for military service, and in times of crisis, these systems allowed governments to call up large numbers of reservists almost immediately. Many soldiers had already completed basic training during earlier periods of service but had returned to civilian life. Mobilization meant being recalled, sometimes with only a few days' notice, leaving behind jobs, families, and unfinished lives. The transition was abrupt. In Britain, the "calling up" of reservists meant that a man could be working in a bank on Friday and, by Monday, be in uniform, learning to fire a Lee-Enfield rifle. This early period (September 1939 to May 1940) became known as the "Phoney War" or *Sitzkrieg* (Sitting War), where soldiers sat in the Maginot Line or the Siegfried Line, dealing with boredom and mud rather than bullets. The process of recruitment and selection varied by country. Some men were assigned based on age, physical condition, and prior experience, while others were placed where manpower was most urgently needed. Not all were sent directly to combat roles. Some were assigned to engineering units, transport services, or support roles essential to sustaining armies. Despite this structure, mobilization often felt rushed and disorganized. Equipment shortages were common, particularly in the early months, and not all units were fully prepared. For many, the transition from civilian life to military service was abrupt, marked by uncertainty about how long the war would last and what their role would be.

179. Training, Equipment, and the First Days in Uniform

Once mobilized, soldiers entered a period of training intended to prepare them for combat, though the available time varied widely. A typical soldier's burden was staggering, as they were required to carry everything needed for survival on their backs. A British soldier's "Full Marching Order" weighed about sixty pounds (twenty-seven kilograms), while a German *Landser* (infantryman) carried nearly seventy pounds (thirty-two kilograms). This weight included the standard rifle, most of which were bolt-action designs, such as the German Karabiner 98k or the Soviet Mosin-Nagant, which required the soldier to manually cycle a bolt after every shot. Training emphasized discipline in the smallest details: keeping boots greased, packing gear to balance the load, and maintaining weapons amid mud and dust. These routines weren't only practical but also helped create a sense of order and control in a vast military system where soldiers often understood little about the larger strategy or the intensity of the combat that lay ahead.

180. "Fit," "Deferred," or Rejected: The U.S. Peacetime Draft and Mass Screening

Before the United States entered combat, Washington began building an army through the Selective Training and Service Act, signed on September

16, 1940: the first U.S. peacetime draft. Men were registered, classified, and either called up, deferred, or rejected. What made this system feel personal wasn't the law; it was the examination line. Induction centers ran recruits through medical and sometimes psychiatric screening that could be invasive and humiliating, with doctors deciding if someone was "fit" for combat, better suited for support work, or unfit entirely. Standards also shifted as manpower demands grew: early strictness could keep out men for issues like poor eyesight or dental problems, but by 1942, the military increasingly accepted "fixable" problems through treatments (glasses, dental work, etc.) because the war was expanding faster than ideal recruitment pools. Meanwhile, classification wasn't just a bureaucracy; it shaped lives: some men felt stigma if rejected, others felt guilt if deferred while friends shipped out, and many entered service convinced it would be brief, until the war made "brief" impossible.

181. Segregated Service and Fighting Two Wars at Once

After the Selective Training and Service Act was introduced by the United States, Black Americans were both allowed and pressured to serve, but they entered a military that was rigidly segregated, meaning Black and white soldiers were kept in separate units and lived in separate housing. Training bases often mirrored the "Jim Crow" laws of the era, which enforced racial separation and meant that Black recruits faced routine harassment and were often restricted to manual labor instead of being given combat roles. This created a bitter contradiction: men were being asked to fight against fascism (a system of government that suppresses freedom) in Europe while they were being treated as second-class citizens in their own country. In 1942, Black newspapers and civil rights leaders launched the Double V Campaign. The "Two Vs" stood for Victory over enemies abroad and Victory over racism at home. This movement encouraged Black Americans to serve their country while simultaneously demanding the full rights of citizenship they were fighting to protect. As the need for more soldiers grew, new opportunities slowly opened up. Specialized units proved their skill in battle, such as the Tuskegee Airmen, the first Black military pilots, who flew dangerous escort missions over the Mediterranean. On the ground, the 761st Tank Battalion (known as the "Black Panthers") entered combat in 1944 and earned high praise for their bravery in the face of the enemy. For these soldiers, the war was a "double struggle," surviving the dangers of the battlefield while carrying the added burden of serving a system that demanded their sacrifice while still questioning their humanity.

182. Orders, Ranks, and the Invisible Structure of Command

Once a civilian entered military service, he became part of a vast structure that extended far beyond the battlefield. The army was organized as a clear hierarchy, designed to control large numbers of men across different fronts and conditions. At the lowest level was the private, responsible for carrying out orders, maintaining equipment, and functioning as part of a small unit. Around ten to twelve soldiers formed a squad, led by a corporal or sergeant, who was often the most direct authority a soldier experienced. Several squads formed a platoon under a lieutenant, while multiple platoons made up a company commanded by a captain. These companies combined into battalions and regiments, and eventually into divisions, corps, and entire armies, each level increasing in size, distance from the front, and responsibility. Above the battlefield, command became more strategic. Generals coordinated movements across entire regions, while national headquarters planned campaigns that could involve millions of soldiers. Civilian leaders, such as presidents or prime ministers, formally held ultimate authority, deciding overall war aims and approving major operations. This structure was designed to create order, ensuring that instructions could be passed from the highest level down to individual soldiers. However, communication wasn't always smooth. Orders could be delayed, misunderstood, or based on outdated information. A decision made far from the front might not reflect the reality on the ground. For soldiers, the system often felt distant and abstract. Most never saw beyond their immediate officers, yet their actions were shaped by a chain of command that stretched far above them, connecting individual experience to the larger direction of the war.

183. Uniforms, Helmets, and the Limits of Protection

A soldier's uniform was designed for function rather than comfort, serving as his only shelter and shield against both the enemy and the elements. Standard issue typically included a wool jacket, trousers, boots, a helmet, and webbing, a system of canvas straps and belts used to carry ammunition, water, and tools. While these items offered some protection, they were limited in what they could do; for instance, steel helmets, such as the German Stahlhelm or the American M1, were mainly designed to protect the head from shrapnel (small, jagged metal fragments from explosions) and falling debris rather than direct gunfire at close range. Boots were perhaps the most critical piece of equipment a soldier owned, as poor foot care could take a man out of action faster than a bullet. Long marches, wet conditions, and freezing weather made specialized footwear essential, from the hobnailed Ammo Boots of the British to the high-topped jackboots of the German infantry. However, uniforms had to adapt to environments they weren't always designed for, such as the thin cotton "drill" uniforms issued to the Afrika Korps for the desert or the thick, padded Telogreika jackets worn by Soviet troops to survive the Siberian cold. Because supplies weren't always consistent, soldiers frequently modified their clothing by adding layers of newspaper for insulation, cutting fabric to make improvised gloves, or using captured enemy gear, like the highly prized Soviet fur caps, to improve their chances of survival. Over time, uniforms became worn, patched, and encrusted with the mud of the front, reflecting the brutal conditions of service. Protection remained partial at best, and every soldier understood that while his equipment could help deflect a piece of rubble or a distant fragment, it offered no guarantee of survival against the heavy machinery of modern war.

184. Bread Bags, Field Kitchens, and the Reality of Rations

As armies began to move, soldiers quickly learned that food was the engine of the army, essential for maintaining both the physical strength and the morale needed to continue fighting. When supply lines functioned properly, meals were prepared by field kitchens, which followed units to provide hot food such as soup, stew, or coffee; German soldiers even nicknamed their horse-drawn field kitchen the "Goulash Cannon" (*Gulaschkanone*). These hot meals offered a brief, precious sense of normal life, but during rapid advances or retreats, these kitchens often couldn't reach the front, forcing soldiers to rely on iron rations and whatever they could carry in small bags attached to their equipment. The composition of these rations varied by nation: American troops primarily used the C-Ration, a heavy canned meal of meat and beans, or the K-Ration, a lighter, waxed-paper pack designed for paratroopers, while in the Soviet Red Army, the staple was *kasha* (a thick buckwheat porridge) and a heavy, dark rye bread that was often so hard it had to be soaked in soup just to be edible. Beyond food, water remained an ongoing concern; canteens often ran dry, and when clean sources were unavailable, soldiers were forced to drink from rivers, puddles, or melted snow, which frequently led to debilitating illnesses. To supplement these meager supplies, troops often gathered local resources, took food from farms, or traded with civilians, because food was ultimately more than just sustenance: it was a psychological lifeline, and the memory of intense hunger stayed with them as clearly as the battles themselves.

185. Cold, Mud, and the Return of Trench Conditions

Although World War II is often remembered for fast-moving battles, many soldiers found themselves in conditions that resembled the trench warfare of the previous war. As fighting slowed in certain areas, especially during the winter months of 1939–1940, troops were forced to dig defensive positions and remain in place for extended periods. These positions were often little more than shallow foxholes or hastily constructed trenches. Rain turned the ground into thick mud that clung to boots and soaked clothing. In colder regions, water froze overnight, making movement difficult and increasing the risk of frostbite. Soldiers slept in these conditions. often without proper shelter, using blankets or whatever materials they could find for protection. Keeping dry became nearly impossible. Wet clothing led to skin infections and "trench foot," a painful condition caused by prolonged exposure to moisture and cold. These environments were physically and mentally exhausting. Soldiers had to remain alert for enemy attacks while dealing with discomfort that never fully went away.

186. The First Encounter with Combat

For many soldiers, the transition from training to combat was sudden and disorienting. Days or weeks of marching could end in moments of violence that felt overwhelming and difficult to process. The first experience of combat was often confusing rather than dramatic. Visibility was limited, orders were shouted or misunderstood, and the source of danger wasn't always clear. Gunfire could come from unseen positions, and explosions could occur without warning. Many soldiers later described their first engagement as chaotic and fragmented. Some focused on simple tasks, loading a weapon, following a command, and staying close to others while trying to manage fear. Training provided basic instructions, but it couldn't fully prepare individuals for the noise, speed, and unpredictability of real combat. Reactions varied. Some froze, some acted automatically, and others relied heavily on the presence of more experienced soldiers. Afterward, the psychological impact often remained. The realization that death was immediate and constant changed how soldiers approached everything that followed. The first encounter wasn't just a battle; it was a shift in perception, in which the abstract idea of war became a direct, personal experience.

187. Replacements: The Most Dangerous Day at the Front

New soldiers didn't usually arrive with their unit. Instead, they were sent forward as individual replacements, often at night, handed over to a squad they had never met. Veterans viewed them with a mixture of pity and distance. Newcomers were called "replacements," "fresh meat," or simply "new guys," and many weren't expected to last long. The first hours were often the most dangerous. Replacements didn't yet know the terrain, the routines, or the instincts that kept others alive. They might stand up at the wrong time, expose themselves, or misunderstand orders under fire. Veterans sometimes avoided learning their names immediately, knowing that many would be killed within days. This created a quiet divide within units. Survival wasn't only about skill but also about experience, and experience was measured in days. A soldier who lasted a week was already considered lucky. Those who survived longer became part of the group, but the constant arrival of replacements meant that units were always changing, always losing, and always rebuilding.

188. Desert Heat, Sand, and Thirst

In North Africa, soldiers fought in an environment that could be as dangerous as combat itself. The desert stretched across vast regions, including parts of the Sahara, where temperatures often reached around 110 degrees Fahrenheit (43 degrees Celsius) during the day and dropped close to freezing at night. These extreme shifts placed constant stress on the body. Soldiers suffered from heat exhaustion under the intense sun and from cold exposure after sunset, often without adequate shelter. Shade was rare, and even metal equipment could become too hot to touch. Prolonged exposure led to burns, dehydration, and fatigue, reducing combat effectiveness even before contact with the enemy. Water was the most critical resource. Supplies had to be transported over long distances, leading to frequent shortages. Rations could be as low as one pint (about half a liter) per day, which had to cover drinking, cooking, and basic hygiene. Washing was often impossible, leaving soldiers covered in dust and sweat. Dehydration became a constant threat, affecting concentration, strength, and decision-making. Food was also affected by the environment, which was often dry and salty, with sand frequently contaminating meals. In this setting, survival depended on endurance as much as training, as the desert itself constantly weakened those fighting within it.

189. Sand, Machinery, and Improvisation in the Desert War

Beyond heat and thirst, sand became a persistent enemy that affected nearly every aspect of warfare. Fine desert dust penetrated weapons, watches, radios, and vehicles, often causing equipment to fail. Rifles jammed easily, and tank engines suffered heavy damage as sand acted like an abrasive, wearing down moving parts. Maintenance became a daily necessity, with soldiers repeatedly cleaning weapons and machinery just to keep them operational. Goggles and scarves were used to protect eyes and lungs, particularly during sandstorms, which could reduce visibility to almost nothing and bring operations to a halt. With little natural cover, soldiers relied on vehicles or shallow dugouts for protection from both the sun and enemy observation. The open terrain made concealment difficult, making movement easily spotted and often dangerous. To cope with these harsh conditions, soldiers improvised. One example was the British "Benghazi Burner," a simple stove made from a biscuit tin filled with sand and petrol, used to heat water for tea. Tea became more than a drink; it was a routine that provided comfort and a sense of normality. In North Africa, survival required constant adaptation, as soldiers learned to manage not only the enemy but also the environment itself, which shaped how battles were fought and how long men could endure.

190. Frozen Fronts and the "White Death"

On the Eastern Front, the winter of 1941 brought some of the coldest temperatures recorded in decades, dropping to around minus forty degrees Fahrenheit (minus forty degrees Celsius). This period, often referred to as "General Winter," became a decisive factor in the fighting. The cold affected not only soldiers but also the technology on which modern armies depended. Synthetic oils used in engines and weapons froze solid, preventing tanks, trucks, and artillery from functioning. Machine guns and rifles could jam or fail completely, leaving soldiers unable to fire when needed. German crews often had to improvise simply to keep equipment operational. Fires were lit beneath vehicles to warm engines, and weapons were cleaned constantly in attempts to prevent freezing. Despite these efforts, many machines became unusable. The failure of equipment slowed movement, disrupted supply lines, and reduced the effectiveness of coordinated attacks. In a war that relied heavily on mechanization, the environment itself became a powerful opponent, limiting both mobility and firepower. The cold turned technology from an advantage into a liability, showing that even advanced military systems could be rendered ineffective by extreme conditions.

191. Survival, Frostbite, and the "White Death"

For soldiers, survival in the extreme cold depended on clothing, adaptation, and endurance. The difference in equipment between armies had serious consequences. Soviet troops were often issued valenki, thick felt boots that provided insulation and allowed circulation, helping prevent frostbite. German soldiers, however, wore tight leather jackboots with metal hobnails, which conducted cold and restricted blood flow. During the first winter alone, over 100,000 German troops suffered frostbite, many losing toes, fingers, or entire limbs. Soldiers improvised constantly to survive. Boots and uniforms were stuffed with newspaper, straw, or animal fur to add insulation. Even simple mistakes could be dangerous. Touching metal with bare skin could cause it to freeze instantly, tearing flesh away when pulled. The landscape itself created additional hazards. Snowstorms produced "whiteout" conditions, erasing visibility and making navigation nearly impossible. Units could become disoriented, leading to separation or ambush. The most feared threat was hypothermia, often called the "White Death." Exhausted soldiers could become numb and disoriented, experiencing a false sense of warmth before losing consciousness. In the absolute exhaustion of the front, thousands of men succumbed to a fatal lethargy, a deceptive feeling of warmth that precedes freezing, falling asleep in their foxholes and simply never waking up.

192. Jungle Warfare and the "Green Hell"

In the Pacific, soldiers encountered an environment so hostile that it became known as the "Green Hell." Unlike the open deserts of North Africa, the jungle was dense, enclosed, and constantly alive with moisture and sound. In places like Guadalcanal and New Guinea, humidity often reached ninety percent, with rainfall exceeding 200 inches (508 centimeters) per year. Rain wasn't an occasional event but a constant presence, soaking clothing, weapons, and supplies day after day. Nothing stayed dry. Uniforms clung to the body, boots remained wet, and equipment rusted quickly. Even after the rain stopped, the thick canopy of the jungle trapped moisture, preventing anything from fully drying. Visibility was extremely limited. Dense vegetation, vines, and thick undergrowth often reduced sightlines to less than ten feet (about three meters). Soldiers could move only slowly, cutting through foliage or following narrow paths. This created an atmosphere of constant tension.

The enemy could be just a few meters away, completely hidden by the jungle. Gunfire often erupted suddenly at close range, leaving little time to react. The noise of insects, birds, and the environment itself masked movement, making it difficult to detect approaching forces. Combat in the jungle was often confused and fragmented, and fought at extremely close distances. Movement through the jungle was exhausting. The ground was often muddy, uneven, and covered in thick vegetation. In some areas, soldiers had to push through kunai grass, which had sharp edges that cut exposed skin. Elsewhere, mud could reach knee or even thigh depth, making each step physically demanding. Carrying equipment under these conditions quickly led to exhaustion. Supply lines were difficult to maintain, meaning that food, ammunition, and medical supplies weren't always reliable. Units often operated in isolation, cut off from immediate support.

193. Disease, Survival, and Psychological Strain

The environment itself caused severe physical damage. Constant moisture led to conditions such as "jungle rot," a painful infection where the skin broke down into open sores due to prolonged exposure to wet conditions. Feet were particularly vulnerable. Soldiers' boots could rot within weeks, and skin that remained wet for long periods became soft, cracked, and easily infected. This condition, similar to trench foot, could disable soldiers even without combat injuries. Clothing wore out quickly, and replacement supplies weren't always available, forcing soldiers to endure deteriorating gear. Disease was one of the most significant threats. Mosquitoes thrived in the warm, wet conditions, spreading illnesses such as malaria and dengue fever. In some units, disease caused far more casualties than combat, sometimes five times as many. Soldiers were required to take Atabrine tablets to prevent malaria, but these caused side effects, including turning the skin a noticeable yellow color. Some soldiers avoided taking the medication due to these effects, increasing their risk of illness. Fever, weakness, and prolonged recovery times weakenedentire units. The psychological impact of jungle warfare was also significant. The constant noise, limited visibility, and ever-present threat of ambush created a sense of isolation and uncertainty. Soldiers could rarely see the larger battlefield and often had little understanding of their position relative to the enemy. The jungle removed the sense of distance that existed in other theaters of war. Combat was immediate, personal, and unpredictable.

194. Mountains, Mud, and the "Vertical War"

The Italian campaign quickly devolved into a grueling "Vertical War" as soldiers were forced to fight their way up the jagged spine of the Apennine Mountains. This geography provided a massive advantage to the German defenders, who occupied the "high ground," turning every mountain peak into a natural fortress. Allied troops, including Americans, British, Canadians, and Poles, had to haul heavy machine guns, mortars, and ammunition crates up sixty-degree slopes on their backs, often while under direct observation and fire from German snipers and artillery positioned thousands of feet above them. The misery of the terrain was multiplied by the weather, specifically the Italian version of "Rasputitsa," a relentless rainy season that transformed the volcanic soil into a thick, glue-like mud. This "mountain muck" was so deep that it swallowed Jeeps up to their axles and rendered tanks useless on the narrow, winding valley roads. Consequently, the high-tech Allied armies had to revert to older methods. Mules became the only reliable form of transport, carrying food, ammunition, and water up steep slopes and bringing wounded men back down. A single division might require over 1,000 mules just to remain supplied, showing how modern warfare could still depend on pre-industrial solutions in extreme terrain.

195. Exposure, Fortifications, and Attrition

During the brutal winter of 1944, the fighting reached its most stagnant and punishing phase. Because the rocky ground was too hard to dig into for traditional foxholes, soldiers were forced to live in sangars, dry-stone breastworks, or small "nests" built above ground from loose rocks. These offered limited protection against small-arms fire but provided almost no shelter from the environment. Men lived for weeks on exposed mountain peaks, enduring freezing rain, snow, and relentless winds that cut through clothing and made rest difficult. In this environment, progress was painfully slow. Military advances were no longer measured in miles but in individual ridges, hills, and ruined farmhouses. Each position often had a number, and capturing a single hill could cost hundreds of lives. Even after taking it, soldiers frequently found themselves facing another, higher position still held by the enemy. This constant uphill struggle turned the Italian campaign into a war of attrition that exhausted even experienced units. The landscape itself became a defensive weapon, demonstrating that terrain and weather could be as decisive as any army or technology.

196. Lice, Latrines, and the Spread of Disease

Life at the front exposed soldiers to constant health risks that weren't directly related to combat. Hygiene was difficult to maintain, especially in static positions where water was limited. Lice, small parasitic insects that live in clothing and bedding, spread rapidly among troops. They caused itching and skin irritation and, in some cases, transmitted diseases such as typhus. Soldiers often spent time picking lice from their uniforms or holding clothes over flames in an attempt to kill them. Sanitation was another major problem. Latrines were usually simple pits dug into the ground, often close to living areas. If not properly managed, they attracted insects and spread contamination. Combined with poor water quality, this led to outbreaks of illness, including dysentery, which caused severe dehydration and weakness. Medical care existed, but resources were limited, and treatment wasn't always immediate. These conditions reminded soldiers that danger didn't only come from enemy fire. Disease, discomfort, and poor hygiene were constant threats that affected entire units.

197. Artillery, Noise, and the Constant Threat from Above

One of the most defining features of the battlefield wasn't direct fighting but artillery fire. Large guns positioned far behind the front lines fired shells over long distances, meaning soldiers could be targeted without ever seeing the enemy. These shells produced explosions that caused both physical destruction and psychological strain. The sound of artillery was constant. Incoming shells could be heard as a distant whistle or sudden rush before impact, giving soldiers only seconds or no warning at all. Explosions threw dirt, metal fragments, and debris into the air, making even well-prepared positions unsafe. The unpredictability made it difficult to feel secure. A position that seemed safe one moment could be destroyed the next. Living under artillery fire created ongoing stress. Sleep was interrupted, communication was difficult, and movement became dangerous. Even when not actively under attack, the possibility of bombardment remained. Over time, this environment affected concentration and morale. Soldiers learned to recognize different sounds and react quickly, but the strain of constant exposure never fully disappeared. The battlefield wasn't only a place of action but also one of waiting, listening, and enduring.

198. Rumors, Misinformation, and the War of Stories

Most soldiers knew very little about the larger war. Information was limited, delayed, or deliberately controlled by high-level commanders. In this vacuum of facts, rumors, often called "latrine rumors" by the troops, spread with lightning speed and were frequently believed as gospel truth. Stories circulated constantly: that the war would end by Christmas, that reinforcements were arriving, or that the enemy was about to surrender. Conversely, dark rumors of secret weapons or massive defeats could shatter a unit's morale in hours. Soldiers relied on fragments to build their worldview: overheard conversations between officers, heavily censored letters from home, captured enemy newspapers they couldn't fully read, or "scuttlebutt" from passing transport units. These pieces were almost always incomplete or incorrect, but they offered a desperate sense of control in a situation where the truth was a luxury. One of the most famous examples of this "War of Stories" occurred during the Battle of the Bulge in 1944, involving "Operation Greif." Under the command of Otto Skorzeny, a small group of German soldiers dressed in captured American uniforms, driving American Jeeps, and speaking English, were sent behind U.S. lines to cause chaos. While their military impact was limited, the rumors they sparked were devastating. Word spread among American troops that thousands of German "spies" were everywhere, led by an elite team tasked with assassinating General Dwight D. Eisenhower. This single rumor paralyzed Allied movement for days. To catch the "impostors," American soldiers began setting up roadblocks and began "testing" each other with questions only a "real" American would know, such as "Who is Mickey Mouse's girlfriend?" or "What is the capital of Illinois?" Even high-ranking officers were detained; General Omar Bradley was famously held for a short time by his own men because he correctly identified the capital of Illinois as Springfield, but the guard mistakenly believed it was Chicago. These stories show that on the battlefield, a well-placed rumor could be just as disruptive as a direct artillery strike.

199. Wounds, Shock, and Immediate Survival

When a soldier was hit, survival depended on what happened in the first few minutes. Wounds varied widely, from small fragments to severe injuries caused by artillery, which was responsible for many of the most serious casualties. Soldiers were trained to carry basic first-aid kits, often including bandages and morphine syrettes, small pre-filled tubes used to inject pain relief. If a man was able, he was expected to treat himself or assist others nearby. The greatest immediate danger was often not the wound itself, but shock and blood loss. Shock could cause the body to shut down, even if the injury wasn't fatal. Fellow soldiers played a crucial role, applying pressure to wounds, offering reassurance, and trying to move the injured to safer positions. This was often done under fire, where helping someone could expose others to the same danger. Training emphasized speed and calm, but in reality, conditions were rarely controlled. Noise, fear, and confusion made even simple actions difficult. A wounded soldier's chances depended heavily on how quickly help arrived. In many cases, survival was determined not by the severity of the injury but by how long it took to reach medical care.

200. Fear, Fatigue, and the Limits of Endurance

Beyond physical danger, soldiers faced a constant mental strain that was often harder to measure but just as damaging. Fear wasn't limited to moments of combat. It existed before, during, and after engagements, shaped by uncertainty and the awareness that danger could come at any time. Even in quiet periods, soldiers remained alert, listening for distant sounds that might signal an attack. Fatigue made this pressure more difficult to manage. Sleep was often interrupted by noise, duty shifts, or the need to remain ready. Long periods without proper rest reduced concentration and slowed reactions, increasing the risk of mistakes. Hunger, cold, and illness added to this exhaustion. Over time, these conditions affected judgment and emotional stability. Some soldiers experienced what was then called "combat fatigue," where the mind became overwhelmed by stress. Symptoms could include shaking, withdrawal, confusion, or an inability to respond to orders. Armies developed systems to manage this, often removing affected soldiers from the front temporarily. However, not all cases were recognized or treated. For many, the pressure built gradually, showing that the battlefield tested not only the body but also the limits of human endurance.

201. Discipline, Punishment, and Control

Military discipline remained strict, even in combat zones. Soldiers were expected to follow orders immediately, maintain equipment, and remain at their posts regardless of danger. Failure to do so could result in punishment, ranging from loss of pay and duties to imprisonment or, in extreme cases, execution. Desertion (abandoning one's post) was one of the most serious offenses. Some armies carried out executions as a warning to others, particularly in the early years of the war. More commonly, punishment took the form of exhausting labor, confinement, or reassignment to dangerous duties. However, enforcement varied. Experienced officers often understood the limits of endurance and sometimes chose to overlook minor violations, knowing that survival depended on morale as much as strict obedience. In other cases, discipline was harshly enforced to maintain control amid chaotic conditions. For soldiers, discipline was both necessary and feared. It provided structure, but it also meant that the line between survival and punishment could be very thin.

202. Camaraderie, Routine, and Small Acts of Normal Life

Despite the harsh conditions, soldiers developed ways to cope with daily life at the front. One of the most important was camaraderie. Living, working, and facing danger together created strong bonds within small groups. Soldiers often relied on each other not only for support in combat but also for maintaining morale during quieter moments. Routine also played a key role. Cleaning equipment, preparing meals, standing guard, and maintaining positions provided structure in an otherwise unpredictable environment. Even simple tasks helped create a sense of control. Humor was another common response. Jokes, stories, and shared experiences allowed soldiers to release tension, even in difficult situations. These small elements, friendship and routine, helped soldiers manage the emotional demands of war. While they didn't remove the dangers, they provided moments of stability, allowing individuals to continue functioning in an environment where normal life had largely disappeared.

203. Nicknames, Identity, and Losing the Individual

As soldiers settled into units, individual identity often shifted. Nicknames replaced formal names, based on personality, appearance, or origin. These names were used more frequently than official ones, especially within small groups. Uniforms, routines, and shared experiences created a sense of collective identity. Soldiers became part of a unit first, individuals second. Personal differences were less important than reliability and cooperation. Over time, the war could blur individuality. Soldiers were known by their role, their position, or their function within the group. This helped units operate efficiently, but it also changed how individuals saw themselves. Identity became tied to survival and belonging. Being part of the group was essential, both practically and emotionally.

204. Letters, Censorship, and the Lifeline to Home

For most soldiers, letters were the primary connection to life beyond the battlefield. Postal systems were organized on a massive scale to move mail between the front and home, often across continents and active war zones. In many armies, soldiers were encouraged to write regularly, and mail was delivered whenever conditions allowed. Some units received letters weekly, while others, especially in remote or active combat zones, might wait weeks or even months. Letters were both personal and controlled. Military authorities censored outgoing and incoming mail to prevent sensitive information from being revealed. Soldiers weren't allowed to mention locations, movements, or details that could compromise security. As a result, many letters focused on everyday topics, health, weather, and small routines, while avoiding the realities of combat. Families at home often received a version of the war that was quieter and less dangerous than what soldiers actually experienced. Writing letters served an important emotional purpose. It allowed soldiers to maintain a sense of identity beyond their role in the war. Receiving a letter could improve morale, while long periods without news could create anxiety and isolation. Some soldiers carried letters with them, reading them repeatedly during quiet moments. In a setting where uncertainty was constant, communication with home became one of the few stable and meaningful connections they could rely on.

205. Alcohol, Cigarettes, and Small Escapes

In a life defined by danger, discomfort, and uncertainty, soldiers relied on small habits to cope. Among the most common were alcohol and cigarettes. These weren't luxuries in the traditional sense; they were part of daily life, used to manage stress, fatigue, and fear. Cigarettes were especially widespread. Many armies issued them as part of regular rations, alongside food and ammunition. Soldiers smoked during rest periods, after meals, and sometimes even in combat zones when conditions allowed. Lighting a cigarette could mark a moment of calm, however brief, or provide something to do while waiting. It also became a form of social exchange. Cigarettes were traded, shared, and used to build connections between soldiers. For some, smoking became a constant habit, a way to steady nerves or pass time in an environment where little was under their control. Alcohol served a different purpose. When available, it was often issued in controlled amounts, such as rum for British troops or vodka for Soviet soldiers. These rations were intended to boost morale, provide warmth in cold conditions, or help soldiers relax after long periods of tension. In some cases, alcohol was consumed before or after combat, dulling fear or offering temporary relief from the realities of the battlefield. Access to alcohol varied. In rear areas or occupied regions, soldiers sometimes obtained additional supplies through trade or requisition. However, strict discipline was usually enforced, and excessive drinking was often punished, especially if it affected performance. Despite this, alcohol remained a common part of military life, particularly during moments away from direct combat. Both cigarettes and alcohol functioned as forms of escape.

206. Death, Burial, and Living Among the Fallen

Death was a constant presence on the battlefield, and soldiers were often exposed to it in ways that were difficult to avoid. Bodies could remain in the open for extended periods, especially in areas of heavy fighting where movement was dangerous. This created a situation where soldiers had to continue their duties while surrounded by the remains of those who had fallen. Whenever possible, units attempted to bury the dead. These burials were often simple and carried out quickly, using shallow graves marked with temporary signs such as helmets, rifles, or wooden crosses. In some cases, identification tags were collected to record who had died, while personal belongings were gathered for sending home. However, conditions didn't always allow for proper burial, and many soldiers remained where they had fallen until later recovery. Living in proximity to death affected morale and mental state. It served as a constant reminder of risk and loss, reinforcing the reality of the situation. Soldiers developed ways to cope, sometimes through routine, silence, or emotional distance. The presence of death wasn't an isolated event but an ongoing part of daily life at the front.

207. Missing, Prisoners, and the Uncertainty of Fate

Not all soldiers who disappeared in battle were confirmed dead. Many were listed as missing, leaving families and units uncertain about their fate. In the confusion of combat, it was often difficult to determine what had happened. A soldier might be separated from their unit, captured, or killed without immediate confirmation. This uncertainty could last for months or years. Capture brought a different set of challenges. Prisoners of war were removed from the battlefield, but their conditions depended on where they were held and how they were treated. Some camps provided basic shelter, food, and medical care, while others were marked by shortages and harsh conditions. Prisoners often faced hunger, illness, and long periods of inactivity, along with uncertainty about when or if they would be released. For those who remained at the front, the knowledge that capture or disappearance was possible added another layer of tension. War didn't always provide clear outcomes. Survival, death, or captivity could all occur without warning, leaving both soldiers and their families dealing with uncertainty long after the fighting had moved on.

208. POW Cages, Stalags, and the Slow Violence of Captivity

Between 1940 and 1945, many British and Commonwealth soldiers became prisoners during major defeats in France, Greece/Crete, and North Africa, often after chaotic surrenders, encirclements, or being cut off from evacuation routes. Many described capture as a shock: weapons taken, identity reduced to a number, then forced marches or transport in crowded trains toward camps across German-occupied Europe. Camps were commonly divided into Stalags (for enlisted men) and Oflags (for officers). Under the 1929 Geneva Convention, enlisted prisoners could be required to work (often farm or industrial labor), while officers were generally not compelled to do so, though reality varied by location and conditions. Even when treatment was "lawful" by wartime standards, hunger, boredom, lice, and exhaustion were constant. Escapes happened, but many prisoners were simply too weak, too watched, or too far from safe borders to risk it, so survival became a daily discipline of routine, makeshift education, and waiting.

209. Rotation, Leave, and Moments Away from the Front

Despite the constant demands of war, most armies recognized that soldiers couldn't remain on the front line indefinitely. Over time, systems developed to rotate units out of combat for short periods of rest. These breaks could take place in rear areas, away from immediate danger, where soldiers were given time to recover physically and mentally. Conditions in these areas varied. Some provided basic comforts such as hot food, medical care, and the opportunity to sleep without interruption. Others were little more than safer zones, still exposed to occasional danger. Even limited rest could make a significant difference, allowing soldiers to clean their equipment, wash, and regain strength. Leave, when granted, allowed soldiers to return home for a brief period. This created a sharp contrast between the front and civilian life. Some found comfort in familiar surroundings, while others struggled to adjust, knowing they would soon return to combat. The experience could feel temporary and distant from the realities of war. These breaks didn't remove the pressures of conflict, but they provided moments of relief. They allowed soldiers to continue functioning over long periods, offering a brief return to normal life before facing the front again.

210. The End of War and the Return to Civilian Life

When the war ended in 1945, the experience of soldiers didn't simply stop. For many, the transition back to civilian life was gradual and uncertain. Demobilization (the process of releasing soldiers from service) took time, and not all units returned home immediately. Some remained in occupied territories, while others waited months for transport to become available. Returning home brought its own challenges. Soldiers had spent years in structured, high-pressure environments, and adjusting to civilian life required a different set of skills. Routines that had once defined daily life were gone, and the sense of purpose tied to military service was often difficult to replace. Physical injuries were visible, but psychological effects were less obvious. Some veterans struggled with memories of combat, loss, and prolonged stress. Others found it difficult to communicate their experiences to those who had not been at the front. At the same time, there was a sense of relief that the conflict had ended. Families were reunited, and societies began rebuilding. The end of the war marked a transition not just for nations but also for individuals who had lived through it. The experience of being a soldier didn't disappear with peace. It remained part of their lives long after the fighting had stopped.

TWENTY

Medical Survival and Innovation

World War II forced rapid advancements in medicine as doctors and scientists worked to treat injuries on a scale never before encountered. New techniques, equipment, and procedures were developed in response to the urgent need to save lives, often under extremely difficult conditions. This chapter explores the medical challenges of the war, from battlefield treatment and evacuation systems to the development of new drugs and surgical methods. It highlights how necessity drove innovation, leading to breakthroughs that would influence medicine long after the war had ended.

211. First Aid, Field Surgery, and the Race Against Time

At the beginning of the war, survival for a wounded soldier depended less on advanced medicine and more on speed and organization. Most armies relied on systems developed during World War I, where the goal was to stabilize a soldier quickly and move him away from the front as fast as possible. Every soldier carried a basic field dressing and, in some cases, morphine to control pain and bleeding immediately after injury. The first stage of care usually took place at a regimental aid post, often located just behind the front line. These were small, makeshift stations, sometimes in tents, barns, or damaged buildings, where medics worked under constant pressure. Conditions were rarely sterile. Mud, blood, and debris were common, and supplies were limited. Doctors focused on immediate survival: stopping bleeding, preventing shock, and preparing the wounded for evacuation. From there, soldiers were moved further back to field dressing stations and field hospitals, where more complex procedures could be performed. However, getting a wounded soldier to these locations was often dangerous and slow. Stretcher-bearers had to carry men across open ground, sometimes under fire, or wait for vehicles that might not arrive quickly. Even in these difficult conditions, the system saved many lives. What mattered most was time. The faster a wounded soldier reached medical care, the greater his chances of survival, making speed the most important factor in early wartime medicine.

212. Blood Transfusions and the Creation of Wartime Blood Banks

One of the most important medical advances during the early years of the war was the development of large-scale blood transfusion systems. Severe blood loss was one of the leading causes of death on the battlefield, and earlier wars had shown that replacing lost blood could dramatically improve survival. During World War II, this idea was expanded into organized national systems. In Britain, doctors such as Janet Vaughan helped establish one of the first large-scale blood banks. Blood was collected from civilian donors, carefully stored, and transported to military hospitals. By 1940, refrigerated blood supplies were being sent to treat casualties during air raids and on overseas fronts. This allowed wounded soldiers to receive transfusions even far from major hospitals. The United States developed similar systems, with a particular focus on blood plasma. Plasma, the liquid component of blood, could be dried, stored for long periods, and reconstituted when needed. Unlike whole blood, it didn't require strict matching of blood types, making it easier to use in emergency situations. This made plasma especially valuable in forward medical units, where time and conditions were critical. The introduction of transfusions significantly improved battlefield survival rates. Soldiers who might previously have died from shock could now be stabilized long enough to reach surgery. However, challenges remained. Blood had to be kept at controlled temperatures, supplies could be limited, and mishandling could be dangerous. Despite these risks, the development of blood banks marked a major turning point.

213. The Arrival of Penicillin and the Fight Against Infection

At the beginning of the war, infection was often more dangerous than the original wound. Even a minor injury could become fatal if bacteria entered the body. Dirt, fabric, and metal fragments carried into wounds created ideal conditions for infection, and without effective antibiotics, doctors relied on older methods such as cleaning, draining, and applying antiseptics. Despite these efforts, diseases like gangrene (tissue death) and sepsis (blood poisoning) were common, and amputation was often the only way to save a life. The introduction of penicillin changed this reality. First discovered in 1928, penicillin wasn't widely available until the early 1940s, when scientists in Britain and the United States developed methods to produce it on a large scale. By 1943, it began reaching frontline medical units, and by 1944, it was widely used by Allied forces. Penicillin works by killing bacteria that cause infections, allowing wounds to heal more effectively. For the first time, doctors could treat infections directly rather than just managing their symptoms. This reduced the need for amputations and dramatically improved survival rates, particularly for soldiers with severe injuries. However, early supplies were limited. Doctors often had to decide which patients would receive the drug, prioritizing those most likely to survive. In some cases, penicillin was even extracted from patients' urine and reused, reflecting how valuable it was. The widespread use of penicillin marked a major shift in wartime medicine.

214. Sulfa Drugs, Infection Control, and the "First Line of Defense"

Before penicillin became widely available, the primary defense against infection came from sulfa drugs, a group of synthetic antibiotics developed in the 1930s. These drugs were among the first effective treatments against bacterial infections and were issued to soldiers as part of their personal medical kits. Each soldier often carried a small packet of sulfa powder, intended to be applied directly to wounds as soon as possible. If a soldier was injured, he or a nearby comrade would sprinkle the powder onto the wound before applying a bandage. This immediate treatment could slow the growth of bacteria, reducing the risk of infection before the wounded soldier reached a medic. Medics also used sulfa drugs in larger quantities at aid stations, combining them with cleaning and dressing wounds. While not as powerful as penicillin, sulfa drugs were widely available and easy to use, making them essential during the early and middle years of the war. In addition to medication, infection control depended heavily on basic practices. Wounds were cleaned as thoroughly as possible, damaged tissue was removed, and dressings were changed regularly. These procedures were often performed in difficult conditions, sometimes in tents or improvised shelters close to the front. Despite these efforts, infection remained a constant threat, especially in environments like jungles or muddy battlefields where bacteria thrived. The combination of sulfa drugs, improved surgical techniques, and later penicillin gradually reduced death rates, but the risk never fully disappeared.

215. Venereal Disease, Discipline, and the Hidden Strain on Armies

Beyond wounds and infection, armies faced another persistent medical problem: venereal disease (V.D.), particularly gonorrhea and syphilis. Soldiers stationed far from home, often dealing with loneliness, boredom, and long periods of inactivity, frequently sought companionship, thereby spreading infection across many theaters of war. During World War I, V.D. had incapacitated tens of thousands of soldiers daily, and although rates were significantly reduced by World War II, it remained a serious issue. By 1944, hundreds of servicemen were still removed from duty each day due to infection. Military authorities responded with a combination of medical treatment, education, and discipline. Soldiers received pamphlets, lectures, and warning posters emphasizing sexual hygiene and the risks of infection. Condoms and chemical prophylaxis kits were distributed, sometimes free of charge, and special "prophylactic stations" were established where soldiers could receive immediate treatment after exposure. Advances in medicine, particularly sulfa drugs and penicillin, dramatically reduced recovery time. A case of gonorrhea that once required weeks of hospitalization could be treated in days. However, the issue wasn't only medical but also disciplinary. In some units, infection could result in punishment, including loss of rank or restricted duties. This created tension between prevention, personal behavior, and military control. Venereal disease became a quiet but constant challenge, affecting manpower, morale, and the daily functioning of armies far from home.

216. Triage and the Hard Decisions of Who Lives

As the number of wounded increased, especially during large-scale offensives, medical teams faced a critical problem: there were often more injured soldiers than they could treat at once. This led to the widespread use of triage, a system that prioritized patients based on their chances of survival and the urgency of their injuries. At regimental aid posts and field hospitals, wounded soldiers were quickly assessed and placed into categories. Those with minor injuries who could return to duty quickly were treated first, as they could be sent back to the front. Soldiers with serious but survivable wounds were also prioritized, as timely treatment could save their lives. Those who were too severely wounded, with little chance of survival, were often given only basic care or pain relief. This system was practical, but it forced doctors and medics to make extremely difficult decisions. In some cases, they had to pass over severely wounded men who were still conscious, focusing instead on those who could be saved with limited resources. These decisions were made quickly, often under pressure, with little time for reflection. Triage changed how medical care functioned on the battlefield. It was no longer just about treating each individual; it was about managing large numbers of casualties and using resources where they could have the greatest impact. While it saved many lives, it also left some behind, not because they were unimportant, but because they couldn't be saved in time.

217. Surgery Without Time: Amputations, Exhaustion, and Battlefield Reality

In large battles, especially during the early and middle years of the war, medical systems were often overwhelmed. Field hospitals received waves of wounded soldiers faster than they could be treated. In these conditions, surgery became a continuous process rather than a controlled procedure. Surgeons worked long hours, sometimes operating for twelve to twenty-four hours without rest, moving from one patient to the next with little pause. The focus was speed and survival, not precision. Sterile conditions were difficult to maintain. Operations were often performed in tents, damaged buildings, or hastily prepared rooms close to the front. Lighting could be poor, especially at night or during blackout conditions, forcing surgeons to work under dim lighting. Supplies were limited, and anesthesia, when available, was sometimes reduced or delayed due to shortages or other urgent needs. In extreme situations, procedures had to begin before full preparation was possible. Amputation was one of the most common emergency operations. Severe limb injuries caused by artillery or crushing wounds left little choice. Removing a limb quickly could prevent infection or death from blood loss. These decisions were made in minutes. The scale of casualties meant that surgeons couldn't treat every injury in detail. They worked to keep as many men alive as possible, often under conditions of noise, exhaustion, and constant pressure. Survival depended not only on skill but also on endurance.

218. Medics Under Fire and the Role of Frontline Care

The first person to treat a wounded soldier was often not a doctor but a combat medic. These individuals operated on the front lines, moving through active combat zones to reach the injured. Medics worked without weapons in many armies, marked by symbols such as the Red Cross to indicate their non-combat role. Despite this, they were frequently exposed to the same dangers as infantry soldiers, including gunfire, artillery, and explosions. Reaching a wounded soldier could mean crawling across open ground or entering areas still under enemy fire. Their tasks were urgent and practical. They stopped bleeding, treated shock, administered pain relief, and prepared soldiers for evacuation. In many cases, the actions taken in these first few minutes determined whether a soldier would survive. Medics also had to decide when it was safe to move the wounded, balancing the risk of further injury against the danger of leaving them in place. The psychological pressure on medics was intense. They worked in proximity to severe injuries, often treating multiple casualties at once, while knowing that they couldn't save everyone. Many were recognized for acts of bravery, receiving medals for rescuing wounded soldiers under fire. Frontline medical care became a critical part of survival. It connected the battlefield to the larger medical system, ensuring that wounded soldiers had a chance to reach more advanced treatment further from the front.

219. Nurses in Field Hospitals: Care, Endurance, and Emotional Strain

Behind the front lines, nurses played a central role in caring for the wounded, often working in field hospitals and casualty clearing stations. These facilities received soldiers directly from evacuation routes, meaning nurses encountered injuries at their most severe. They assisted in surgery, changed dressings, managed infections, and monitored patients recovering from major trauma. Conditions were demanding. Hospitals were often overcrowded, especially during major offensives, with large numbers of wounded arriving within short periods. Nurses worked long shifts, sometimes for days at a time, with little rest, moving continuously between patients. Their role extended beyond medical care. Nurses provided reassurance, comfort, and human connection in a setting where many soldiers were far from home and facing pain or death. They wrote letters for the wounded, helped identify the dead, and supported men struggling with fear or shock. The emotional toll was significant. Nurses were exposed daily to severe injuries and loss, often forming brief but intense connections with patients who didn't survive. Despite these conditions, their work was essential to recovery. They maintained the continuity of care between surgery and healing, ensuring that wounded soldiers received ongoing attention in an environment where survival depended on both medical skill and constant support.

220. Jeeps, Ambulances, and the Race Against Time

Once a soldier received initial treatment at the front, the next step was evacuation, and speed became critical. The faster a wounded man could reach a surgical unit, the greater his chances of survival. This led to the widespread use of motorized evacuation systems, especially ambulances and jeeps adapted for carrying casualties. In earlier wars, wounded soldiers were often transported by horse or on foot. In World War II, motor vehicles became the backbone of evacuation. Jeeps were modified with stretcher racks, allowing two to three wounded men to be transported at once, even across rough terrain. Larger ambulances could carry more patients, but they required usable roads, which were often damaged or under fire. The journey itself was dangerous. Roads could be targeted by artillery or aircraft, and vehicles sometimes had to travel at night without headlights to avoid detection. In muddy or mountainous terrain, vehicles could become stuck, forcing stretcher-bearers to carry the wounded on foot over long distances. Time was everything. Medical teams aimed to move casualties from the front line to surgical care within hours. Delays increased the risk of infection, shock, and death. As a result, evacuation routes were planned carefully, and drivers often worked continuously, moving back and forth between the front and rear areas. The use of motorized transport transformed battlefield medicine. It allowed wounded soldiers to reach advanced care much faster than before, significantly improving survival rates, especially during large-scale operations.

221. Air Evacuation and the First Use of Helicopters

As the war progressed, a new method of evacuation emerged: air transport. Fixed-wing aircraft were increasingly used to move wounded soldiers from forward airstrips to hospitals further behind the lines. These flights were faster than ground transport and could bypass damaged roads or difficult terrain. Planes were often fitted with stretchers, allowing multiple patients to be transported at once. Medical personnel accompanied the wounded, providing care during the flight. Although conditions were basic, air evacuation reduced travel time from days to hours, greatly increasing survival rates for seriously injured soldiers. Near the end of the war, an even more experimental development appeared: the helicopter. Early models, such as the *Sikorsky R-4*, were used in limited numbers, particularly in the Pacific theater. These aircraft could land in areas inaccessible to planes or vehicles, including jungle clearings and mountainous terrain. Helicopters were slow and could carry only one or two patients at a time, but they demonstrated a new possibility: direct evacuation from the battlefield. In some cases, wounded soldiers were lifted out of areas that would have been impossible to reach by ground. Although still rare, these early helicopter evacuations marked the beginning of a major change in military medicine. They showed that rapid, direct extraction from combat zones was possible, a concept that would become standard in later conflicts.

222. Flight Nurses and Air Evacuation: Care in Transit

As air evacuation expanded, a new role emerged: the flight nurse. These nurses were trained to care for wounded soldiers during transport in aircraft, where conditions were far from stable. Planes often flew at low altitudes, in cold, noisy environments, with limited space and equipment. Wounded men were secured on stretchers, sometimes stacked in tiers, with little room for movement. Flight nurses monitored vital signs, administered medication, managed bleeding, and provided oxygen when available. They worked in difficult conditions, where turbulence, noise, and limited lighting made even simple tasks challenging. Communication was often reduced to gestures due to the sound of engines. Flights could last several hours, and patients were often in critical condition. Nurses had to respond quickly to changes, stabilizing soldiers who might deteriorate during transport. The goal was to keep them alive long enough to reach fully equipped hospitals further from the front. Air evacuation significantly reduced travel time, and the presence of trained medical staff during flights improved survival rates. For many soldiers, these flights marked the transition from immediate danger to recovery. Flight nurses became a vital link in the chain of care, ensuring that treatment continued even in transit, under conditions that required both medical skill and adaptability.

223. Burn Injuries, Aircrew Survival, and the "Guinea Pig Club"

One of the most severe injuries of the war came from burns, particularly among airmen. Pilots and bomber crews faced extreme risks: when aircraft were hit, fuel ignited instantly, turning cockpits into enclosed fires. Those who survived often suffered extensive burns to the face, hands, and upper body, injuries that were both life-threatening and permanently disfiguring. Early in the war, survival rates for severe burns were very low. Infection, shock, and fluid loss often led to death within days. Treatment was painful and limited, involving basic dressings and morphine for pain. Many doctors initially believed that patients with large-area burns couldn't survive. This changed through the work of surgeons such as Archibald McIndoe, working with the Royal Air Force. At Queen Victoria Hospital in England,

McIndoe developed new methods of treatment, including improved skin graft techniques and better management of infection and fluid loss. He also emphasized psychological recovery, recognizing that disfigurement affected identity as much as the body. Patients under his care formed a unique social group known as the "Guinea Pig Club," named after the experimental nature of their treatments. Members supported each other through long recoveries, often undergoing dozens of operations. They also engaged with local communities, helping reduce stigma around disfigurement. These advances significantly improved survival rates. Burn victims who would have died earlier in the war were now able to live, though often with lasting physical and emotional scars.

224. Plastic Surgery, Reconstruction, and Rebuilding Faces

Beyond survival, one of the greatest medical challenges of the war was reconstruction, helping soldiers live with injuries that changed their appearance and function. Explosions, shrapnel, and burns often caused severe damage to the face, including the loss of noses, jaws, or eyes. Plastic surgery, still a developing field, advanced rapidly during the war. Surgeons developed techniques to rebuild damaged areas using skin grafts and "flap" procedures, where skin and tissue were moved from one part of the body to another while maintaining a blood supply. These operations were often performed in stages, requiring multiple surgeries over months or years. For many patients, recovery wasn't just physical. Facial injuries affected speech, eating, and social interaction. Some soldiers were reluctant to return home, fearing how they would be perceived. Hospitals began to address these concerns, encouraging patients to socialize and rebuild confidence alongside physical treatment. Artificial replacements, or prosthetics, were also developed for missing features such as eyes, noses, or parts of the jaw. While not perfect, these helped restore some appearance and function. Dental reconstruction became particularly important, allowing soldiers to eat and speak more normally. These medical efforts transformed survival into long-term recovery. Soldiers who might previously have lived isolated lives were given the chance to reintegrate into society. The techniques developed during this period became the basis for modern reconstructive and cosmetic surgery, showing that medicine wasn't only about saving lives but also about restoring them.

225. Combat Fatigue" and the Recognition of Psychological Collapse

As the war intensified, armies began to face a problem they couldn't ignore: soldiers who were physically unharmed but no longer able to fight. Early in the war, these men were often labeled as cowards or accused of lacking discipline. Terms like "shell shock" from World War I were still used, but understanding remained limited. By 1941–1942, especially on the Eastern Front, in North Africa, and later in Italy and France, the scale of psychological breakdown became impossible to dismiss. Soldiers exposed to constant artillery fire, exhaustion, and fear began to show clear symptoms: shaking, confusion, inability to speak, paralysis without injury, or complete withdrawal. Some wandered aimlessly; others couldn't follow orders or even recognize their surroundings. This condition became known as "combat fatigue" or "battle exhaustion." Studies showed that even well-trained soldiers had limits. In some units, it was estimated that up to one in four soldiers would experience some form of psychological breakdown if exposed to combat long enough. Armies began to change their approach. Rather than punishing these soldiers, the medical staff was instructed to treat them as casualties. The key principle became "PIE" treatment: Proximity (treat near the front), Immediacy (treat quickly), and Expectation (expect recovery). Soldiers were given rest, food, and reassurance, often just for a few days, before being returned to duty. This approach had mixed results, but it marked a major shift. War was no longer seen as a test of will alone. It revealed that the human mind, like the body, could be pushed beyond its limits.

226. Psychiatric Units, Forward Treatment, and the Strain of Endurance

By the later years of the war, psychiatric care became more organized and structured. Dedicated forward psychiatric units were established close to the front lines, designed to treat soldiers before their condition worsened. The idea was simple: remove the soldier briefly from combat, provide rest, food, and calm, and then return him to his unit as quickly as possible. These centers were deliberately kept close to the battlefield so that soldiers didn't feel permanently removed from their role. Doctors believed that sending men too far to the rear made them less likely to return to duty. Treatment focused on simplicity. Soldiers were encouraged to sleep, eat, and talk about their experiences. In some cases, mild sedatives were used. The emphasis wasn't on deep therapy but on restoring basic functioning. Despite these efforts, the strain of continuous warfare remained overwhelming. Campaigns like Normandy, the Eastern Front, and the Pacific involved months of sustained combat with little relief. Soldiers rotated in and out of the line, but the cumulative effect of fear, loss, and exhaustion was constant. Some soldiers recovered and returned to their units. Others were evacuated further back and didn't return to combat. The war showed that psychological injury wasn't rare or exceptional; it was a common consequence of prolonged exposure to violence. These experiences influenced postwar medicine, contributing to later understanding of conditions such as post-traumatic stress disorder (PTSD).

TWENTY-ONE

Animals in War

Animals played a significant and often overlooked role in World War II. They were used for transport, communication, detection, and even direct participation in military operations. From horses and dogs to pigeons and dolphins, animals became part of the war effort in ways that were both practical and, at times, unexpected. This chapter examines the contributions of animals in the conflict, highlighting their roles on the battlefield and behind the lines. It also considers the risks they faced and the reliance that human forces placed on them during critical moments. It was a war in which not only humans but also animals were drawn into the demands and dangers of global conflict.

227. Horses in a "Modern" War

At the beginning of World War II, despite the presence of tanks and motor vehicles, horses remained essential to military operations. Germany alone relied on over 600,000 horses during the invasion of Poland in 1939, and by 1941, this number would grow to more than one million. The Wehrmacht (German Defense Force) was often perceived as fully mechanized, but in reality, much of its supply system depended on horse-drawn transport. Horses were used to pull artillery, wagons, and supply carts, especially in areas where roads were poor or damaged. In Eastern Europe, where infrastructure was limited, motor vehicles frequently broke down or became stuck in mud. Horses, by contrast, could move across rough terrain and required no fuel, making them more reliable in certain conditions. However, their use came at a high cost. Horses were vulnerable to exhaustion, extreme weather, and enemy fire. They required food and water, which placed additional strain on supply systems. During harsh winters or long campaigns, many died from overwork or starvation. In some cases, they were slaughtered to feed troops when supplies ran low. Although often overlooked, horses remained a crucial part of early war logistics. Their presence highlighted the contrast between modern weapons and traditional methods, showing that even in a mechanized war, older forms of transport still played a vital role.

228. Carrier Pigeons and the Lifeline of Communication

Before secure radio communication became widespread, carrier pigeons played a critical role in military operations. These birds were used by many countries, including Britain, Germany, and the United States, to carry messages across enemy lines. Their ability to return to their home lofts over long distances made them a reliable form of communication, especially when other systems failed. Pigeons were often used in situations where radio signals could be intercepted or jammed. A small message was placed in a capsule attached to the bird's leg, and the pigeon was released. It would then fly back to its base, sometimes covering distances of over 100 miles (160 kilometers). Because they flew at high speeds and were difficult to track, pigeons were less vulnerable to interception than human messengers. Their use was particularly important for isolated units. Soldiers cut off behind enemy lines could send information about their position, request assistance, or report enemy movements. In some cases, pigeons helped coordinate rescue operations or artillery support. However, the role was dangerous. Pigeons were often targeted by enemy forces, and many were lost during missions. Despite this, thousands were successfully delivered. Some birds became well-known for their service. One notable example from World War II was a pigeon named Winkie, who was awarded the Dickin Medal for her service. In February 1942, a damaged Royal Air Force bomber crashed into the North Sea during a mission. The crew released Winkie in the hope that she would return to her home loft and alert authorities. Although she carried no written message, her arrival time allowed officials to estimate the aircraft's location. A rescue mission was launched, and the crew was found shortly afterward. Winkie's flight demonstrated how even in an age of advancing technology, simple and natural methods of communication could still be vital to survival.

229. War Dogs as Messengers, Guards, and Lifesavers

Dogs were used extensively by nearly every army during the war, trained for a wide range of roles that combined instinct, intelligence, and loyalty. Germany, the Soviet Union, Britain, and the United States all developed specialized dog units, with tens of thousands of animals serving alongside soldiers. One of the most important roles was message carrying. In situations where radio communication was unreliable or dangerous, dogs could be sent between positions with written messages. Unlike human runners, they were smaller, faster, and less visible, making them harder to target. They could navigate terrain under fire, moving through trenches, forests, or ruined buildings. Dogs were also used as guard animals, particularly around camps, supply depots, and prisoner enclosures. Their hearing and sense of smell made them highly effective at detecting intruders, often alerting soldiers before any human could notice movement. In occupied territories, guard dogs were sometimes used in patrols, reinforcing control over civilian populations. Perhaps most valued were rescue dogs, especially on the Eastern Front and in areas of heavy fighting. These dogs were trained to search for wounded soldiers on the battlefield. Using their sense of smell, they could locate men buried under debris or lying unconscious in difficult terrain. Some carried small medical packs, allowing wounded soldiers to treat themselves, while others were trained to return to handlers and signal when they had found someone. For many soldiers, these animals were more than tools. They became companions in an environment defined by danger and uncertainty. A trained dog could mean the difference between life and death, whether by delivering a message, providing a warning, or finding a wounded man who might otherwise have been left behind.

230. Anti-Tank Dogs and the Brutal Experiments of War

One of the most controversial uses of animals during the war occurred in the Soviet Union, where dogs were trained for anti-tank missions. Faced with the rapid advance of German armored units during Operation Barbarossa in 1941, Soviet forces developed a desperate strategy to counter tanks. Dogs were trained to carry explosives on their backs and run underneath enemy tanks. The idea was that the explosive charge would detonate on contact, destroying the vehicle. Training often involved conditioning the dogs to associate tanks with food, encouraging them to run toward them during battle. In practice, the system proved deeply flawed. Dogs trained with Soviet diesel-powered tanks sometimes became confused when confronted with German tanks, which used different engines and smells. In some cases, they ran back toward the Soviet lines, creating danger for their own troops. Others panicked under fire or failed to reach their targets. Despite these problems, the program was used in combat, particularly in 1941 and 1942. Some tanks were reportedly destroyed, but the overall effectiveness was limited. The approach also raised serious ethical concerns, as it involved the deliberate sacrifice of animals in dangerous and often chaotic conditions. The use of anti-tank dogs reflected the extreme pressures of the Eastern Front. As losses mounted and resources were stretched, military planners turned to unconventional methods, even those that were unreliable or controversial. It showed how war could push both human and animal lives into roles shaped by urgency, desperation, and survival.

231. Mine Detection Dogs and the Hidden Danger Beneath the Ground

As the war progressed, landmines became one of the most persistent and deadly threats on the battlefield. Millions were laid across Europe, North Africa, and Asia, often hidden beneath soil, sand, or vegetation. These devices didn't distinguish between soldiers and civilians, and long after battles ended, they continued to kill and injure anyone who stepped on them. To counter this, armies increasingly relied on trained dogs to detect explosives. Dogs were trained to identify the scent of explosives such as TNT, even when buried underground. Handlers would guide them slowly across suspected areas, watching for specific behaviors, such as stopping, sitting, or pawing the ground, that indicated a possible mine. This method allowed soldiers to clear paths more safely than manual probing alone, which required individuals to search inch by inch with metal rods, often at great personal risk. Mine detection dogs were used by both Allied and Axis forces, but became especially important during and after major offensives, when large areas needed to be secured quickly. In Italy, France, and later Germany, they helped clear roads, fields, and abandoned defensive lines. Their work didn't end with combat; after the war, dogs continued to assist in clearing mines, allowing civilians to return to farmland and rebuild communities. Despite their effectiveness, the work was dangerous. A single mistake could be fatal. Many dogs were injured or killed during operations, but their ability to detect hidden threats saved countless human lives. Their role highlighted how war extended beyond visible danger, where survival often depended on finding what couldn't be seen.

232. Mascots, Companions, and the Emotional Survival of Soldiers

Beyond their official roles, animals became an important part of soldiers' emotional lives. Units often adopted mascots, which could include dogs, cats, goats, birds, or even more unusual animals such as monkeys or bears. These animals weren't trained for combat; they served a different purpose: providing comfort, familiarity, and a sense of normalcy in an environment dominated by stress and uncertainty. Mascots were often found locally or brought in from other areas and quickly became part of the unit. Soldiers named them, fed them, and cared for them collectively. In many cases, these animals moved with the unit, traveling through different fronts and becoming symbols of shared experience. Some mascots were even given unofficial ranks or uniforms, reflecting their integration into military culture. Animals also played a role in daily routines. A dog greeting soldiers returning from patrol, a cat in a trench, or a bird in a cage could provide small moments of calm. These interactions helped reduce stress and offered a distraction from constant danger. For soldiers far from home, animals could serve as a reminder of ordinary life, something familiar in a situation that was otherwise unpredictable. The loss of a mascot could affect morale significantly. Just as soldiers formed bonds with each other, they formed attachments to these animals. Their presence showed that survival wasn't only physical but also emotional. In a war defined by destruction, these small relationships provided moments of connection, helping soldiers endure the psychological strain of prolonged conflict.

233. Unusual Animal Roles and the Story of Wojtek the Bear

Not all animals in the war fit standard roles. Some became famous for their unusual duties, blurring the line between mascot and working animal. One of the most well-known examples is Wojtek the bear, who served with Polish forces during the war. Wojtek was found as a cub in Iran by Polish soldiers who had been released from Soviet camps and were making their way to the Middle East. The soldiers adopted him, raising him within their unit. As he grew, Wojtek became part of daily life, eating, playing, and even mimicking human behavior, such as drinking from bottles and carrying objects. During the Italian campaign in 1944, Wojtek's role became more practical. He was trained to carry heavy crates of artillery shells, particularly during the Battle of Monte Cassino. His strength and ability to move across difficult terrain made him useful for transporting supplies under challenging conditions. To officially include him, the Polish unit even enlisted him as a soldier, giving him a rank and service number. Wojtek became a symbol of the unit, appearing on their insignia as a bear carrying a shell. His presence boosted morale and created a sense of identity among the soldiers, especially those who had experienced displacement and hardship before reaching the front. Other unusual animal roles also appeared during the war. Experiments were conducted with dolphins and sea lions for naval detection, while some armies attempted to train animals for sabotage missions, with mixed and often unsuccessful results. These efforts reflected both innovation and desperation, as militaries explored unconventional methods to gain an advantage. The story of Wojtek, however, stands out for a different reason. He wasn't just a tool of war but a companion who shared the experience of the soldiers around him. His story highlights how, even in the most mechanized conflict in history, animals remained a part of the human experience of war.

TWENTY-TWO

Daily Life in World War II

For civilians, World War II transformed everyday life in profound ways. The war reached into homes, workplaces, and communities, reshaping routines and expectations. Rationing, blackouts, and constant uncertainty became part of daily existence, while governments mobilized entire populations to support the war effort. This chapter explores life on the home front, including the social and economic changes brought about by the conflict. It looks at how ordinary people adapted to extraordinary circumstances, balancing fear, responsibility, and the need to continue living under the pressures of war. It was a time when the line between civilian and combatant blurred, and survival required resilience far from the battlefield.

234. The First Changes: Queues, Coupons, and Quiet Fear

When war was declared in September 1939, daily life didn't collapse overnight, but it changed immediately in subtle and visible ways. In Britain, France, and Germany, governments moved quickly to control food supplies, anticipating shortages long before they fully appeared. Rationing systems were introduced or prepared, requiring civilians to register with local shops and receive ration books filled with coupons. These coupons limited how much sugar, butter, meat, and fuel a person could buy each week. Even before strict rationing fully took effect, people began queuing outside shops, uncertain how long supplies would last. In Britain, for example, rationing officially began in January 1940, but people were already stockpiling goods such as canned food, tea, and flour by late 1939. Long lines formed outside grocers and butchers, and shop shelves could empty quickly after deliveries arrived. In Germany, the government had already begun managing food supplies years earlier, preparing the population for a controlled wartime economy. Citizens were expected to accept limits as part of their duty to the state. Clothing also began to change. New production shifted toward military needs, meaning civilian goods became harder to find. People were encouraged to repair old clothes rather than replace them. Shoes, in particular, became valuable, as leather was increasingly reserved for the military. Despite these changes, much of daily life still continued. People went to work, children attended school, and shops remained open. However, there was an underlying sense of uncertainty. The war had begun, but for most civilians, it was still distant. The real impact had not yet arrived, but the first signs were already visible in ration books, queues, and the quiet awareness that normal life would not last.

235. Blackouts and the Transformation of the Night

One of the first major changes to civilian life was the introduction of blackout regulations. Beginning in 1939, cities across Britain and later other European countries were required to eliminate all visible light at night to make it harder for enemy aircraft to locate targets. This transformed daily routines in ways that were immediate and unavoidable. Streetlights were turned off or heavily dimmed. Windows had to be covered with thick curtains or blackout fabric so that no light could escape. Even a small crack of light could result in fines or warnings from local authorities. Cars were required to use covered headlights that allowed only narrow beams to shine downward, making driving slow and dangerous. Public transport continued, but movement at night became more difficult and disorienting. For civilians, the blackout made ordinary activities more complicated. Walking through the streets after dark became hazardous, with many people stumbling, falling, or getting lost. Accidents increased sharply. In Britain alone, thousands of injuries and deaths were attributed to blackout conditions, including traffic accidents and falls. Inside homes, the blackout changed the rhythm of daily life. Families gathered in single rooms with covered lamps, often going to bed earlier than before. Social life was reduced, and evenings became quieter. The absence of visible light created a constant reminder of the threat from above, even before large-scale bombing began. The blackout wasn't just a safety measure; it was a psychological shift. It marked the moment when civilians understood that the war could reach them directly. Darkness became part of daily life, and with it came a growing awareness that the boundaries between the front line and the home front were beginning to disappear.

236. Evacuation, Separation, and Families Divided

As the threat of bombing increased in 1940, particularly in Britain, governments began large-scale evacuation programs to protect civilians, especially children, from expected air attacks. This led to one of the most emotional and disruptive changes in daily life: the separation of families. In Britain, "Operation Pied Piper" began in September 1939, evacuating over 1.5 million people, mostly children, from cities like London, Birmingham, and Liverpool to rural areas. Children were often sent away with labels attached to their coats, carrying small bags with clothing, gas masks, and ration books. Many were accompanied by teachers or strangers rather than their parents. The experience varied widely. Some children were welcomed into rural homes and treated kindly. Others faced difficult conditions, living with families who resented the burden or treated them as unpaid labor. Many children experienced homesickness, fear, and confusion, having been separated suddenly from their families. Parents who remained in cities lived with constant anxiety, unsure of when they would see their children again. Letters became the main form of contact, but delays and uncertainty made communication difficult. Some families were reunited quickly when early bombing didn't meet expectations, while others remained separated for years. Evacuation changed the structure of family life. Homes were left half-empty, schools were disrupted, and communities were divided between those who left and those who stayed. For many civilians, the war was no longer something distant. It had already altered the most basic relationships, separating parents from children and turning everyday life into something unfamiliar.

237. Air Raids, Sirens, and Living Under Bombardment

By 1940, the war reached civilians directly as large-scale bombing campaigns began, most notably during the Blitz in Britain between September 1940 and May 1941. Daily life became structured around the possibility of air raids, which could begin at any time, often at night. The warning system became part of everyday routine. Air raid sirens signaled incoming aircraft with a rising and falling wail, sending people rushing to shelters. These shelters varied. Some families had small backyard shelters, such as the Anderson shelter, made of corrugated steel and partially buried in the ground. Others relied on public shelters or underground stations, including the London Underground, where thousands of people slept on platforms during bombing raids. Nights were often interrupted by explosions, anti-aircraft fire, and the constant noise of aircraft overhead. Sleep became irregular, and exhaustion was common. Families sometimes spent entire nights in shelters, returning to damaged homes in the morning. Daily routines had to continue despite this. People went to work, children attended school, and services continued to operate even after heavy bombing. However, the threat was always present. Buildings could be destroyed overnight, streets could change completely, and familiar places could disappear. The psychological impact was significant. Civilians lived in fear that they could be targeted without warning. The distinction between soldier and civilian became blurred. Survival depended not on training or weapons, but on luck, timing, and the ability to endure repeated disruption.

238. Rationing Deepens and the Rise of Substitutes

By 1941, the war had expanded, and supply shortages became more severe. Rationing systems tightened across Europe, and civilians had to adapt to living on limited, often poor-quality food. What people ate began to change significantly, shaped by availability rather than preference. In Britain, rationing expanded to include meat, butter, sugar, cheese, and eggs. Weekly allowances were strictly limited. For example, a person might receive only a few ounces of butter or sugar per week. Eggs were rare, often replaced by powdered eggs imported from overseas. Meat was limited, and cheaper cuts became more common. As shortages increased, substitutes became part of daily life. Coffee was replaced by alternatives made from roasted barley or chicory. Butter was replaced by margarine. In Germany, ersatz (substitute) products were widely used, including synthetic coffee and bread mixed with fillers such as potato or other grains. Cooking habits changed as well. Governments issued recipes to help people make meals from limited ingredients. In Britain, dishes like "Woolton pie," made from vegetables rather than meat, became common. People learned to stretch small amounts of food across multiple meals. Food became more than just nutrition. It was a daily challenge. Planning meals required careful use of ration coupons, and shortages couldn't always be avoided. The experience of eating changed from choice to necessity, with civilians adapting to whatever was available.

239. Cold Homes, Fuel Shortages, and Improvised Heating

By 1942, shortages were no longer limited to food. Fuel, coal, wood, and oil became increasingly scarce across both Allied and Axis countries, forcing civilians to rethink how they heated their homes. Governments prioritized fuel for factories, railways, and the military, leaving ordinary households with reduced allocations. In Britain, coal was rationed, and many families were limited to heating only one room in the house during winter. This "living room" became the center of daily life, where families ate, worked, and slept together to conserve warmth. Bedrooms were often left unheated, and people went to bed wearing multiple layers of clothing, sometimes including coats, hats, and gloves. In Germany and occupied Europe, the situation could be even harsher. Bombing had disrupted supply lines, and coal shortages became severe, especially in cities. Civilians burned whatever they could find: broken furniture, wooden fences, books, and even floorboards. Public buildings and schools were sometimes closed during the coldest periods because they couldn't be heated. Improvised solutions became common. People sealed windows with paper or cloth to reduce drafts. Blankets were hung over doorways to trap heat. Hot water bottles, when available, became essential for surviving cold nights. The cold wasn't just uncomfortable; it affected health, especially among the elderly and children. Illnesses increased, and for many, winter became one of the hardest periods of the war. Survival depended not only on avoiding bombs but also on enduring the long, cold months with limited resources.

240. Transport, Bicycles, and the Slowing of Everyday Movement

As fuel shortages worsened in 1942, transportation systems began to change dramatically. Petrol (gasoline) was heavily rationed or reserved entirely for military use, meaning that civilian travel became limited, slower, and often more difficult. Private car use nearly disappeared in many countries. In Britain, most civilian cars were taken off the road, either because fuel was unavailable or because vehicles were requisitioned for military purposes. Public transportation, such as buses and trains, continued to operate but was often overcrowded, unreliable, and subject to delays caused by military priorities. Bicycles became one of the most important forms of transport. Across Europe, people relied on them for commuting, carrying goods, and traveling between towns. In countries like the Netherlands, Denmark, and France, bicycles were already common, but during the war, they became essential. People adapted them creatively, adding baskets, trailers, or wooden platforms to carry food, firewood, or supplies. In occupied areas, movement was often restricted by checkpoints and regulations. Civilians needed permits to travel between regions, and railways were closely controlled. Journeys that once took hours could take an entire day or might not be possible at all. Even small trips required planning. Visiting relatives, going to work, or accessing markets became more complicated. Distance felt larger, and everyday movement slowed down. The war reshaped not just what people did, but how they moved through their world, turning simple travel into a challenge.

241. Clothing Shortages and the Culture of Repair

By 1942 and into 1943, clothing became another major area of shortage. Textile production had shifted toward military uniforms, parachutes, and equipment, leaving fewer resources for civilian clothing. Governments introduced rationing systems to control the use of fabric and ensure fair distribution. In Britain, clothing was rationed using coupons, similar to food. Each person received a limited number of coupons per year, which had to be used carefully. A new coat or pair of shoes could consume a large portion of a person's allowance, meaning that most people avoided buying new items unless absolutely necessary. As a result, repair and reuse became part of daily life. Clothes were patched, altered, and reused as long as possible. Old garments were taken apart and remade into new ones. Children's clothes were passed down between siblings, often modified to fit. Women were encouraged to "make do and mend," a phrase used in government campaigns to promote conservation. Materials also changed. Synthetic fabrics and lower-quality materials were used more frequently. Some clothing was made from unusual sources, including repurposed curtains or blankets. Shoes, in particular, became difficult to replace, leading people to repair soles repeatedly or wear damaged footwear. Appearance shifted as well. Fashion became simpler, more practical, and less varied. Bright colors and decorative elements were less common, replaced by functional designs. Clothing reflected the reality of wartime life: limited, practical, and often worn.

242. Hygiene, Water Shortages, and Everyday Improvisation

As the war continued, maintaining personal hygiene became increasingly difficult, especially in heavily bombed or occupied areas. Water supplies were often disrupted by damaged infrastructure, and soap and cleaning products became scarce. Bathing became less frequent. In many places, people relied on public bathhouses, which operated on limited schedules and were often crowded. At home, families used small amounts of water for washing, sometimes heating it manually and sharing it among multiple people. Soap was rationed or difficult to obtain. In some countries, it was replaced with lower-quality substitutes that were less effective. People improvised, using whatever was available to stay clean. Clothes were washed less often, and maintaining cleanliness required effort and creativity. Hair and grooming also changed. Women often cut their hair shorter to make it easier to manage without regular washing. Men shaved less frequently when razors and blades were scarce. Personal appearance became secondary to practicality. Despite these challenges, hygiene remained important for health. Poor sanitation could lead to illness, especially in crowded urban areas or shelters. People developed routines to manage with limited resources, showing how even basic activities required adaptation during the war.

243. Boredom, Waiting, and the Rhythm of War

Not every moment of civilian life was filled with danger. Much of wartime life was defined by waiting, uncertainty, and long periods of boredom. The pace of daily life slowed, shaped by shortages, restrictions, and limited entertainment. Work continued for many, especially in factories, offices, and farms. However, outside of work, options were reduced. Travel was limited, entertainment venues were restricted or closed, and curfews were sometimes imposed. Evenings were often quiet, especially during blackout conditions. People found ways to fill the time. Reading, knitting, and listening to the radio became common activities. Radios were an important source of news and entertainment, broadcasting music, speeches, and updates from the front. However, in occupied territories, listening to foreign broadcasts could be dangerous or illegal. Community activities also played a role. Neighbors gathered to share news, help each other, or simply talk. Small routines, cooking, repairing, and cleaning provided structure to days that might otherwise feel uncertain. At the same time, waiting carried emotional weight. People waited for news from the front, for letters from loved ones, and for signs that the war might end. This waiting was often filled with anxiety, as information was limited and outcomes were unclear. The war wasn't only experienced in moments of crisis. It was also lived in the spaces between, in the long, quiet periods when uncertainty became part of everyday life.

244. Black Markets, Barter, and the Shadow Economy

By 1943, official rationing systems in many countries could no longer meet the needs of civilians. As shortages worsened, a parallel economy emerged: the black market. This underground system became essential for survival, even though it was illegal and often harshly punished. In Germany, France, Italy, and other parts of occupied Europe, ration cards provided only minimal food. Meat, butter, eggs, and sugar were often unavailable through official channels. As a result, people turned to unofficial sources, buying food directly from farmers or traders willing to operate outside government control. Barter became common. Instead of money, people exchanged goods. Clothing, jewelry, cigarettes, and even family heirlooms were traded for food. In cities, civilians would travel to the countryside carrying suitcases of items to exchange for bread, potatoes, or meat. These journeys were risky, as authorities often tried to prevent unauthorized trade. Prices on the black market were high, often far beyond what ordinary people could afford. This created inequality. Those with valuable items or connections could access better food, while others relied on official rations and went hungry. Despite the risks, the black market became a normal part of life. For many civilians, it wasn't a matter of choice but necessity. Survival increasingly depended not on official systems but on informal networks, negotiation, and luck.

245. Bombing Intensifies and the Destruction of Cities

By 1943, the scale of bombing in Europe had increased dramatically. Allied air forces began sustained bombing campaigns against German cities, while German bombing had earlier targeted cities like London. Civilians found themselves living under constant threat from the air. In Germany, cities such as Hamburg experienced devastating air raids. In July 1943, bombing created a firestorm, where intense heat and wind combined to produce fires that spread uncontrollably. Entire neighborhoods were destroyed, and tens of thousands of people were killed in a matter of days. Daily life became organized around the expectation of air raids. Sirens warned of incoming aircraft, giving civilians time to move to shelters. People slept in basements, bunkers, or public shelters, often crowded with neighbors. Nights were frequently interrupted, leaving people exhausted. Buildings were damaged or destroyed, leaving many homeless. Families were forced to move repeatedly, staying with relatives or in temporary housing. Streets were filled with rubble, and essential services such as water, electricity, and transport were often disrupted. Children were sometimes evacuated from cities to safer rural areas. In Britain, this process had begun earlier, but similar evacuations occurred in Germany later in the war. Families were separated for long periods, adding emotional strain to physical danger. Bombing changed the nature of civilian life. The home, once a place of safety, became a potential target.

246. Displacement, Refugees, and the Movement of Civilians

By 1944, the war was no longer confined to distant fronts. As armies advanced across Europe, millions of civilians were forced to move, either to escape fighting or because they were ordered to evacuate. In Eastern Europe, entire communities fled ahead of advancing armies. Civilians traveled on foot, by cart, or by overcrowded trains, carrying only what they could take with them. These journeys were often chaotic, with limited food, shelter, or protection. In Western Europe, the Allied invasion of Normandy in June 1944 brought fighting directly into towns and villages. Civilians were caught between armies, forced to leave their homes or shelter in place as battles took place around them. Cities damaged by bombing became difficult to live in. Housing shortages forced people into crowded conditions, sometimes sharing space with strangers. Public buildings, schools, and churches were used as temporary shelters. Refugees faced constant uncertainty. They often didn't know where they were going, how long they would be gone, or whether they would be able to return home. Families were sometimes separated during these movements, adding to the confusion and stress. The war created a large population of displaced people, individuals who were no longer connected to a stable place of living. Movement became a defining feature of civilian life, as millions searched for safety in a landscape shaped by conflict.

247. Hunger, Collapse, and the Limits of Survival

As the war approached its final phase, conditions in many areas deteriorated further. Supply systems broke down, infrastructure was destroyed, and food became increasingly difficult to obtain. In parts of Europe, especially in areas affected by fighting or occupation, hunger reached severe levels. One example is the Dutch "Hunger Winter" of 1944–1945, when food shortages in the Netherlands led to widespread malnutrition and starvation. People ate whatever they could find, including tulip bulbs and animal feed, to survive. In Germany, constant bombing and disrupted transport made it difficult to distribute food. Rations decreased, and shortages became more severe. Cities struggled to maintain basic services, and everyday life became increasingly unstable. Fuel shortages worsened as well, making heating and cooking difficult. Many homes were damaged or destroyed, leaving people exposed to the elements. Winter conditions added to the hardship. The collapse of systems meant that survival depended on individual resourcefulness. People relied on remaining supplies, local networks, and whatever could be improvised. The structures that had once supported daily life, transport, distribution, and administration were no longer reliable. By this stage of the war, civilian life was defined by endurance. The focus shifted from adaptation to survival as people faced the final, most difficult months of the conflict.

248. Liberation, Ruins, and the Return to Uncertainty

When the war in Europe ended in 1945, civilian life didn't return to normal immediately. Instead, many people found themselves in cities that had been heavily damaged or destroyed, with limited resources and uncertain futures. Buildings lay in ruins, and infrastructure such as roads, railways, and utilities needed to be rebuilt. Many people were homeless, living in temporary shelters or damaged buildings. Food shortages continued, and rationing remained in place in many countries even after the fighting ended. At the same time, liberation brought relief. Occupied territories were freed, and restrictions imposed by occupying forces were lifted. People who had lived under control or fear began to rebuild their lives. Families attempted to reunite, but not all were able to do so. Many people had been displaced, captured, or killed, and the process of finding loved ones could take months or years. The end of the war marked a transition rather than a resolution. While the fighting had stopped, the effects of years of conflict remained visible in cities, communities, and individuals. Civilian life moved from survival in wartime to the challenges of rebuilding in peace.

TWENTY-THREE

Atrocities and Occupation

World War II was marked not only by combat but also by acts of violence and oppression carried out against civilian populations. Occupied territories faced harsh control, forced labor, and systematic persecution, while millions suffered under policies that led to widespread suffering and loss of life. This chapter examines the realities of occupation and the atrocities committed during the war, including the treatment of prisoners, the impact on civilian populations, and the systems of control imposed by occupying forces. It also considers the responses of those who resisted, collaborated, or struggled to survive. It was a conflict that revealed the darkest aspects of human behavior, leaving scars that would endure long after the fighting ended.

249. The Invasion of Poland and the Systematic Targeting of Civilians

When Germany invaded Poland in September 1939, violence against civilians began immediately alongside military operations. German forces carried out executions aimed at eliminating Polish leadership, intellectuals, and professionals in an operation later known as the Intelligenzaktion. By the end of 1939, an estimated 50,000–60,000 Polish elites had been killed. Entire communities were subjected to arrests, forced removals, and executions. Villages suspected of resistance were destroyed, and civilians were often shot in reprisal for attacks on German troops. At the same time, Nazi racial policies began to reshape the country. Polish Jews, numbering over three million people, faced immediate restrictions, including forced labor, property confiscation, and segregation. Poland was divided between Germany and the Soviet Union. In the Soviet-controlled east, mass deportations took place, with hundreds of thousands of people sent to labor camps. One of the most notable crimes was the Katyn massacre (1940), where approximately 22,000 Polish officers and officials were executed by Soviet forces. From the beginning, occupation meant not just control of territory but the deliberate dismantling of society.

250. Ghettos and the Systematic Isolation of Jewish Communities

As Nazi control expanded in Eastern Europe, Jewish populations were forced into segregated urban districts known as ghettos. Beginning in 1940, cities such as Warsaw, Łódź, and Kraków saw entire neighborhoods sealed off with walls, fences, and guarded entrances. The Warsaw Ghetto, the largest, confined over 400,000 people into an area of just 1.3 square miles (about 3.4 square kilometers). Conditions inside ghettos were severe. Overcrowding was extreme, with multiple families often sharing single rooms. Food rations were set far below subsistence levels; in some cases, official allocations provided as little as 200–300 calories per day. Starvation became widespread, and disease spread quickly due to poor sanitation and lack of medical care. Typhus outbreaks were common. Despite these conditions, daily life continued in limited ways. Schools operated secretly, and informal economies developed as people traded goods to survive. Smuggling, especially by children, became essential to bring in food at great personal risk. Many were caught and shot. The ghettos weren't intended as permanent settlements. They were part of a larger system of control that isolated Jewish communities, making them easier to exploit and, later, to deport.

251. The Invasion of the Soviet Union and Mass Shootings by Einsatzgruppen

When Germany launched Operation Barbarossa in June 1941, the war in the East quickly became one of unprecedented brutality. Following the advancing German army were special SS (*Schutzstaffel*, or "Protection Squadron") units known as *Einsatzgruppen*, tasked with eliminating perceived enemies of the Reich, particularly Jewish communities, political officials, and intellectuals. Unlike later camps, the killings in 1941 were carried out in open spaces, forests, ravines, and fields. Victims were often gathered under false pretenses, told they were being relocated or registered. They were then taken to isolated areas, forced to dig or stand near mass graves, and shot in large groups. Local collaborators were sometimes involved in identifying or guarding victims. One of the most well-known massacres occurred at Babi Yar, near Kyiv, in September 1941, in which over 33,000 Jews were killed in two days. Across Eastern Europe, similar actions took place repeatedly, resulting in the deaths of more than one million people in what historians later described as the "Holocaust by bullets." These killings also affected those carrying them out. Some German soldiers reported psychological strain, leading commanders to seek more "efficient" methods of mass murder. The experience of 1941 would directly influence the later development of industrialized killing systems in camps.

252. The Siege of Leningrad and Civilian Starvation as a Weapon of War

In September 1941, German and Finnish forces surrounded the Soviet city of Leningrad (modern St. Petersburg), beginning a siege that would last 872 days. Rather than storm the city, the German strategy focused on cutting it off completely, preventing food, fuel, and supplies from entering. The aim wasn't only military defeat but also the collapse of the civilian population through starvation. By the winter of 1941–1942, conditions inside the city had become catastrophic. Food rations dropped to as little as 4.4 ounces (about 125 grams) of bread per day, often mixed with sawdust or other substitutes. Fuel shortages meant that homes couldn't be heated, and temperatures fell far below freezing. Water systems failed, forcing civilians to collect ice or water from frozen rivers. Hunger became the central reality of daily life. People collapsed in the streets, too weak to move. Bodies were often left where they fell because families lacked the strength to bury them. Reports of cannibalism, though rare, were documented as desperation grew. Despite these conditions, the city didn't surrender. Civilians continued to work in factories, maintain defenses, and transport supplies across the frozen "Road of Life" on Lake Ladoga. By the time the siege was lifted in 1944, over one million civilians had died, making it one of the deadliest sieges in history.

253. From Mass Shootings to Industrialized Killing

In the early years of the war, Nazi Germany's persecution of Jews and other targeted groups relied heavily on mass shootings carried out by mobile killing units known as *Einsatzgruppen*. However, these methods were seen by Nazi leadership as inefficient and psychologically difficult for those carrying them out. By late 1941, plans were underway to create a more centralized system of killing. This shift was formalized in January 1942 at the Wannsee Conference, where officials coordinated what they called the "Final Solution," the plan to systematically eliminate Europe's Jewish population. This marked a turning point in the Holocaust. Killing was no longer carried out mainly in open spaces but was reorganized into a system designed for scale, secrecy, and efficiency. The focus moved from localized massacres to a coordinated effort across occupied Europe, laying the foundation for the extermination camps that would soon follow.

254. Extermination Camps and the Systematic Murder of Millions

Beginning in 1942, Nazi Germany established a network of extermination camps in occupied Poland, including Auschwitz-Birkenau, Treblinka, Sobibor, and Belzec. Unlike concentration camps, which were used for imprisonment and forced labor, these facilities were designed specifically for mass killing. Victims were transported to the camps in sealed freight trains from across Europe. These journeys could last several days, with little or no food, water, or sanitation, and many died before arrival. Upon reaching the camps, prisoners were subjected to a rapid selection process. Those considered able to work were sent to labor, while the majority, including children, the elderly, and many women, were sent directly to gas chambers. These chambers used gases such as carbon monoxide or Zyklon B to kill large groups at once. The process was organized with a high degree of efficiency. Bodies were removed, valuables were taken, and remains were burned or buried. Personal belongings were sorted and redistributed, often sent back to Germany. Victims were frequently misled about their fate, told they were entering showers or undergoing disinfection. By the end of the war, approximately six million Jews had been murdered, alongside millions of others, including Roma, Soviet prisoners of war, disabled individuals, and political prisoners. The scale, organization, and intent behind these killings made the Holocaust one of the most systematic and devastating acts of mass violence in modern history.

255. Forced Labor Across Occupied Europe

As the war intensified, Nazi Germany faced a growing need for labor to sustain its military and industrial production. To meet this demand, a vast system of forced labor was created across occupied Europe. Millions of civilians were taken from their homes and transported to Germany or forced to work in their own countries under German control. By 1944, an estimated seven to eight million foreign laborers were working within the

German economy. In Western Europe, workers were often recruited through pressure or deception, but as the war continued, forced conscription became more common. In France, the Service du Travail Obligatoire (STO) required young men to work in German factories. In Eastern Europe, the system was far harsher. Civilians, including teenagers, were seized in raids and transported under guard. These workers, often referred to as *Ostarbeiter* (Eastern workers), faced strict controls, poor living conditions, and limited rights. Workers were housed in overcrowded camps or barracks, received minimal food, and were subject to strict discipline. Movement was restricted, and contact with local populations was often forbidden. Many were forced to work long hours in factories producing weapons, vehicles, and other military supplies. Resistance or attempts to escape could result in severe punishment or execution. Forced labor became a central part of the German war effort, linking occupation policies directly to industrial production. It demonstrated how civilian populations were exploited on a massive scale, turning human lives into resources for sustaining the war.

256. Reprisals, Partisans, and the Violence of Occupation

As resistance movements grew across occupied Europe, German forces responded with increasingly harsh reprisals against civilian populations. Partisan groups operated in countries such as Yugoslavia, Poland, Greece, and the Soviet Union, carrying out sabotage, ambushes, and intelligence gathering. These actions disrupted German control but also led to severe consequences for civilians. Occupation authorities often applied collective punishment, targeting entire communities for the actions of a few. Villages suspected of supporting resistance were burned, and inhabitants were executed or deported. In some areas, German policy followed strict ratios; for every German soldier killed, dozens or even hundreds of civilians could be executed in retaliation. Several massacres became widely known. In 1942, the Czech village of Lidice was destroyed after the assassination of Reinhard Heydrich. All men were executed, women deported, and children either killed or sent to German families for "re-education." In France, the village of Oradour-sur-Glane was destroyed in 1944, with over 600 civilians killed. These reprisals were intended to discourage resistance but often had the opposite effect, strengthening opposition and increasing support for partisan groups. For civilians, the line between battlefield and home disappeared. Everyday life was shaped by the constant risk that violence could occur without warning, making occupation a condition of fear and uncertainty.

257. The Liquidation of Ghettos and Uprisings

By 1943, Nazi policy moved toward the complete liquidation of Jewish ghettos across occupied Eastern Europe. Ghettos that had existed for years as sites of forced labor, starvation, and confinement were systematically emptied. Their populations were deported to extermination camps such as Treblinka and Auschwitz or killed on the spot. This marked a final phase in the destruction of Jewish communities that had once formed a central part of urban life in cities like Warsaw and Łódź. In some ghettos, resistance emerged despite overwhelming odds. The most well-known example was the Warsaw Ghetto Uprising in April 1943. When German forces entered to carry out deportations, Jewish fighters, many armed only with pistols, homemade explosives, and limited ammunition, launched an organized resistance. For nearly a month, they fought German troops using the narrow streets, buildings, and underground passages of the ghetto. The uprising was eventually crushed. German forces systematically destroyed the area, burning buildings and using heavy weapons to eliminate resistance. Approximately 13,000 Jews were killed during the fighting, and tens of thousands more were deported to camps. The ghetto was left in ruins. Although militarily unsuccessful, such uprisings demonstrated that resistance existed even in the most extreme conditions. They became symbols of defiance, showing that even in a system designed to eliminate entire populations, some chose to resist despite knowing the likely outcome.

258. Bombing Campaigns and the Destruction of Cities

As the war progressed, large-scale bombing campaigns became a central part of strategy, bringing the war directly into civilian areas. Both the Allies and Axis powers targeted cities to disrupt industry, transport, and morale. Bombing raids increasingly focused on urban centers, where factories and civilian populations were concentrated. In Germany, cities such as Hamburg, Cologne, and Dresden were heavily bombed. One of the most destructive raids occurred in Hamburg in July 1943 during Operation Gomorrah. A combination of high-explosive and incendiary bombs created a firestorm, where intense heat generated hurricane-like winds that fed the flames. Entire neighborhoods were destroyed, and approximately 40,000 people were killed in a matter of days. Bombing campaigns blurred the line between military and civilian targets. While factories and transport networks were primary objectives, residential areas were often affected, leading to large numbers of civilian casualties. People lived with the constant threat of air raids, spending nights in shelters, basements, or underground stations. The destruction of cities changed the nature of the war.

259. Death Marches and the Collapse of the Camp System

As Allied forces advanced into German-occupied territories in 1944 and 1945, the Nazi regime began evacuating concentration and extermination camps in an attempt to prevent prisoners from being liberated. Tens of thousands of prisoners were forced onto long marches toward the interior of Germany in what became known as "death marches." These marches took place in extreme conditions, often during winter, with little food, water, or rest. Prisoners, already weakened by starvation, disease, and forced labor, were required to walk long distances under guard. Anyone who fell behind, collapsed, or was unable to continue was often shot on the spot. The routes were chaotic and poorly organized. Columns of prisoners moved along roads crowded with refugees, retreating troops, and collapsing infrastructure. In some cases, trains were used, but these were often overcrowded and lacked basic necessities, leading to further deaths. It is estimated that tens of thousands of prisoners died during these evacuations. The marches revealed the extent of brutality within the camp system, even as it was collapsing. Rather than abandon the camps, authorities chose to move prisoners under conditions that ensured many would not survive. For those who did survive, liberation often came shortly afterward, as Allied forces reached the camps and encountered the remaining prisoners and evidence of the system that had operated across occupied Europe.

260. The Firebombing of Cities and the Destruction of Urban Life

As the war entered its final phase, aerial bombing intensified to unprecedented levels, turning entire cities into targets. Allied bombing campaigns aimed not only at military and industrial sites but also at breaking the enemy's ability to sustain war. One of the most devastating attacks occurred in Hamburg in July 1943 (Operation Gomorrah), where firestorms created by incendiary bombs killed an estimated 37,000 people. By 1944–1945, similar tactics were used repeatedly across German cities. The bombing of Dresden in February 1945 became one of the most controversial events. Over several days, waves of British and American bombers dropped high-explosive and incendiary bombs, creating a firestorm that destroyed much of the city. Estimates of the death toll vary, but tens of thousands of civilians were killed. In Japan, the scale of destruction was equally severe. The firebombing of Tokyo on the night of March 9–10, 1945, killed an estimated 80,000–100,000 people in a single raid, making it one of the deadliest air attacks in history. The city, largely built of wood, burned rapidly, and many victims died from fire or suffocation. For civilians, bombing transformed daily life into a constant state of fear. Air raid sirens, shelters, and blackout routines became part of survival. Cities that had once been centers of life were reduced to ruins, showing how modern warfare extended destruction far beyond the battlefield.

261. Hiroshima and the First Atomic Bomb

On August 6, 1945, the United States dropped the first atomic bomb used in warfare on the Japanese city of Hiroshima. The bomb, code-named *Little Boy*, was released from the B-29 bomber *Enola Gay* and detonated approximately 1,968 feet (600 meters) above the city. In a matter of seconds, an immense explosion and flash of heat destroyed much of Hiroshima. Temperatures at the center of the blast reached several thousand degrees Fahrenheit, with some estimates exceeding 7,000 degrees Fahrenheit (3,900 degrees Celsius), igniting fires across the city and vaporizing buildings and people close to the impact point. An estimated 70,000–80,000 people were killed instantly. Many victims died from the blast itself, while others were burned by the intense heat or crushed by collapsing structures. In the days and weeks that followed, tens of thousands more died from severe injuries and radiation exposure. Survivors often suffered burns, blindness, and radiation sickness, with symptoms including nausea, hair loss, and internal bleeding. The destruction of Hiroshima demonstrated a new level of warfare. Unlike conventional bombing, a single weapon could destroy an entire city. The use of the atomic bomb was partly intended to force Japan to surrender quickly, but it also reflected a broader context of escalating violence, including earlier firebombing campaigns that had already devastated Japanese urban areas.

262. Nagasaki, Radiation, and the End of the War

Three days after Hiroshima, on August 9, 1945, a second atomic bomb, code-named *Fat Man*, was dropped on the city of Nagasaki. The original target was Kokura, but poor visibility led the bomber to divert to Nagasaki. The bomb detonated over the city, causing widespread destruction, though the surrounding hills limited the blast compared to Hiroshima. An estimated 40,000–70,000 people were killed by the end of 1945. As in Hiroshima, many deaths weren't immediate. Survivors suffered from burns, injuries, and radiation sickness, which continued to claim lives in the following months and years. Radiation exposure became one of the most defining features of atomic warfare. People who had survived the initial explosion developed long-term illnesses, including cancers and chronic conditions. These survivors became known as *hibakusha*, many of whom faced not only health problems but also social stigma. The atomic bombings occurred alongside other pressures on Japan, including the Soviet Union's entry into the war against Japan on August 8, 1945, and continued conventional bombing. Facing these combined threats, Emperor Hirohito intervened to accept surrender. On August 15, Japan announced its surrender, with formal documents signed on September 2, 1945. The bombings marked the beginning of the nuclear age. They introduced a form of warfare capable of mass destruction on an unprecedented scale, shaping global politics and military strategy for decades to come.

263. Total Loss, Lasting Wounds, and the Invisible Scars of War

By the end of World War II, the scale of human loss was unprecedented. It is estimated that between seventy and eighty-five million people died worldwide, representing roughly three to four percent of the global population at the time. Civilians made up the majority of these deaths, killed not only in combat zones but also through bombing, starvation, disease, forced labor, and systematic murder. The Soviet Union alone lost an estimated twenty-four to twenty-seven million people, while China suffered around fifteen to twenty million deaths. Germany lost approximately six to seven million people, including civilians, and Japan lost around 2.5–3 million. The Holocaust accounted for the murder of approximately six million Jews, alongside millions of other victims, including Roma, disabled individuals, and prisoners of war. Beyond those killed, millions more were permanently injured. Modern warfare, especially the use of artillery, explosives, and mechanized weapons, caused widespread physical trauma. Soldiers and civilians alike lost limbs, suffered severe burns, or were left with long-term disabilities. Advances in battlefield medicine meant that more people survived injuries that would previously have been fatal, but often with lasting consequences. Amputations became common, and many survivors required lifelong care, prosthetics, or assistance. The psychological impact of the war was equally significant, though less visible. What was then referred to as "combat fatigue" or "shell shock" is now recognized as post-traumatic stress disorder. Soldiers who had experienced prolonged exposure to combat often suffered from anxiety, nightmares, emotional numbness, and difficulty returning to civilian life.

Civilians, especially those who endured bombings, occupation, or imprisonment, experienced similar effects. At the time, understanding of these conditions was limited, and many struggled without formal support. The end of the war didn't mark the end of its consequences. Physical injuries, psychological trauma, and the loss of millions of lives continued to shape societies long after the fighting stopped, leaving a legacy that extended far beyond 1945.

TWENTY-FOUR

The End & the Long Shadow

The conclusion of World War II marked the end of large-scale fighting, but it did not bring an immediate return to stability. The destruction left behind was immense, and the consequences of the war would continue to shape the world for decades to come. Nations faced the challenge of rebuilding, while new political tensions emerged in the aftermath of the conflict. This chapter explores the final stages of the war and its lasting impact, including the reshaping of borders, the rise of new global powers, and the beginning of a new era defined by both recovery and uncertainty. It highlights how the effects of the war extended far beyond its official end. It was a conclusion that marked not just the end of a conflict but the beginning of a transformed world whose influence continues to be felt today.

264. Germany's Collapse and the Division into Occupation Zones

After Germany's surrender in May 1945, the country ceased to function as a unified state. Its government had collapsed, its cities were heavily damaged, and its infrastructure was in ruins. The Allied powers, the United States, the Soviet Union, Britain, and France, divided Germany into four occupation zones, each controlled by one of the victors. Berlin, although located deep within the Soviet zone, was also divided into four sectors, reflecting the shared control over the former capital. Occupation authorities faced immediate challenges. Millions of soldiers had to be disarmed, prisoners of war processed, and Nazi institutions dismantled.

Denazification programs were introduced to remove former Nazi officials from positions of power, though implementation varied widely between zones. In the Soviet-controlled areas, land reforms and political restructuring began quickly, while in the western zones, efforts focused on rebuilding administrative systems and stabilizing the economy. For civilians, occupation meant uncertainty. Laws changed, currencies lost value, and authority shifted overnight. Food shortages remained severe, and many relied on rationing or black markets to survive. The division of Germany, initially intended as a temporary measure, would later become a central issue in the emerging Cold War, shaping Europe for decades to come.

265. Displaced Persons and the Largest Migration in European History

The end of the war didn't bring immediate stability to millions of people across Europe. Instead, it triggered one of the largest population movements in modern history. By 1945, an estimated thirty to forty million people were displaced, including former prisoners of war, forced laborers, concentration camp survivors, and civilians fleeing advancing armies or destroyed homes. Many of these individuals were referred to as "Displaced Persons" (DPs). Allied authorities established camps to house them temporarily, but conditions were often crowded, and resources were limited. Some people were able to return home, but for others, this was impossible. Borders had shifted, governments had changed, and in some cases, returning meant facing persecution or arrest. One of the largest forced migrations involved ethnic Germans living in Eastern Europe. Between 1945 and 1950, around twelve to fourteen million Germans were expelled or fled from countries such as Poland, Czechoslovakia, and Hungary. These movements were often chaotic and violent, with many dying from exposure, disease, or attacks during the journey. For survivors of the Holocaust, displacement carried an additional burden. Many had lost entire families and communities, with no homes to return to. Some emigrated to countries such as the United States, while others moved to Palestine, contributing to tensions that would later shape the Middle East. The war's end didn't restore stability; for millions, it marked the beginning of another uncertain journey.

266. The Nuremberg Trials and the Question of Justice

After the war, the Allied powers faced a major question: how to deal with the leaders responsible for the conflict and its crimes. Rather than executing them without trial, they chose to establish an international tribunal in the German city of Nuremberg. Beginning in November 1945, leading figures of Nazi Germany were put on trial for crimes against peace (starting the war), war crimes, and crimes against humanity (including mass killings and persecution). Twenty-two major Nazi officials were tried, including Hermann Göring, Joachim von Ribbentrop, and Albert Speer. The trials presented extensive evidence, including documents, films, and witness testimony, revealing the scale of atrocities such as the Holocaust. For many people around the world, this was the first time the full extent of Nazi crimes became widely known. The outcomes varied. Twelve defendants were sentenced to death, others received long prison terms, and a few were acquitted. The trials established an important legal precedent: individuals, including political and military leaders, could be held personally responsible for actions carried out by the state. However, the trials were also controversial. Some critics argued that they represented "victor's justice," since only Axis leaders were prosecuted. Despite this, the Nuremberg Trials marked a turning point in international law, shaping future efforts to address war crimes and human rights violations. They demonstrated an attempt to replace revenge with legal accountability, even in the aftermath of a global conflict.

267. The Occupation of Japan and the Remaking of a Nation

Following Japan's surrender in August 1945, the country came under Allied occupation, led primarily by the United States under General Douglas MacArthur. Unlike Germany, Japan wasn't divided among multiple powers; instead, it remained under a single occupation authority, which allowed for more centralized reforms. The occupation aimed not only to demilitarize Japan but also to transform its political system. The Japanese military was dismantled, war industries were reduced, and a new constitution was introduced in 1947. This constitution included a key provision, Article 9, in which Japan renounced war as a sovereign right and agreed not to maintain traditional military forces. Political reforms also expanded democratic rights. Women were granted the right to vote for the first time, and efforts were made to reduce the power of large industrial and political groups. At the same time, war crimes trials were held in Tokyo, similar to those in Nuremberg, prosecuting Japanese leaders for their role in the war. For ordinary civilians, the occupation years were difficult. Cities had been heavily bombed, food shortages were common, and the economy struggled to recover. However, the reforms laid the foundation for Japan's postwar recovery. Within a decade, the country began to rebuild its economy and political system, eventually becoming one of the world's leading industrial powers. The occupation of Japan showed a different model of postwar reconstruction, focused not only on control but also on long-term transformation.

268. Hiroshima, Nagasaki, and the Long Shadow of Radiation

After the atomic bombings of Hiroshima and Nagasaki, destruction didn't end with the explosions. Survivors, later known as *hibakusha* ("bomb-affected people"), continued to suffer long after the cities were rebuilt. Many experienced severe burns that healed slowly or left permanent scars, known as keloids. Others developed symptoms of radiation sickness, including hair loss, bleeding, fatigue, and weakened immune systems. In the months and years that followed, doctors began to observe higher rates of leukemia and other cancers among survivors. These illnesses often appeared years after exposure, making the long-term effects difficult to fully understand at the time. Children exposed to radiation faced particular risks, and concerns also arose about genetic damage, though research later showed more limited hereditary effects than initially feared. Social consequences were also significant. Many hibakusha faced discrimination, as others feared radiation could be contagious. Survivors often struggled to find employment or marriage partners due to stigma. At the same time, Hiroshima and Nagasaki became symbols of nuclear destruction. Memorials, survivor testimonies, and peace movements grew in the postwar years, shaping global debates about nuclear weapons. The atomic bombings didn't end with 1945; they marked the beginning of a new era in which the effects of war could last across generations.

269. Europe in Ruins and the Struggle to Rebuild

By the end of the war in Europe, much of the continent lay in ruins. Major cities such as Berlin, Warsaw, and Dresden had been heavily bombed or fought over, leaving vast areas destroyed. In Warsaw, for example, around eighty-five percent of the city had been reduced to rubble. Infrastructure, including railways, bridges, and factories, was severely damaged, making transport and production difficult. For civilians, daily life was shaped by shortages. Food, fuel, and basic goods were limited, and rationing continued in many countries well into the late 1940s. In the harsh winter of 1946–1947, often called the "Hunger Winter" in parts of Europe, freezing temperatures and poor harvests worsened conditions. People relied on black markets, barter, or aid from occupying forces and international organizations. Reconstruction required both physical rebuilding and economic support.

270. The "Iron Curtain" and the Division of Europe

In March 1946, former British Prime Minister Winston Churchill delivered a speech in Fulton, Missouri, where he declared that an "Iron Curtain" had descended across Europe. This phrase described the growing division between Western Europe, influenced by the United States and democratic systems, and Eastern Europe, increasingly controlled by the Soviet Union. Although the war had ended less than a year earlier, the alliance between the Western Allies and the Soviet Union was already breaking down. In Eastern Europe, countries such as Poland, Hungary, Romania, and Bulgaria were gradually brought under Soviet influence. Communist parties, often supported by Soviet troops still stationed in the region, took control of governments. Elections were manipulated, opposition parties suppressed, and political systems reshaped along Soviet lines. These states became part of what would later be called the Eastern Bloc. In the West, countries moved toward reconstruction and democratic governance, often supported by American economic aid. The ideological differences between the two sides, capitalism versus communism and democracy versus one-party rule, became more pronounced. Churchill's speech didn't create this division, but it publicly acknowledged it. The wartime alliance had given way to suspicion, competition, and a growing sense that Europe was entering a new kind of conflict, one defined not by direct fighting but by political and ideological rivalry.

271. Decolonization and the Collapse of European Empires

The end of World War II didn't simply reshape Europe; it transformed the global balance of power, accelerating the collapse of European colonial empires. Before the war, countries such as Britain, France, the Netherlands, and Belgium controlled vast territories across Asia, Africa, and the Middle East. However, the war weakened these powers economically and militarily, making it difficult to maintain control over distant colonies. At the same time, the war had changed expectations. Millions of colonial soldiers had fought in the conflict, often in Europe, North Africa, and Asia. They had seen the vulnerability of imperial powers and returned home with new ideas about independence and self-determination. Wartime propaganda, which emphasized freedom and resistance against tyranny, also created contradictions that couldn't easily be ignored by colonized populations. In Asia, independence movements gained momentum quickly. India achieved independence from Britain in 1947, followed by the partition into India and Pakistan, which led to mass migration and violence affecting millions.

In Indonesia, nationalist forces declared independence from the Netherlands in 1945, leading to a four-year conflict before it was recognized in 1949. In Vietnam, resistance against French colonial rule escalated into a prolonged war. In Africa, the process unfolded more gradually, but by the late 1950s and 1960s, many territories were gaining independence. Countries such as Ghana (1957), Algeria (1962), and Kenya (1963) emerged from colonial rule, often after periods of conflict and negotiation. Decolonization wasn't a single event but a global transformation. It reshaped political borders, created new nations, and led to both hope and instability. The legacy of colonial rule, including economic inequality and political tensions, would continue to influence these regions long after independence. In this way, World War II not only ended empires in Europe but also triggered their decline across the world, redefining the international order.

272. The Marshall Plan and the Economic Divide

In June 1947, the United States introduced the European Recovery Program, commonly known as the Marshall Plan, aimed at rebuilding the economies of war-torn Europe. The program provided over $12 billion (more than $100 billion in modern terms) in aid to Western European countries. This assistance included money, raw materials, machinery, and food, helping nations restore industry, rebuild infrastructure, and stabilize their economies. The plan wasn't only economic but also political. American leaders believed that poverty and instability could lead to the spread of communism. By supporting economic recovery, they hoped to strengthen democratic governments and reduce the appeal of Soviet influence. Countries such as France, West Germany, Italy, and the Netherlands benefited significantly, experiencing faster recovery and improved living conditions. The Soviet Union viewed the Marshall Plan as a threat. It rejected the offer of aid and pressured Eastern European countries to do the same. Instead, the Soviet Union established its own system of economic cooperation within the Eastern Bloc. This decision deepened the division of Europe into two separate economic and political spheres. The Marshall Plan contributed to recovery in the West but also solidified the emerging Cold War (1947–1991), a decades-long ideological and geopolitical struggle in which cooperation between former allies was replaced by competition, mistrust, and proxy conflicts.

273. The Berlin Blockade and Airlift

By 1948, Germany had become the central point of tension between the former Allies. As the Western Allies began to rebuild their zones and introduce a new currency to stabilize the economy, the Soviet Union viewed this as a threat to its influence. In June 1948, Soviet forces blocked all road, rail, and canal access to West Berlin, attempting to force the Western Allies out of the city. This blockade cut off more than two million civilians from supplies, including food, fuel, and medicine. Instead of withdrawing, the United States and its allies responded with the Berlin Airlift. For nearly a year, cargo planes flew into West Berlin around the clock, delivering essential goods. At its peak, a plane landed every few minutes. Over 2.3 million tons of supplies were delivered, keeping the city alive through the winter. The operation demonstrated both technological capability and political determination. In May 1949, the Soviet Union lifted the blockade. The crisis marked one of the first major confrontations of the Cold War and showed that while direct war was avoided, the conflict between East and West would continue through pressure, strategy, and symbolic standoffs.

274. The Division of Germany into East and West

Following the Berlin Crisis, the division of Germany became permanent. In May 1949, the Western occupation zones were formally merged to create the Federal Republic of Germany (West Germany), with a democratic government supported by the United States, Britain, and France. In response, the Soviet Union established the German Democratic Republic (East Germany) in October 1949, creating a separate socialist state aligned with Moscow. This division reflected the broader split of Europe. West Germany developed a market-based economy and integrated into Western political and military structures, while East Germany adopted a centrally planned economy under a one-party communist system. Berlin remained divided as well, becoming a focal point of tension between the two blocs. For ordinary Germans, the division meant families separated, different political systems, and limited movement across borders. Over time, this separation would become more rigid, eventually leading to the construction of the Berlin Wall in 1961. The division of Germany symbolized the long-term consequences of World War II. What began as a military occupation evolved into a political boundary that would shape Europe for decades, turning Germany into one of the central front lines of the Cold War.

275. Early Memorials and the First Efforts to Remember

As reconstruction progressed, societies began to create physical memorials to the war. In many countries, these took the form of monuments dedicated to fallen soldiers, resistance fighters, or victims of bombing. These memorials often focused on sacrifice, heroism, and national unity, reflecting how governments wanted the war to be remembered. However, the way the war was remembered varied widely. In Western Europe, emphasis was often placed on resistance and liberation, while collaboration and complicity were less openly discussed. In Eastern Europe, memory was shaped by Soviet influence, highlighting the role of the Red Army and framing the war as a struggle against fascism. Other aspects of the war, including certain atrocities, were downplayed or controlled. The Holocaust, in particular, wasn't immediately central to public memory. While evidence of the camps had been revealed at the end of the war, a broader understanding developed slowly. Many early memorials referred to victims in general terms, without specifically identifying Jewish persecution or other targeted groups. Despite these limitations, the 1950s and 1960s marked the beginning of public remembrance. Cemeteries, monuments, and commemorative ceremonies created spaces where the dead could be acknowledged. These early efforts laid the foundation for later, more detailed and critical engagement with the past.

276. Trials, Testimony, and Confronting the Past

By the 1960s, a new phase of memory began, marked by legal trials and the growing importance of survivor testimony. One of the most significant moments was the trial of Adolf Eichmann in 1961, held in Jerusalem. Eichmann, a key organizer of the deportation of Jews during the Holocaust, was captured in Argentina and brought to trial. For many people around the world, this was the first time they heard detailed, personal accounts of the Holocaust from survivors. The trial was widely broadcast and reported, bringing individual experiences into public awareness. Survivors spoke not only about death and destruction but also about daily life in ghettos and camps, the loss of families, and the struggle to survive. These testimonies challenged earlier narratives that had minimized or generalized the suffering of specific groups. In Germany and other countries, similar processes began. Trials of former officials and collaborators forced societies to confront their own roles in the war. Younger generations, who had grown up after the conflict, began asking questions about what their parents and communities had done. This period marked a turning point. The war was no longer remembered only as a story of victory or defeat. It became a subject of moral examination, where responsibility, guilt, and memory were openly discussed. The past could no longer be ignored, and the voices of survivors became central to understanding what had happened.

277. Memory Culture, Education, and "Never Again"

From the 1970s onward, the memory of World War II became more institutionalized, particularly through education, museums, and public commemorations. The Holocaust, in particular, came to be recognized as a central event in understanding the war. Schools began to teach its history more systematically, and memorial sites such as former concentration camps were preserved and opened to the public. Museums and archives collected documents, photographs, and personal testimonies, ensuring that the experiences of victims were recorded and accessible. Films, literature, and academic research also played a role in shaping how the war was understood by new generations. The phrase "Never Again" became a guiding principle in many countries, reflecting a commitment to prevent similar atrocities in the future. This idea influenced the development of international human rights laws and organizations, including the United Nations' efforts to define and prevent genocide. At the same time, memory remained contested. Different countries emphasized different aspects of the war, and debates continued about responsibility, interpretation, and commemoration. However, the overall trend moved toward greater openness and recognition of the war's human cost. By the end of the 20th century, World War II was no longer just a historical event. It had become a central reference point for discussions about violence, human rights, and the responsibilities of states and individuals. The memory of the war continued to shape global perspectives long after the last battles had been fought.

TWENTY-FIVE

Conclusion

World War II is often remembered through its largest events, battles, leaders, and the dates that mark its beginning and end. These provide structure, a way to understand a conflict that stretched across continents and involved millions of people. But as this book has shown, the reality of the war is found just as much in the details.

In the unexpected decisions that changed the course of entire campaigns. In the inventions created under pressure, sometimes saving lives and sometimes destroying them. In the experiences of ordinary people, soldiers, civilians, prisoners, and workers who faced situations few had ever imagined possible.

These moments can be surprising. Some are difficult to believe. Others are deeply unsettling. Yet each reveals something essential about the nature of the war.

World War II was not only fought on battlefields; it reached into homes, hospitals, factories, and laboratories. It relied not only on weapons and strategy but also on endurance, improvisation, and the ability of individuals to adapt under extreme conditions. The facts explored in these pages show how unpredictable the conflict could be. Plans failed. Accidents altered outcomes. Small actions had consequences far beyond their immediate moment. At times, survival depended as much on chance as on skill or preparation. They also show the scale of human suffering.

Behind every statistic were real lives, families separated, communities destroyed, and individuals forced to make impossible choices. The war tested the limits of what people could endure, and it exposed both the best and the worst of human behavior. There were acts of courage and cooperation. There were also acts of cruelty, exploitation, and indifference. Often, these existed side by side. The end of the war brought relief, but it did not erase what had happened.

Many of the technologies developed during the conflict continued to shape the modern world. Political tensions that emerged in its aftermath have influenced decades of global relations. The lessons learned about power, responsibility, and the consequences of unchecked ambition remain relevant today.

The events of World War II are not as distant as they may seem. The systems, alliances, and conflicts that define the present have been shaped, in part, by what took place during those years. Understanding the war means looking beyond the well-known milestones and considering the details that reveal how it was lived.

The facts in this book are not just curiosities or isolated stories. They are reminders of how quickly stability can give way to crisis, of how technology can be used in ways both beneficial and destructive, and of how individual choices, even small ones, can have lasting consequences. Above all, they are reminders of the human dimension of war.

World War II was not inevitable, and its outcomes were not guaranteed. It was shaped by decisions, by circumstances, and by people, each acting within the limits and pressures of their time. To study these facts is not only to learn about the past. It is to better understand the present and to recognize the importance of the choices to be made in the future.

Bonus!

Thanks for supporting me and purchasing this book! I'd like to send you some freebies. They include:

- The digital version of *500 World War I & II Facts*

- The digital version of *101 Idioms and Phrases*

- The audiobook for my best seller *1144 Random Facts*

Scan the QR code below, enter your email and I'll send you all the files. Happy reading!

Check out my other books!